A MOTION FOR INNOCENCE:
And Justice for All?

Shaun Webb

AMY,
THANK YOU SO MUCH +
BLESSINGS! ENJOY!

The events in this book are based on a true story. All names have been changed to protect the innocent and guilty alike.

Manufactured in the United States of America.

A special thank you to my Editorial
Consultant: Lynn Gillard

ISBN: 978-1475073348
ISBN-10: 1475073348

Published by Shaun Webb through *In Motion, LLC*.

Thank you to Donna Gundle-Krieg for her Reporting
expertise.

First printing- April 2010
Second printing- April 2011
Third printing- April 2012

Afterword © by Shana Rowan, advocate for nationwide sex
crime legislation reform.

To: My daughter Alycia.

"I can't get my hands on the guy that murdered my daughter, so I've made it my job to make the rest of these sexual offenders and predators' lives miserable, as miserable as I can." –Mark Lunsford

"We're talking about Romeo and Juliet here, not some 36-year-old pervert following around a 10-year-old." -- Mark Lunsford, responding to his son's arrest for a sex crime

A Motion for Innocence
And Justice for All?

In Motion Publishing, LLC
Michigan

Intro

My name is Sean West and I would like to share a story with you. It deals with my experience in going through the criminal justice system. I'm telling this story to help give people knowledge about how the justice "system" worked, or did not work, which applies here.

I feel it is my responsibility to share everything that happened to me. I will include daily logs, diaries, court documents and interviews that encompass the beginning accusation of sexual abuse brought against me through to my trial, and the aftermath. I hope to help you understand my plight.

I will talk about the people who mean the most to me, and the people who hurt my family so severely. You'll be shocked by the details of how unsympathetic of a "system" we have.

I will share with you exactly how awful *I* believe our courts function. From my lawyers, to the State's Prosecutors, to Circuit Court Judges, and even right down to the police, you will read for yourself about my perception of the damaged Halls of Justice.

While reading, remember one thing; **this could happen to you**. If you don't think so, I wouldn't be surprised. I didn't think so either, until I was placed in a precarious situation that I didn't see coming.

1

*

Many citizens don't realize how far-reaching the effects of a sex assault claim are. Our prison population has more than *doubled* (and counting) within the last twenty-five years. One out of every thirty-one people in the United States has a felony on their record; some deserved and some not; many are for sex offenses.

Court has turned into an ugly game between a prosecutor and a defendant, with the defendant playing the role of pawn. Money also plays a major role in court cases. Whoever loses pays big cash so the "incarceration corporation" stays afloat.

The people in charge will tell you that our legal system is the best in the world and that they rarely get it wrong. Trust me, they get it wrong, and more than rarely. "Best in the world" is also very questionable.

It's not only the accused who suffers and spends time in jail. It affects families and friends along with everyone else who may be close to the accused.

I'm hoping this book serves as an educational tool and possibly an aid to help deter false sex assault accusations and convictions. Something needs to be done. If we continue at the rate in which we are going, *every US citizen* will have been, or have a family member jailed. It's no joke; the prison system is a big business.

*

You may notice prayer during this story. Please understand that I don't think God comes down with a bolt of lightning and makes everything okay. I pray because I have faith and I believe God can help you emotionally when times are tough. Man is the perpetrator of many bad occurrences that happen to people all over the world. God is there to help. We should use prayer more often.

*

I'm also *not* attempting to skew or change your personal view of our court system. The experience that I encountered has left a very nasty taste in *my* mouth. If, after reading this, your opinion changes, bravo. If not, that's fine too. I'm a firm believer in "two sides to every story." Don't take my word for it, read it for you. Do some research and see if what I say isn't true.

Shaun Webb

I.

Shaun Webb

Love, Marriage and Work

It started on August 12th. My wife Nikki and I were enjoying the last week of our summer vacation together. It was a sunny Friday afternoon and life was working out well for us. I had what I considered a great job as a building maintenance man at St.Paul Parish in White Lake, Michigan. I was close to home, which was beneficial, and given the responsibility for the upkeep of the Church and School. Nikki was looking forward to her tenth year of teaching at St. Paul School. We met each other working together at the facility and were married. I was headed into my ninth year of service.

*

Nikki had spent her life teaching kids and found it to be very challenging and rewarding. This woman was very friendly and got along with most everyone. She had the ability to calm people with her easygoing presence and soft-spoken demeanor. Her teaching experience had been second, fourth, and eighth grade.

Dealing with the kids and their parents could be difficult, but Nikki did it with enthusiasm and pure compassion.

I was more high-strung than Nikki was, but we complemented each other well. My job at the facility was a source of pride. Taking care of the ENTIRE campus is a huge task that I completely cherished in every way. It was like my own home, and I treated it accordingly. My sense of responsibility was the best.

Nikki and I lived in a modestly comfortable ranch home in Waterford Township, just four or five miles from our work. It had a decent size lot, with a nice front yard and a few trees, plus the wooded lot we owned next-door. Our backyard was fenced in because of my Siberian husky, who constantly tried to think up new ways to escape and explore. We loved doing outdoor gardening together; growing flowers, trees and plants of all varieties. Nikki even had her own veggie garden, which she grew each summer. I was the lawn hawk. I took care of our grass; keeping it green and lush throughout the warm seasons. My lawn was the best in the neighborhood, in my humble opinion. I took it as a challenge to keep it in the nicest shape possible. Simple pleasures, like sitting in our swing in the backyard on a warm summer day, reading or watching nature were all things we did at our home.

Animals were another of our loves. Owning a dog and cat was a tremendously rewarding experience. Bird and squirrel watching also topped our list of leisurely activities. We thoroughly enjoyed the outdoors. We looked forward to it, and to each other, every day. We also caught a few concerts and movies together. Walking every day (we always held hands) supplied us with more quality time and exercise. Both of us worked as a team in keeping things fresh and new so we could enjoy our marriage fully. Our communication skills were excellent. We loved talking to each other and had no trouble expressing ourselves. It was a short life, so we thought

8

we should take advantage of our time. You never knew when you or your significant other would be gone.

*

After meeting, we fell in love quickly and it blossomed. Our love continued to blossom each day. It took me a while, but I finally worked up the courage to ask Nikki out on a date. Her beauty intimidated me and I felt that I had to step cautiously so I wouldn't scare her away. It was like approaching a timid deer; you didn't want to run 'em off.

We were both divorcees and began chatting with each other at work. This progressed to my bringing her coffee in the morning and both of us getting to the school earlier and earlier so we could talk before starting our jobs. I found her to be a perfect combination of smart and beautiful. Nikki had pretty auburn colored hair and soft, happy brown eyes. I was smitten with her. She was so pleasant and confident. The anticipation rattled around in my head and body each morning as I looked forward to seeing her.

Our talking turned into dating, which in turn, led to marriage. Never will I forget our first kiss. We went hiking up a rather large hillside in a park. Upon reaching the top, I couldn't catch my breath. It was a combination of butterflies in my stomach and being completely out of shape. (I think out of shape had more to do with it). Nonetheless, I summoned the courage to pull her close to me, and kiss her. She kissed me back, so I knew I hadn't crossed that line in the sand. This officially started our dating life together, which went on for a

9

few months. When I felt it was the right time and worked up more courage, I asked her to marry me.

I proposed to her in the schoolteacher's lounge. I knew the local UPS delivery driver, and for a few bucks, he delivered the engagement ring to the building for me. It was in a postal box, so she was none the wiser to my little trick. She opened the package in the presence of the entire staff, not sure what she had just received. She assumed it was a school related item. After seeing what was there, she looked at me with glassy eyes and said yes. Another line in the sand successfully crossed. I felt like a valiant prince, chin high, who had just won his life's love. We were building something special together. Nikki and I were married in a beautiful outdoor ceremony at Hess-Hathaway Park in Waterford. I would never stop loving this woman. She was the companion I'd always wanted.

"Being deeply loved by someone gives you strength, while loving someone deeply gives you courage."
-Lao Tzu

Curiosity (Did it really kill the cat?)

On that sunny Friday afternoon, Nikki and I were out
running errands, and returned home somewhere around three
in the afternoon. It was natural for us to come in, hang up the
car keys, hug and feed our pets, and then check the answering
machine.

When we heard that Detective Mike Smart from the White
Lake Police Department had left a message, asking me to call
him back, I instantly thought there was a problem at the school
or church. I was right, but the problem was not at all what I'd
expected.

*

I had dealt with the White Lake Police on many different
occasions while doing my job. Alarm calls in the middle of
the night, police presence at the church's annual fall fair, and
conversing with them at the various school functions they
were involved in. I felt as though we had built a decent
rapport.

Detective Mike Smart was a thirtyish, average looking
person of medium height and weight. He didn't wear his hair
in typical cop fashion, meaning it wasn't a flat top or of
extreme shortness. Mr. Smart carried himself like a normal

everyday man. You couldn't tell that he was an authority figure of any kind. I would converse with him from time to time, especially when he worked at the fairgrounds during our fall festival. I had also dealt with Mr. Smart in his uniformed police officer days when he would respond to alarm calls and other situations that arose at St. Paul. We seemed to get along well and I was not the least bit intimidated or afraid of him. There was no reason to be.

I called Mr. Smart right away. He told me he needed to talk about an incident involving the school, but wanted to do it face to face, not over the phone. I asked him to tell me what was going on, but he wouldn't. He requested that I come to the station at noon on Saturday and we would talk about the situation. I begrudgingly agreed and hung up.

My thinking was that this talk would involve questions about theft or property defacement at the school. I dialed the Principal to see if she knew anything about what might be happening, but could not reach her. Upon speaking with Nikki, I decided to drive up to the station right away. I had a good reason why I thought this would be questioning about thievery in the school.

"Being hurt personally triggered a curiosity about how such beliefs are formed."

-Philip Zimbardo

Suspicion and Theft

In March, I had been plowing snow in the parking lot at or around three in the morning and needed to stop for a restroom break. I entered the school building and was surprised to see the alarm disarmed. This piqued my senses, causing me to enter the facility with more care than usual. In retrospect, I should have called the police and let them handle it, but I didn't think that it would be a big problem. Due to all the crime going on in the world, I guess thinking it was no big deal could get you killed. Luckily for me, it didn't.

I walked around the first corner after entering the vestibule and jumped with fright when I found myself suddenly face to face with David Carowitz, one of the building janitors. It was a good thing it was Carowitz and not some person with a gun. Had it been, I suspect I wouldn't be sharing this story.

Sweat was rolling off the man's face. I asked what he was doing in the school at three in the morning. He stated that he was checking the work of his janitorial team from the night before. This team included his girlfriend, Sara Joan Radison, his girlfriend's fifteen year-old daughter Blair Radison and Blair's aunt, Bonnie.

*

I met all of these people when they began cleaning the
school. Carowitz seemed like a nice person. He would
sometimes exchange pleasantries with my wife when he saw
her in her classroom. He also enjoyed feeding carrots to our
pet hamster, which lived in Nikki's room during the school
year. I would converse with him from time to time if we ran
into each other. We exchanged jokes and laughs when we'd
see each other.

Carowitz was overweight, but not to the extreme. I figured
him in his late forties or early fifties. He wore a black
mustache and beard with a speckle of gray, giving it a salt and
pepper look. His girlfriend, Sara Joan Radison, was
significantly overweight and always wore a bandana on her
head to catch the sweat that worked up while she cleaned. I
had a chance to speak with Sara Joan on occasion, and I found
her to be cordial and friendly. Bonnie, Sara Joan's Sister, was
usually, but not always, working with them. A short, blond-
haired woman of middle age and average build, she was also
cordial when I would see her. Bonnie and Blair would make a
couple trips out to my garage office for supplies, which I
thought was of no real consequence. Little did I know.

My office was located about five hundred feet from the
school building with the church sitting in between the two
buildings. I used this area to do repairs, make phone calls and
store the company plow truck. It also housed all the
equipment and props for the fall fair. I had a desk, a phone
and a workbench. A small office met my needs for the job. If
I needed a moment of quiet, this was the spot for it. It was my
domain, my area of retreat. There were two windows on each

side of the garage, but the previous maintenance man, to dissuade would-be thieves, had boarded them up. It was a good idea to keep valuables hidden from sight. *(Note):* I didn't board those windows up.

*

Allow me to introduce my future tormentor to you: Blair Radison. This was Sara Joan's daughter. Blair was a freshman or sophomore in high school. She was rather tall and thickly built. Standing around 5'9" or 5'10" tall and weighing in at around 170 or 180 pounds, she was a big girl. Blair had blond hair just past her shoulders, and owned a child's face. I would occasionally see her at the playground with other kids, or sitting in the car while her mom and Carowitz worked. Blair would help in the school from time to time, but I think she was merely along for the ride. Perhaps her mom needed to keep an eye on her. If that was the case, she wasn't doing a very good job of it.

I spoke to Blair on a few occasions, but as you will find out, not as extensively as would be suggested. I originally thought Blair to be nice, but my first impressions are usually positive. You have to earn my mistrust.

That's all I knew of these folks. They worked for an outside contractor hired by St. Paul called Tornado Clean.

*

I wasn't skeptical about Carowitz checking the work because I had never had any reason to doubt this man's word.

15

We both shrugged it off and moved on, me to relieve myself; Carowitz out the door. I checked the building to make sure no one else was present, set the alarm, and then went about my business of plowing snow. I found it odd that he would want to check things at three in the morning, but perhaps he couldn't sleep. I forgot about it quickly.

The next day, I had a request for toilet paper to be placed in a school restroom. When I went to retrieve some out of the locked supply closet, the entire stock was cleaned out. Everything from toilet paper, paper towels and garbage bags were gone. I knew we were fully stocked with at least twenty boxes of each product, as I had received the order only a week or so earlier. This amount of supplies would typically last about two-and-a-half months. This raised my suspicions about Carowitz's presence the night before, but I wasn't going to start blaming people for theft without adequate proof, at least not at that point.

I continued my daily activities but kept my eyes opened wider due to these strange discoveries. My boss, Gail Pritchett, told me that there were possible thefts occurring in the school. She told me that kindergarten graduation cap tassels, paper clips and even the school flag had been reported missing. I explained to Gail what I had discovered earlier and she told me to write a report and give it to her. This report was stored in my employee file for safekeeping.

*

Gail was the building superintendent at St. Paul and for all intents and purposes, my boss. We had an excellent working

16

relationship and got along very well. She trusted me and I shared that trust about her. When she asked me to do something, I did it without argument or fanfare. I was free to express my opinion and she respected that. Gail, however, had the bottom line and I didn't challenge it. I very much enjoyed working for her. I felt as if I was her right-hand man. Her husband Bruce owned and ran a business called Premo Cooling. Often times, Bruce's employees would assist me at St. Paul. My friend Danny Davis was one of the most popular choices to work with me at the parish.

*

In May, I again noticed that newly ordered supplies were missing. This time I called Tornado Clean and explained to Cassie, a Tornado Clean supervisor, that I believed theft was occurring and that her team was, at least, partly responsible.

I wasn't as gentle as I should have been.

"Cassie, items in the school are coming up missing, and I think your people may have something to do with it."

As you can imagine, that elicited a lot of anger and outrage.

"How dare you out and out blame us. You'll be hearing from my boss," she told me.

"I'm not blaming anyone in particular," I explained, "I simply have reason to believe that your people may have done this or been involved."

In my explanation, I told her about my meeting with Carowitz in March, but she didn't seem to be listening. My thinking was that she was too angry from my initial accusation. My call with Cassie ended, and thirty seconds later, I received a call from Cassie's boss, who was hot.

"I'll pull my team and resign on the spot," he screamed.

I tried to calm him.

"Take it easy. Let me tell you why I think this."

Like Cassie, he wasn't listening. He hung up on me. I'd wish later they would have, in fact, quit, but for now, they were still here and they were *right*. I shouldn't have blamed them, but I thought a dose of fear would help solve this problem. I believed this company was responsible, but I couldn't prove it. When you can't substantiate that a crime had been committed, it was best to keep your opinions to yourself. Incidentally, the owner also called Gail and threatened to quit, but she calmed him down and asked me to issue an apology for my actions. I did.

Gail explained to me that, "you can't go around flinging accusations".

I agreed wholeheartedly. Gail has been around the block once or twice and knows proper etiquette.

There were no more thefts after that, perhaps because I moved the supplies to my office in the garage. I also think my accusation may have scared them. I started noticing other strange occurrences.

*

In late May-early June, before the end of the school year, I would find odd scenes upon opening the school in the morning. These oddities included the roof hatch left open. There were dirty pictures; depictions of oral sex, along with

18

male and female genitalia, drawn on the dry erase boards in the religious education supply room. I alerted the school principal, Mrs. Lindsay, and religious education director, Jillian, to these anomalies and they were noted. What else could I do? I certainly wouldn't point fingers again. As a matter of point, Jillian's keys had come up missing just weeks earlier, so our suspicions already pulsed. Somebody had those keys and it would all make sense in the near future.

The school year ended on June 10th, and we started our summer vacations. The janitorial team wouldn't be needed again until late August. It was not surprising that with their absence throughout the summer, no more drawings, open roof hatches or petty thefts occurred.

"I don't know how to defend myself: surprised innocence cannot imagine being under suspicion."

-Pierre Corneille

Shaun Webb

An Accusation

I arrived at the police station at about five P.M.. and asked the front desk if Mr. Smart was still in the building. Mike came out fifteen minutes later and met me with a handshake and a half-hearted smile. He seemed to be a bit miffed that I'd shown up despite agreeing to Saturday at noon, but as far as I was concerned, that was too bad. He called and I came because my attention was needed. I didn't like pushing off until later what can be taken care of right now. This situation was no different. I hoped the meeting wasn't too serious, but important enough to warrant my attention.

Perhaps this would confirm my suspicions about the theft in the school. It could be that the people or persons who were stealing weren't this cleaning crew at all, but someone we knew on a closer level. Obviously, I didn't want that to be the case. I would be saddened if it was someone to whom I was close. There was no denying that I felt some pride and maybe even a little protective of the facility.

*

Mr. Smart politely led me into his office, asked me to sit down and came right out with it.

"Do you know Blair Radison?"

I told him no.

"She works in the school as a janitor," he stated with a lift of his right eyebrow.

"Oh," I said, "Yeah, I know Blair."

I thought for sure he had said Brian, not Blair. His speech was low and he had his mouth turned downward. He was looking at me from what seemed like the top of his head. I felt a hint of trepidation with his technique.

"Well," said Smart, "There's been a criminal complaint filed. You are not under arrest and may leave anytime you like."

"Whoa! Time out!" I thought.

You had to be in my shoes to understand the feeling. It was instant anxiety with my heart in my throat. I felt threatened. It sounded like it was about to be *me* as the subject line. I felt like a hunted buck, helpless and exposed, with Smart lining me up in his crosshairs. Sudden warmth starts from your toes and moves to your head very quickly. The heartbeat races, the adrenaline flows, and its fight or flight. I was stunned. What was this man going to tell me? What were the next words coming out of his mouth going to be? I wasn't prepared for them.

*

He continued his interview. He explained to me that Blair's mom overheard a phone call between Blair and her friend. Smart said that Mom thought Blair and I had been fooling around in a sexual manner. Completely taken aback and stunned, I nervously asked Smart to go on. I had a look of pure surprise on my face.

"Blair said you touched her breasts and nipples."

"Don't even joke about shit like that. No. I did not," I told Smart.

I kept saying it repeatedly.

"NO, NO, NO, NO."

It was important that I try to keep my cool because I was truly frightened. My heart continued racing and my head began to ache. I felt as if I was having trouble breathing.

"Calm it down, Sean, calm it down." I told myself.

The questioning in a criminal matter that *directly* involved me? Never has anything even remotely comparable to this ever happened in my life. I was having a bad dream, I hoped. I was scared. I was the accused. I never thought I'd get questioned about something so taboo, revolting and hideous. This subject matter was a stigma in the eyes of society and now that stigma, fairly or not, was being applied to me.

I needed some space to clear my head and calm down, so I stood up and walked back and forth in Smart's office. I polished off my bottle of iced tea and wanted more to drink. I felt like I needed an IV for re-hydration, so I refilled my bottle with water. Smart continued to ask questions, and I continued emphatically denying the bogus allegations. I couldn't believe the nonsense. There were more questions and more denials. Anger was starting to seep into my emotions. Smart asked me if I was a smoker. I told him, "yes and I need a cigarette."

We headed outside and he walked with me to my truck. Despite the fact that I couldn't breathe, I still wanted to smoke. I thought being outside would relieve some of the tension that was building up. It didn't.

"Is that your pick-up truck?" he asked with curiosity.

"Yeah, it's my truck."

"Nice truck," he said.

I barked back at him, probably sounding irritated, even though his comment really didn't bother me much.

"It's just an old truck. Who cares?"

Smart calmly replied, his hands pretending to gently push me over.

"Take it easy, I was just asking."

I apologized, "Sorry, I'm a little scattered right now".

I would find out later how much my truck would come into play. We smoked a couple of cigarettes, he asked more questions and I continued my categorical denials. We finished smoking; I put my cigarettes back in the truck, shut the door; and brainlessly locked my keys inside. "Great," I thought, "get your head together, Sean, your acting like a fool."

"Are you nervous, Sean?" Smart inquired with another raised eyebrow.

"Hell yeah I'm nervous, wouldn't you be?"

My voice was cracking.

"Yeah, I guess I would be", was his obvious response.

He told me he'd ask a police officer to fetch my keys with a jimmy bar. We went back to his office and continued the conversation.

He started asking deeper questions. "Did you piss these people off? Do they have a vendetta against you?"

I answered no, but I thought it was time to stop talking.
I've seen enough cop shows to know when you've said
enough, or too much. Continuing to talk would get me is
more trouble, and there was plenty to go around already. I had
an idea that this was not going to disappear.

He looked at me and said something else that both
surprised me and ticked me off.

"Blair seemed pretty convincing at the Pontiac Care House
interview we had today."

This time he took on a more confident air. My eyes were
squinted, my lips locked and my ire up. She had already been
to the Pontiac Care House and since Blair seemed so
convincing, she must have been telling the truth. She was not.
This began to stink of a set-up to me. I didn't know all the
circumstances at that point, but I did know something smelled
like a dirty rat.

Smart told me to go home and sleep on it, then come back
the next day. Sleep? That was out of the question. I knew I
wouldn't be back, so I gave him one more comment on the
way out the door.

"Sir, I do not care how convincing you say or think Blair
was. I'm more convincing because I'm telling the truth."

I left with my chin raised, but my spirits were sinking. I
was demoralized.

"I can't let this get in my head." I thought, "I must stay
calm and collected. I can't be weak. Take a nice long, deep
breath."

Everything from my thinking to my body felt unbalanced.
I had shaky knees, racing heartbeat and the inability to keep

still. My concentration was hindered, but I was able to safely drive back home.

> *"There is one, and only one, thing in modern society more hideous than crime, namely repressive justice."*
>
> *-Simone Weil*

Shock and Awe No

I went home and explained to my wife what had happened at the police station. That was difficult because I was numb and knew it was going to be difficult. She took it well, or as well as you could realistically expect. The tears flowed, but she didn't believe the accusations from the second I told her. Nikki asked me questions. I answered them as honestly as I could.

"Why is this happening?" I don't know.

"Where did this come from?" I don't know.

"Who would do this to us?" That was the only question I did know the answer to.

She hugged me tight. I could feel the fear in her touch. She rubbed her forehead and cheeks repeatedly and asked the same questions. The frustration was showing in her reddened face. She clutched her mid-section, nauseated with the news. We prayed about it. We tried very hard to understand. The question "Why?" played over like a broken record in my mind.

*

I thought that Blair might've had a crush on me, and I had mentioned that to Nikki near the end of the school year. That

27

idea came from the way she looked and talked to me. Her eyelids were fluttering while she used a soft voice.

"Hi Sean, it's good to see you," she would say in that flirty manner with her head leaned to one side.

Maybe she thought I was "cute" and had a crush on me. Who knew for sure except her? Nikki and I both laughed about it. What I didn't know, or think about, was to what extent Blair's puppy love stretched. Why did she have a crush, if that's what it really was? It didn't make sense.

Blair had visited my wife on numerous occasions while cleaning in the school and they had chatted about many things; school, sports, and her after school activities. It was idle chat. Nikki also spoke with Carowitz and the others from time to time without the slightest hint of any misconduct involving Blair and myself. Nikki never remembered any details from the conversations because she didn't soak it in. That's not to say she didn't care; she simply talked with so many people every day. She couldn't possibly store it all in her mind. Nikki would be in an asylum if she took in every word from every parent, student, boss or friend

*

After Nikki and I talked and prayed, we decided I should call my superiors and tell them about the situation. For the rest of the evening we sat in disbelief. It was a weak, squeamish feeling of despair and confusion. Nobody could describe it. You would have to experience it to get a proper feel. Calling Fr. Patrick, the parish head priest, was as hard as any other part of this situation. I had come to gain a great deal of respect from him due to my diligence and work ethic. I also had a great amount of respect for him in return. He was a stand-up gentleman filled with honesty and integrity. Fr. Patrick was the head priest at St. Paul from the day I was hired. He still held the post as of January 2011. I had done all of his handyman work around the rectory (his home) and always treated his living area as if I was taking care of my own.

Our relationship was difficult for me at first. He was very high strung and wanted things done NOW.

"We have to do this NOW Sean," he would say, arms flailing and eyes looking around. "Why isn't this done yet, Sean?"

It took me some time to get used to his way and understand it. He didn't miss much of what was going on around him. He was always looking, thinking and figuring. I didn't care for him when I first started the job, but as I grew to know him, I understood his focus much better. I figured out that he was one of the kindest individuals I'd ever had the honor of meeting. He was always very respectful and understanding.

By the way, being Head Priest, he had the final say at the parish, even above Gail. He was number one on top of the ladder at the facility. He answered only to the archdiocese. He may not have always showed it, but he had the bottom line. He worked closely with Gail though, and took her opinions very seriously.

*

I phoned Father Patrick and told him the horrible news. He was every bit as stunned as I expected. He couldn't believe it.

"Is this true, Sean?" He had to ask.

I told him what I'd found out so far and explained to him, "This story had no merit and should be considered erroneous".

Fr. Patrick instructed me to stand by while he conferred with his superiors. I only had to wait about thirty minutes for his return call.

Upon speaking with Gail and members of the archdiocese, Fr. Patrick instructed me to go on paid administrative leave until the matter was resolved.

"I'm separating all parties until we straighten this out," he told me.

The crew from Tornado Clean was also asked to stay away from the school until the problem resolved. Fr. Patrick pointed me to Doylan and Hearn's law firm, a well-respected firm throughout the archdiocese, and recommended by the archdiocese.

Nikki and I had no experience in the legal system. The Catholic Church had been fighting allegations for years. It seemed logical for us to follow their recommendations. Who better to take advice from than those who had lived it?

Fr. Patrick and Gail didn't give me any hint as to whether they thought innocence or guilt. They simply wanted me to follow the proper protocol and let the system naturally run its course. They would question me extensively later.

*

I called Bert Doylan at about 8:00 that night and made an appointment for 9:00 the next morning.

Bert asked me, "Do you want me to represent you?" I answered "yes". He had to ask me that question first, because he could not help me until I agreed to his counsel. Bert also told me to keep quiet. "Don't talk," he commanded.

I had to call my friend, though. "Call your buddy," he told me", then keep quiet."

*

I called my best friend Danny, who worked with me often at the church, and told him what had happened. He was shocked.

"Oh Sean, I'm so sorry."

By the sound of his voice, I could tell he felt bad for me. I let him know that Detective Smart would be getting ahold of him for some questioning because I'd said that he would vouch for me.

"No problem, whatever I can do to help."

I told him I was very afraid that I could go to prison. He tried to soften the blow for me.

"No Sean, you won't go to jail."

God bless you Danny, but you didn't know that. You couldn't know that. I did understand him wanting to make me feel better.

This ended one of the worst days of our lives. That was too much drama for anybody to endure in one day. It was only a precursor of what was to come.

*

The following is an actual copy of the police report. Please note that I did not tamper with or edit the report. The only differences are the names and locations. The report is as Det. Smart wrote it. **All grammatical errors fall squarely at his feet.**

WHITE LAKE TOWNSHIP REPORT OF INCIDENT

Police Report from White Lake Police Department

1. David Carowitz (Stepfather)

Dispatched:
To the White Lake Police Department for a susp. circ. report. I arrived at 1100 hours.

Incident:
David Carowitz and Sara Joan Radison responded to the White Lake PD to file a report of a possible criminal molesting of Sara Joan's sixteen year-old daughter Blair. According to the allegations made, the incident occurred at St. Paul's Church from December through January. Blair was also fifteen years-old at the time of the incidents.

Person: David Carowitz

Carowitz stated that he has lived with Sara Joan and her daughter Blair for the last three years. Carowitz

32

stated Blair was like a daughter to him and she views Carowitz as her father. Carowitz stated that last night he was talking to Blair about something that was bugging her. Carowitz stated that Blair confided in him that Sean West, a custodian at St. Paul church, molested her back in December. Carowitz said that Blair told him that she did not allow West to have sexual intercourse with her, but West did fondle her vagina and breasts. Carowitz stated during his talk with Blair, that he believes more than just touching had occurred between the two of them, but could not get Blair to explain any further. Carowitz stated once Blair had told him about this, he advised Sara Joan Radison, who is Blair's mom. Carowitz and Radison then came up to the police station to file a report. Carowitz stated he, Blair and sometimes Sara Joan help clean the church and school at night. Carowitz stated West is also a custodian at the school and that's how they know West.

Person: Sara Joan Radison (mother)
Radison has nothing further to add to this report.
Person: Blair Radison (victim)
Blair was not interviewed or talked to during the taking of this report.
Person: Sean Albert west (suspect)
West has not been contacted at this time.
Arrest: None.
Vehicle: None.
Follow-up: Contact West.
Disposition: Open.
Other: Contact West / Check on his children.

2. Blair Radison (15 Year-old victim)

ADDITIONAL INFORMATION:
By Detective Mike Smart

I made Pontiac Care House interview for Blair on 8-12-05 at 12:00. I called Mrs. Radison and advised her of the date.

On 8-12, the Pontiac Care House interview took place. Ginny from Pontiac Care House interviewed Blair. Haley from the Prosecutors office, and I observed the interview. Keri from Pontiac Care House assisted with the process.

Blair Radison was brought to Pontiac Care House by her mother Sara Joan Radison her Step-father David Carowitz, and her biological Father John Radison. we spoke to family members prior to Blair's interview, without Blair present. Mr. Carowitz retold me how he learned of the incident from Blair; it was consistent with the statement he made in the original police report. Mr. Carowitz stated Blair began to tell and over three hours she told him about the entire situation. Mr. Carowitz believes Blair told him last Friday or Saturday, he then told Blair's mother, Sara Joan. Both Mr. Carowitz and Mrs. Radison stated there has not been any contact Blair and Mr. West since the incident. Mr. Carowitz states that he and Mrs. Radison work for a company, Tornadoclean, that cleans St. Pauls school, they normally clean the school every week night during the school year, Blair would go with them on Wednesdays, Thursdays, and Fridays, to

34

help. Mrs. Radison stated that Blair does not go to church or school at St. Pauls. Mr. Carowitz stated that Mr. West does have a garage area at the school/church that he uses as an office. Mr. Carowitz stated that Blair had just recently told him of the situation and he had no prior knowledge.

Blair was brought to an interview room by Ginny. Haley and I observed the interview through one way glass, none of Blair's family members were present.

Ginny began by talking to Blair about her education; she stated she was going to be a sophomore at the high school in the fall. Ginny explained to Blair the function of Pontiac Care House. Ginny explained to Blair the importance of telling the truth, and Blair agreed to tell the truth. Ginny asked Blair to tell her what happened.

Blair stated that her step-father and mother work cleaning the St. Paul school and she would, sometimes go with them and help them, she started doing this when she was thirteen or fourteen years old. Blair stated that she met Mr.West (Sean) when she started going to the school with her step-father and mother. Blair stated that she thought Sean was strange at first, when Ginny asked why, Blair stated because he had a lot of tattoos. Blair stated that Sean would often say "Hi" to her in the school when she was vacuuming, one day he stopped and they talked. After that they would talk occasionally when she was at the school.

One day Sean asked her to come to his office in the garage, they talked, he showed her his truck, which she liked because she,"loves pickup trucks" and she said he was being nice. Blair stated that she would go to Sean's office when she was at the school, she would talk to him about her problems with her father and other things. Blair states that Sean began saying to her, "you have great looking tits", then say he was just kidding around. Blair states that Sean then began to ask her if he could "touch her titties", she told him no, but he kept asking and telling her, "you might like it", Blair stated that Sean told her he loved her and that he wouldn't ever hurt her. Blair stated that she liked Sean and thought he was her friend, she got sick of telling him "no" so she let him touch her "boobs". Ginny asked Blair when the first time of touching was; she said she thought November of last year. Ginny asked if it was before Thanksgiving, Blair said yes, Ginny asked if it was after Halloween, Blair stated it was. Ginny asked Blair to tell her more about the first touching. Blair stated that she was in the office with Sean talking, he got then said "you are so gorgeous and so sweet, I love you", she said "thank you", he said "can I touch your tits?", she said "no", then said "OK",. Blair stated that Sean rubbed her "boobs" over her shirt in a circular motion. When he was done he said, "it felt good, my dick is hard", and asked her if it felt good, she told him "it felt weird", because she had never done that before. Sean then told her he loved her and would never hurt her.

Blair stated that a little before Christmas, Sean began asking her to touch him and to let him touch her other places. She told him she was not comfortable with this. Blair stated that Sean keep telling her, it was OK, he loved her, and it would be OK. Ginny asked what other touching occurred, Blair stated that Sean would grab her hand and put it on his penis. Ginny asked her what she felt, she said, "kind of scared and kind of confused". Blair then stated that Sean would "suck on her boobs sometimes and pinch her nipples'. Ginny asked her how that started, she stated that he had asked her to lift up her shirt, she did and he started taking off her shirt, she then told him "no", he asked her again and she said "fine". Blair then said, that Sean would always tell her , he loved her, he wouldn't hurt her, and not to tell anyone or he'll go to prison. Ginny asked Blair how he would "suck on her boobs", she said, he undid her bra then licked around her boobs and on her nipples. Ginny asked if he "sucked on her boobs more than once, she said, "yes'.

Ginny asked if he ever touched her anywhere else, she said he would smack her on the butt and squeeze her butt, "he thought it was hot". Ginny asked if he ever touched her anywhere else, she said, "down there", and pointed toward her middle. Ginny asked when this happened, she said the end of January or the beginning of February, she stated that she was getting more comfortable with him. Ginny asked how it started, Blair said that Sean asked to feel "down there" through her jeans, after she let him, the next time he asked to fell over her underwear, and she let him. He then asked to touch her "down there" under her underwear, and she let him. Ginny asked Blair to tell her more about when he touched her under her underwear, she stated that he "went in easy", and asked her if she liked it, he then rubbed her,"down there". Ginny asked her if his fingers stayed outside her body or if they ever

37

went inside her body, she said, his fingers went inside her body "a little bit, I think." Ginny asked how many times this happened Blair said, it happened twice, but most of the time it was over her jeans.

Ginny asked Blair to tell he about her touching him, she stated that she would be standing with her hands behind her back, he would pull out her hand and force her to touch him, Ginny asked her how this made her feel, she said "scared and confused".

Blair stated that after he told her that he thought someone saw her coming in or out of the garage, and told her not to come around for a while. Ginny asked her if it stopped after that, Blair said, no after a couple weeks it went back to normal.

Ginny asked Blair to tell her more about him making her touch him, and asked where did he make you touch, she said, "his penis and all around it", and he would say, "you can't tell anybody, Ginny asked if he took his clothes off, Blair said, no he would pull his pants down a little bit, Blair stated that he would hold her wrist the whole time and control her hand, Blair said, her hand "was like dead wieght", Ginny asked if this happened more than once, she said yes, Ginny asked when was the last time. she said, April, I think.

Ginny asked if the touching happened all the time, Blair stated that it wasn't all the time, sometimes they just talked, it most often happened when she was stressed out about problems with her father. Ginny asked Blair who she told about this first, she said her step-father, then said she told her friend, Michelle about it in March. Ginny asked if she had ever seen Sean drinking alcohol in the office, she said yes, Ginny asked if she ever drank. she said no, Sean offered her beer but she thinks it's "nesty" because of the smell. Ginny asked if Sean ever did anything else, Blair said that he smoked and she didn't like it she was always bugging him to quit, when he was asking her to let him touch her, he would say "if you let me rub your pussy, I'll quit smoking", but he never did quit. Ginny asked if they ever exchanged notes or gave each other anything, Blair said "no', Ginny asked if he ever took pictures of her, she said "no". Ginny then ended the interview. Blair did appear truthful and acted in a manner that would be suspected under these circumstances.

2. Sean West (suspect)

ADDITIONAL INFORMATION:
By Detective Mike Smart

On 8-12 I went to the St. Paul church/school looking for Mr. West, but he was not there. I called Mr. West at his home and left a message on the machine for him to call me. Mr. West called me shortly after. I advised him that I needed to speak to him, but did not tell him what it was regarding, I told him I would rather speak in person. Mr. West agreed to come in on 8-13 at 1300 hrs. to speak to me. At approx. 1715 hrs. on 8-12 as I was leaving for the day, Mr. West came to BPPD. he stated that he need to talk to me, he couldn't wait tell tomorrow to find out what was going on. Mr. West has worked at the St. Paul Church/School for several years and I have spoke to him many times in the past. Mr. West is normally the point of contact for incidents on church/school property and as a police officer I have met Mr. West several times. When we met Mr. West appeared friendly and helpful, which is his normal attitude towards me, from my experience.

I asked Mr. West to come into my office and have a seat. I explained to Mr. West that I was investigating a criminal complaint, he did not have to speak to me and he was free to leave anytime, he said "OK'.

I asked Mr. West if he knew Blair Radison, he said he didn't, I said Blair, her step-dad cleans the school, he said "oh yeah, sure I know Blair". I asked Mr. West how long he knew Blair, he said three or four years, maybe less. I asked what their relationship was, Mr.West stated "friends", and stated that he thought she might have a crush on him.

Mr.West asked what was going on, I told him that Blairs mother had overheard her talking on the phone to her friend about him, and she is afraid that they are more than just friends. Mr.West stated, "no chance, I never touched that girl", he went on to say that he never laid a finger on her, not a hug, not a kiss, not a thing. I asked Mr.West if Blair had ever been in his office, he said "yes a couple times, but never with the door shut", he went on to explain that the only kids that had been in his office with the doors shut were boys that do community service at the church, and that he won't let girls do community service

40

there because he doesn't want any chance of false allegations.

Mr. West appeared very upset, he kept repeating that he couldn't believe this was happening. I explained to Mr. West that Blair had had gone to a Pontiac Care House interview and what that entailed. I told Mr. West that Blair stated that he had touched her breasts, and nipples. he said "nope I never touched her". Mr. West asked if he could stand up, I told him for sure he could do what ever he wanted. Mr. West appeared upset, he was pacing around in my office, making statements including: I can't believe this was happening, I would never do anything like this, she is only a kid I have a daughter I would never do that, I am going to prison or jail over something that never happened.

Mr. West finished the bottle of tea he had brought with him and asked if he could have some water, we walked to the kitchen, he filled his bottle with water, and we returned to my office. Mr. West kept saying he couldn't believe she would say that. I asked him, why would she say that, he stated he didn't know why. I asked him if they had a falling out or if she was mad at him, he said no. Mr. West stated that he thinks she has a crush on him and she would talk about her problems and how she didn't like her father. Mr. West stated again that Blair has never been in his office with the door closed, he stated that his friend Danny, from Premo Cooling had been around in the afternoon and seen her there before, with the door open. I asked Mr. West if he ever stays after work, watches TV and drinks beer in the office, Mr. West said, never his wife

41

can confirm and vouch that he is home right after work
every day, I asked if there is a TV in the office, he said
there was, "it's on a lot," I asked if there was any reason
Blair would be angry with him, he said that sometimes she
would come to the office and knock on the door and he
wouldn't answer because he was too busy to talk to her,
that could have made her mad. Mr.West stated that he
hadn't even seen Blair since the end of May or beginning
of June when school got out and her step-father quit
cleaning.

Mr.West stated that he wanted a cigarette, we walked
out by his vehicle, a pick-up truck, and smoked a cigarette.
While we were outside Mr.West kept reiterating that he
never touched Blair and he couldn't believe this was
happening.

I asked Mr.West if he ever drank beer in front of Blair,
he said no he doesn't drink at work. I asked him if there
was any beer in his office that she might of seen and made
an assumption, he stated that he has empty cans in a
bucket from the fair in the garage, but no full cans.
Mr.West stated that sometimes when he goes to the store
he buys beer for home and leaves it in his truck until he
goes home. I asked if Blair had ever been in his truck, he
said no, then said that once she was getting supplies from
the garage for her step-father and he put them in his truck
and they drove over to the school so she didn't have to
carry them. I asked if he had any beer in his truck that
day, he said yes, possibly. I asked where it would be, he
said behind the seat in a bag, I asked if it was possible she
saw it when she was in his truck, he said it was possible.

While putting his cigarettes back in his vehicle, Mr.West locked his keys inside. As we were returning to my officer I asked officer Collins to unlock Mr.West's vehicle and bring him the keys, which he did.

When we returned to my office Mr.West continued saying that he couldn't believe she would say that. I asked him if she had ever come on to him, he said she hadn't. Mr.West stated that he did think she had a crush on him, and for the last year had been dressing in more "belly shirts and stuff", he said, I don't know what word, more... I said "provocatively", he said "yes, provocatively". I asked if Blair ever talked to him about boys, he said yes she had a boyfriend, I asked , did she talk sexual talk about him, he said no. I asked if she was ever flirtatious with him, he stated no. Mr.West stated that some times in the hall when she was vacuuming he would pull out the power cord, and they would have "tickle fights", but nothing flirtatious, just the kind of stuff he would do with his daughter. I stated you mean,"just messing around, horse play", he said yes.

Mr.West continued that he couldn't believe this was happening. I told Mr.West that we should talk tomorrow and that he could sleep on it, he could come in tomorrow at 1300 hrs. and we could talk some more. Mr.West left, I did not find any inconsistancies in his statement or anything to suggest he was being untruthful, his reaction seemed appropriate to the circumstances.

On 8-13 I received a call from Bert Doylan, Attorney, informing me that Mr.West had retained him as his attorney and that all future contacts with Mr. West would be through him.

3. Father Patrick (St. Paul Parish)

ADDITIONAL INFORMATION:
By Detective Mike Smart

On 8-13 I contacted Father Patrick, the Pastor of St. Paul church and informed him of the investigation. Father Patrick was already aware there was an investigation because Mr.West told him he had been questioned. I informed Father Patrick that if he had future questions to feel free to contact me. Father Patrick indicated that he would not talk to the police, only representatives from the archdiocese. I told him okay and left.

4. Danny Davis (Contractor)

ADDITIONAL INFORMATION:
By Detective Mike Smart

On 8-20 Danny Davis from Premo Cooling came to BPPD to speak to me at my request. Danny stated that he formally worked for Premo Cooling and had worked at the St. Paul's church/school often. Mr. Davis states that depending on how busy he was on other jobs, he would work ay St. Paul's anywhere from once a week to everyday of the week some weeks. I asked if he knew Sean West, he stated he did, they worked together at St. Paul's and were friends. I told Mr. Davis that Mr.West said they were best friends, and asked if that was true, he said it was. I asked if they did things together outside of work, Mr.Davis stated yes, their wives were friends also and they sometimes did things as couples. I asked Mr.Davis if he knew Mr. Carowitz, he said he did not. I asked if he knew Sara Joan Radison, he said he did not. I asked if he knew Blair Radison, he said he did not. I asked Mr. Davis if Mr.West ever spoke about Blair, he said no.

I asked Mr.Davis if he ever worked on projects with Mr.West, he stated that he sometimes worked alone and sometimes together with Mr.West. I asked if they ever worked in the garage, he said yes there was a workbench in there. I asked if Mr.West had an office in his garage, he stated, yes there is a desk. I asked if there was a television, he stated there was. I asked if they ever hung out and watched TV, he said yes during their lunchbreak. I asked if ever after work, he said no. I asked if they ever drank beer in the office, he said no. I asked if they ever went to lunch together, he said yes they would go for sandwiches or pizza, and bring food back. I asked if he ever saw Mr. West purchase beer on their lunch break, he said no. I asked if he ever saw anyone else in the garage/office besides Mr.West, he said Father Patrick would sometimes stop in, and a man named "Bruce", who works for the church and was working on the bleachers, would sometimes us the workbench. I asked Mr.Davis if he ever saw anyone from the cleaning crew in the office getting supplies, he said no. I asked Mr.Davis if he ever saw a teenage girl from the cleaning crew around the office, he

45

said no. I asked if he ever saw any teenagers in the office, he said no, I asked what about the kids doing community service, he said no, Mr.West didn't let them in the office.

I asked Mr.Davis if Mr.West had ever spoke to him about extramarital affairs, he said, no he has never know of Mr.West being unfaithful to his wife. I asked Mr.Davis if Mr.West ever spoke about a young girl having a crush on him, he said no. I asked him, when does Mr.West usually work, he said in the daytime, except in the winter he sometimes comes in to plow snow in the evening. I asked Mr.Davis when he last worked at St. Paul's, he stated that Friday, 8-12 was his last day at Premo Cooling and he worked at the church, he found a better job in another city, and has been working there since. I asked him when he last spoke to Mr.West, he stated he spoke to him on the phone on 8-14. I asked him what Mr.West had told him, he said that a girl had accused him of something he didn't do and he had to talk to the police. I asked if Mr.West mentioned that he might have to talk to the police, he said yes, I asked if he told him anything to say, he said no, Interview was concluded.

*(Please note that Danny was also asked if I kept my truck inside the garage and Danny answered no. This was not included on the report.)

5. Michelle Rollins (Blair's Friend)

ADDITIONAL INFORMATION:
By Detective Mike Smart

On 8-23, Melanie Rollins, brought her daughter Michelle, Blairs friend, to BPPD to see me. Michelle will be a sophomore at her high school this upcoming fall. I asked Michelle if she knew Blair Radison, she said she did, they are friends. I asked her how she knew Blair, she said they have been friends since the sixth grade, when they went to the intermediate school I Oakland together. I told her that Blair said they were best friends and asked if that was true, she said it was. I asked Michelle if she knew Blairs parents, she said she knew her mother, step-father and father, she stayed at Blairs home and done things with her family, and Blair has stayed at her home and done things with her family.

I asked Michelle if she knew what she was here to talk about, she stated she did. I asked her when Blair first said something to her, she said Blair had stayed the night, during the school year, sometime this spring. I asked her what Blair had told her, she stated that Blair told her "that some guy at the school where her mom works, wanted her to have sex with him, but she kept telling him no." I asked if she said anything else, Michelle said that Blair told her he grabbed her, I asked if she said where, she said she couldn't remember, I asked if Blair said who he was, she said a janitor at the school. I asked if she ever said his name, she said she thought Blair had told her Sean. I asked Michelle if she knew anything else about him, she said he was old, I asked how old, she said she wasn't sure, but he was married and had a kid. I asked Michelle if Blair told her where this happened, she said, "the school I think, but I'm not sure". I asked Michelle if Blair ever told her what

47

the man said to her, she said, she couldn't remember exactly but Blair told her he"sweet talked her", I asked her if she could remember anything else, Michelle stated that Blair asked her what she did when she was raped, she told her she went right to her mother and told her. Michelle then got upset and stopped talking about it, I asked Michelle if she thought Blair was telling the truth, Michelle said, "she would never lie to me, she has never lied to me that I know of its not in her hart". I told Michelle that Blair said they first talked about it in March, does that sound right, she said yes.

I asked Michelle if they ever talked about this again, she stated that Blair told her step-dad, who told her she had to tell her mom, and she talked to Blair before she told her mom. I asked Michelle what she said, she told her that she didn't want to tell anyone, because she didn't want his daughter to see him go to jail. Michelle states that she told Blair that she should tell her mom, because if he did that to her he could be doing it to other girls. Michelle states that Blair told her mom and they went to the police. I asked Michelle if she could remember anything else, she said no. Interview was concluded.

Police Report Complete

This investigator graduated from college to become a cop and he couldn't put together a proper sentence. The same was true of the grammar and spelling. I suppose Language Arts and English were not pre-requisites for becoming a cop.

*

48

My advice; do not talk to the police except through your lawyers. I simply stated *why*, *how* and *no* to the questions posed? That was still too much information. I offered more detail than I should have, but I had nothing to hide. Keep quiet, hire your attorney and then tell *them* your story in full. Do not get fooled into thinking the police are your friends or better yet, trying to "help" you. They couldn't care less about your situation. It doesn't matter who you are, what you do or who you know. (Unless you have lots of $$$) They say they're looking for the truth. I didn't believe that. I felt that they were looking for a conviction to enhance their own records.

*

I would like to clear up the "Tickle Fight" quote.

One day in the hallway of the school I pulled the plug on Blair's vacuum. I also did this to Carowitz, Sara Joan and Bonnie. Blair came out of the room, tickled me from behind and laughed.

I firmly asked her not to do that. "Blair, please don't tickle me, I can't stand being tickled."

She apologized.

I hated tickling, even by my own wife. When I was a young boy, my father would pin me down on the floor and relentlessly tickle me until I couldn't breathe. Since then, it drove me crazy and made me nervous.

The "tickle fight" quote belonged to Smart, but it was presented to look like *my* assessment. This was from the

White Lake PD report. It was amazing how every little detail was used against me. I wanted to make sure that point wasn't neglected. Incidentally, Smart offered the term "provocatively." I simply agreed with his choice of word. By no means did I ever use either of the terms during our talk on that sunny Friday in August.

> *"Whatever hysteria exists is inflamed by mystery, suspicion and secrecy. Hard and exact facts will cool it."*
> *-Elia Kazan*

Help Us!

I had been in contact with Doylan and Hearns, a legal firm in Farmington Hills, Michigan recommended by Fr. Patrick on the evening in question. I had no idea who they were. What I did know we had to move quickly and get the ball rolling so there would be ample time to mount an effective defense, if needed. I was to meet with Bert Doylan on Saturday morning about nine. He was right on time.

*

Bert was a short, round man with dark hair who struck me as looking unkempt when I first saw him. It was a little surprising that he was a lawyer, but I didn't know what a lawyer was supposed to look like. I did notice that his vanity license plate read "LAW HOUR," so I asked him about it.

"I run the Law Hour program on the radio every Sunday at 2:00," he said with aplomb, bordering on arrogance.

This gave me a touch of confidence right off the bat, so my comfort level improved. If you have a law program on the radio, you must be doing something right. To me, that's an impressive accomplishment.

*

Upon entering the building, Bert led me to a large glass room with a huge wooden conference table in the center. Feeling tiny at this giant table, we sat down, and I explained my situation to him.

"What's going to happen, Bert?" I nervously inquired.

"I'm not sure yet, you'll have to be patient and see if the state brings charges."

Neither one of us knew what, if any, charges would be filed against me. However, he did tell me that if it was Criminal Sexual Conduct in the third degree or higher, it would be a minimum fifteen years in prison if convicted.

"I'm not going to lie. You could go away for a long time, Sean."

Can you imagine receiving that kind of information? What a frightening prospect. I have never been in any kind of legal trouble in my life, and boom, you're rocked. My anxiety level went up a notch.

"Breathe; relax and breathe," I told myself. This helped me to calm down.

Bert did two things at this meeting. First, he asked a *substantial* retainer to use him as my lawyer and secondly, he called Mr. Smart and told him that he was to make no contact with me except through his firm. In all, it took fifteen minutes to complete our meeting. I was sent home and told to wait and see if any charges were to be brought against me.

He told me; "Go rent a good movie and relax."

It was easy for him to say. My very first experience with the system cost us around two thousand dollars ($$$$), and this was only the beginning. Money has a lot more to do with the justice system than I ever imagined. As the days went on and the fees mounted, my cynicism would reach all-time highs. What a way to learn.

"The only people who benefit from lawsuits are lawyers. I think we made a couple of them rich."
-Gavin Rossdale

Shaun Webb

54

It's All in The Details

The couple of weeks following my meeting were tough, but with each day, I felt better. I was off work now, so I could catch up on a few chores around the house. The only problem was, when I would get busy with something, such as cutting grass or painting, I would get obsessed with the accusations against me and become angry. Calming down wasn't easy, because I wanted to know why Blair accused me of such a shocking crime. I decided to start my own investigation into the falsehoods. I formed timelines as to when Blair and I would be working at the same time.

As I uncovered more facts, I bugged Nikki relentlessly about it. "Look at this, Nikki. Look at that Nikki. Can you believe all this stuff?"

I would tell her whenever I found the slightest discrepancy. It drove her up the wall, as she was both embarrassed and upset about the allegations, but she kept her patience and listened attentively. I found out a great deal by scratching away at the surface, unearthing startling data.

*

Out of the two years that Blair had worked at the school, our schedules crossed a grand total of thirty-three times. Out of these thirty-three, no were for more than an hour, and I ran into Blair approximately ten times. I went over this with Nikki. I continued driving her mad. It was ridiculously easy how I could sit by myself and uncover these details and statistics. I couldn't help but share the news with her.

Blair claimed that these "touching meetings" were between 4:45 p.m. and 5:15 p.m. My work schedule ran from 8 a.m. to 5 p.m. and I rarely, if ever, ran late. Many times, I came in thirty minutes or so early. The only time I would stay after hours was if there was an emergency repair needed or snow clean up. In either case, it left me far too busy to visit anyone, including my own wife, who worked five hundred feet from my office.

"Can you believe it, Nikki?" I was a pestilence.

Since I would go home at five p.m., I would have to check and alarm the parts of the building not in use. I would begin this sequence between 4:30 and 4:40 p.m. *every single day.* It took me between twenty and twenty-five minutes to finish the procedure, pick up my truck outside the garage, and pull to the front of the building so I could walk the secretaries out to their cars.

In the ten or so times I actually saw Blair, she would say hi, ask about my job, request supplies, or talk about her school. We were never close, only cordial. She knocked on the large garage door a couple of times if she was bored, but I was either on the phone or in a meeting with someone, so I wouldn't answer. My eyes would roll if I knew it was her. I told Blair that if she saw me around the facility, she was more than welcome to talk to me, but she was not to come to the garage unless she needed supplies or had an important work related message.

"Blair, I have a lot of work to do. I can't always drop what I'm doing if you want to talk."

I also let her know that any repair requests for the school were to be left in my school mailbox.

"I'm sorry, Sean, it's just so boring around here," she would whine.

There was a rare time when I would occupy my office for more than thirty minutes at a time. I had a great deal of work to do. I did keep the garage locked when I was both in it and away from it. If I did answer for anybody, it was by opening the extra-large front door, which faced the church building and parking lot on that side of the campus.

On three or four occasions, Blair and/or Bonnie would walk out to the garage and ask for supplies, which I kept stored in my office since the "stealing" incident in March. They would knock on the big front garage door and call my name to see if I was inside. If I heard Bonnie's voice, I figured it was a supplies need and not boredom on Blair's part. I would open the door *all the way*. I would receive their request and deliver the supplies to the school at a suitable time. This is when I believe Blair and/or Bonnie saw my collection of empty beer and pop cans that I gather from the grounds. They were in a large garbage can, and when full, I would return them for a refund. I had every right to collect and cash. There were no full containers.

*

On one particular day, I saw Blair outside sitting on the sidewalk. She appeared to be sad. I asked if she was okay. She decided that that was a good time to explain to me how she didn't get along with her father.

"I hate my dad, he's a jerk," she pouted.

Her face turned downward, as if the end of the world was imminent. I was polite, and I listened. Afterwards, I told her that not all of us sometimes got along with our parents but you just keep working on it.

I told her, "I don't always see eye to eye with my parents, and I'm thirty-eight years old." I then added," You'll get over it; it happens all the time. You're young and life is just starting. Don't get so worked up about the silly stuff."

She talked for a few more minutes about her relationship with her father, saying that she wanted to break off her relationship with him.

"Good grief," I thought with a sigh, "what a drama."

I told her that I was not a psychiatrist, just a maintenance man. "I'm not able to tell you anything different except to try and work it out."

I shrugged my shoulders, and then went on my way. The entire conversation lasted ten minutes. What else was there to say?

In retrospect, I should not have stopped to talk with her. I should've completely distanced myself. However, I'm a friendly person by nature. If I mislead someone into thinking I like them as more than friends, I apologize. It was not my intent. A sympathetic ear was not a sexual advance.

*

As I continued to put together stats and lists, I would have to laugh aloud at the lunacy of the whole situation. How could anyone come close to believing this trash? My step-dad, Warren, called me after looking over the police report and discounted her story on the spot. Warren often helped me with the fair and other jobs around the parish, and knew this not to be true. He was there often, and worked with me in the garage and other buildings like those that Danny did. He also mentioned that the police report contained too many strange or inconsistent occurrences and quotes. Moreover, he knew me, and if he thought for one second that I would pull something like that, there'd be hell to pay. He wouldn't hesitate to tell me I'd get whatever I deserved if I were messing around with *any* children.

All the fact-finding made me sad because I would never hurt anyone intentionally. I especially would not harm a child. It was both emotional and logical. I wasn't so ignorant as to put myself in jeopardy, and I'm not keen on going to any jails or prisons, thus sacrificing my family or job. My point was that I wasn't a pedophile. I didn't get any kind of a sexual charge out of children.

"People should be allowed to document evidence of criminal wrongdoing. Where is the expectation of privacy if someone is conspiring to commit crime?"
-Linda Tripp

59

Shaun Webb

60

The Statue Incident

Adding to all the lunacy that had already happened, we had an event that I called "the statue incident." This involves the toppling of the St. Paul statue situated in front of the church.

I was questioned on Friday, August 12th, and put on administrative leave that evening. Carowitz, Blair, Bonnie and Sara Joan also were informed that they would not be working at the school again until the matter was resolved.

On Monday, August 15th, Fr. Patrick called me and told me to come up to the church, because something bad had happened.

"We have a huge problem," he said briskly. "Get up here fast, Sean."

When I arrived, I couldn't believe my eyes. The St. Paul statue was lying across the church entrance/walkway with the head disconnected and sitting on the other side of the parking lot, about one hundred feet away from the body. I knew at that moment exactly what had happened. I couldn't prove it, but I'll say it anyway. The cleaning crew, most notably Carowitz, brought their truck to the facility at night, wrapped a large rigging strap around the statue, connected it to their truck and ripped the statue down off its pillars. I would've bet my LIFE on it.

61

"I believe that's exactly what happened here, Father. Those creepy people did this."

Father Patrick nodded to me. He didn't agree nor disagree. I found it extremely funny that this happened so soon after they were asked to stay away from the facility. Father had no choice but to call me in because the damaged stone needed to be moved. This statue stood fifteen feet high and weighed one thousand pounds. Father Patrick supervised me the entire time I was present.

Since the damaged statue had to be stored out of the way, I used the tractor and my own rigging straps to lift it out to the garage for investigative storage, and then I went back home. It took me thirty minutes to move it into the garage and leave the property. Fr. Patrick was devastated. He couldn't believe that someone could be that nasty. Our local news covered the event that evening. I watched on television and could see the hurt in Father's eyes as he talked about it.

"I can't believe someone or someone's could be so cruel," he declared.

It broke my heart too.

*

The White Lake Police Department looked it over, dusted it for prints and declared it "Property damage done by kids."

I would ask Smart about it later, but he blew it off as a kid's prank.

"C'mon Mike, you don't really think that, do you?" I asked. I also told him I wouldn't be surprised if the cleaning crew were behind it. For some reason, he didn't want to hear that.

"Drop the subject," he insisted, "there's no reason to talk about it any further."

I gave him a sarcastic laugh and before I walked away, I asked about my investigation.

"It's still in the works and that's all I'll say about it."

"Fine," I blurted. "I'm outta here."

Never before the allegations surfaced had that statue ever been touched. Since being repaired and placed in its spot, nothing further had happened. I felt as if Smart didn't want anything disrupting his "investigation" against me.

I mentioned this situation to my lawyer. He said without proof, it didn't matter. He couldn't do anything about it. It was up to the White Lake PD to check it out and decide if there was a reason to charge anyone with property defacement. The cleaning crew was never questioned.

"Your own soul is nourished when you are kind; it is destroyed when you are cruel."
-King Solomon

Shaun Webb

Charged

I continued to think; "could anyone ever believe any of this nonsense?" I figured that if the system worked, as I believed it did, truth would prevail and the nightmare would soon be finished. It wouldn't be a problem gaining acquittals on all charges, if any were filed. I was badly mistaken.

*

My next meeting with the Bert came on August 28th. I was contacted by Bert and told that "yes, I'd been charged." I was to meet with him NOW. I called Nikki at school, picked her up, and we headed to his office together.

Upon arriving, we met with Bert. We were introduced to his assistant, Michael Casper and told Michael would be doing all of the "behind the scenes" work while Bert would handle all of the courtroom appearances.

"Don't you two worry," Bert said, pointing at us, "Michael is a top notch attorney."

Little did I know how much responsibility Mr. Casper would be handed. Michael carried himself well, and he was from a family of lawyers, so litigation was branded into him from a young age. He kept a very neat, clean appearance and I never saw him without a freshly shaven face. He was in his early thirties and had a wife plus kids.

"Pleased to meet you, Sean," Michael said with an outstretched, welcoming hand. "I think I can really help you."

Understand that that was our first "legal experience" and we had no idea what to expect or how to move forward. That was what we paid these men to do, help get us through smoothly. We had to put our trust into someone, so why not this firm? Michael and I would work closely together.

Bert explained to Nikki and me the charges: Three counts of Criminal Sexual Conduct.

Count 1: CSC 3rd degree (victim 13-15) this count was for digital penetration (finger to vagina).

Count 2: CSC 4th degree (victim 13-15) this count was for hand to breast.

Count 3: CSC 4th degree (victim 13-15) this count for mouth to nipple (Breast).

"Count one was a felony punishable by up to fifteen years in prison and a five thousand dollar ($$$$) fine. Count two and three were high court misdemeanors (Low court felonies?) punishable by *no more* than two years in prison and a five hundred dollar ($$$) fine." Bert explained that to us with a straight face and a deep, resonating voice.

All told, I faced twenty years in prison if found guilty on all counts. The ice water that ran through my veins when I heard the numbers was nightmarish. It was like a bad dream from which you wish you'd awaken. My wife and I paid the firm another five grand ($$$$) and I was told to turn myself in

66

to the White Lake PD on the following Monday. Bert had two last words of advice for me. "Lose some weight and let your hair grow, Sean. How you appear is half the battle. Oh, and don't drink any alcohol either."

I chastised him for being overweight himself and complained about the hair issue. I was frustrated and needed to vent. My hair was already short, but it was too much so for his liking. Finally, after throwing my hands in the air, Nicki and I walked out stunned, silent and devastated.

"Squeeze human nature into the straitjacket of criminal justice and crime will appear."

-Karl Krause

Shaun Webb

(Cardiac) Arrest

On Monday, I took my second trip to the White Lake PD. I would be arrested and formally charged at the Clarkston 51st District Court. I had no idea how this worked or what to expect. I went in with a straight face and kept my mouth shut. One of my cop "buddy's," Lanny, who had often stopped by to talk to me at St. Paul, saw me at the door. I asked him what the hell was going on.

He shrugged his shoulders and said, "Sorry man, an accusation was made."

What a nice friend. He couldn't get away from me fast enough. He wanted nothing more to do with me. I wore a label now: A scarlet letter, guilty until proven innocent and a pedophile. I was quickly finding out whom my real friends were.

*

Mr. Smart met me. "Mornin' Sean, follow me." It was 8:30 as I was led to a room in the back of the police station.

Officer Dannon, the officer who took the complaint from the family, was my arresting officer. I was printed, photographed for mug shots and asked about distinguishing marks on my body. I felt humiliated and dirty from this

69

process. Dannon did these tasks with a half-smirk on his face. I told him about ten tattoos that I had on my body, but I didn't tell him about one in particular that I felt would vindicate me fully when used in court. After the booking, he placed me in a jail cell within the station and I sat there for about an hour. Around ten, Smart came in and took me from the cell. He handcuffed me in front of my body.

"I trust you Sean, that's why I'm cuffing you in front." He told me.

He placed me in the back of his unmarked police vehicle, which sat in a garage near the rear of the facility. The detective's next move scared me.

I saw Smart open what looked like a mailbox on the wall of the garage and pull out a rather large revolver. I felt hot and shaky. I knew he wasn't going to shoot me, but it clued me in to the seriousness of the situation.

"Why would someone need a gun to transport me to district court?" I nervously inquired. "I've never hurt a fly in my life and don't intend to now."

Smart tried to calm me. "It's procedure, I guess."

It also reeks of intimidation, effective intimidation. I believe scaring the pants off suspected felons was accepted police wide. Perhaps they can coerce a confession of some sort, or maybe it makes them feel better about themselves. Either way, I didn't have to look down the barrel of Smart's gun, but I was definitely looking down the barrel of many years in jail. It's frightening all the same.

We left White Lake PD and headed for district court in Clarkston, which was a mile or two from the station. On the trip, Smart offered me a smoke. I greedily accepted and smoked it down in three minutes flat, maybe less, because of the adrenaline flowing through my body.

He wanted to talk fantasy football.

"How about that kicker? I have him on my team."

I didn't give half a damn, "but fine," I thought, "anything to break the tension." The cheerleader in me reacted.

"Yeah, Mike, he's a real winner. You can't go wrong with him."

Smart offered me another smoke. I accepted and nodded my head in agreement when he spoke. I didn't really hear him; I only wanted to get this trip to the court finished. I didn't talk about the case at all, nor did he ask about it.

"Just because someone gets arrested doesn't mean what they are doing is wrong. Some laws are unfair and unjust.
-Tim Robbins

Shaun Webb

The Bearded Liar

After arriving at the courthouse, Smart led me into a cell, uncuffed my hands and told to have a seat inside. The large steel door slammed behind me, and I stood face to face with about ten seriously dirty looking men who were staring back at me. I was quivering on my insides, but had a seat, closed my eyes, tilted my head back against the brick wall and waited.

One of the men tried to talk to me, "Whatcha in for, dude?"

I wasn't in the mood for carrying on any conversations. Staying silent, I glanced at him, and then shut my eyes again. Those fellows acted as if it was another day in the park, laughing, talking but not making any sense at all. There was no concern or fear in their mannerisms. They were loud and obnoxious. I was scared and looked strangely out of place in their company. The steel door re-opened and ten more men, all in chains, walked in.

The arresting cop loudly barked his orders, "All of you face the wall and don't move."

We did as told while the men were released from their shackles. It was eerie listening to the clings and clangs of the chains as they were allowed to drop to the floor. Glares and stares were prevalent around the room. I continued to feel very uncomfortable. An hour later, the bail bondsman called me out of the cell. In that one hour of sitting, twenty more

73

men joined the crowd. The entire cell was wall-to-wall men. It was like a revolving door, but there was no exit, only an entry.

*

A man with a snow-white beard and bad breath took me to the side. He asked a series of questions.

"Do you drink or use drugs? Do you have kids? Where is your wife? Why are you here?"

He had such a mechanical way of inquiring. The only yes answer was to the drinking. I told him that I drank a beer or two when I would get home from work. I opened my mouth much too wide.

He asked, "When did you first drink beer?"

His nasty breath wafted straight in my face. The man was three or four inches away from me. It was like a drunk at the summer party that invaded your personal bubble of space. He definitely could've used a stick of gum.

"At age eighteen or nineteen, I guess," is how I answered.

"OK, come with me," he ordered.

This bearded man would be another in my growing list of people teaching me another lesson in "the legal systems" manipulation of the truth to fit their needs.

*

Smart recuffed me and led me into the Magistrate's area where my attorney, Bert was waiting for me. Mr. Smart, who was ever the more assiduous in this setting, placed me in a seat next to him.

"How ya doing, Sean?" Bert asked with a smile and an extended hand. "How's it going? Are you alright?"

My eyebrows furrowed tightly together and I spoke, "Oh just fine Bert, as you can see by the handcuffs on my wrists and the setting we're in."

Here's a piece of advice for defense attorneys; Don't ask your clients those questions when they're standing next to you in court wearing handcuffs. No, we are not doing well at all, and want to go home! It wasn't as if I was in a good mood.

I stood shaking my head and frowning. After thirty minutes, the Magistrate called us to the front. They didn't read the charges, per Bert's request. My rights were read, and I was asked how I pled.

"Not guilty," Bert said with an aura of invincibility as he was facing the back of the court while leaning on the lectern with his elbow.

Bert whispered to me to keep my eyes on the Magistrate, so I did.

The next question came; "Any request for Bond?"

This is when the man with the snow-white beard piped in; "Mr. West says that he has been drinking one or two beers a day since he was eighteen."

"That's not what I said to him," I thought. I was very angry, but this was another example of how the crooked wheel turns.

I looked at Bert and whispered, "It's not what I said Bert, he's not being truthful."

Bert told me not to worry about it, that it was par for the course.

"Par for what course?" I whispered, "it's plain dishonest."

"The state requests a $25,000 personal bond for the Defendant," the bearded liar said. "We also request random drug and alcohol testing for him until his trial."

What? Why random testing? I was no addict. I didn't even use drugs. I would find out that it would cost five bucks ($) every time you were called in to be tested, which was at least twice a week. What a wonderful way for the state to make a few extra dollars. Judging from the lines I would wait in, it was quite a lucrative operation.

"Granted" the Magistrate droned, "The Preliminary hearing will be set for one month from today."

*

After finishing with my plea in front of the Magistrate, Smart led me back out into the hallway. He uncuffed me once we entered the vestibule area and took me to a window to sign paperwork. This area was no different from the Secretary of State's office, or any other municipality that functioned as a business. Afterward, because I had a personal bond, I would be released under own recognizance.

There was one more meeting with the bearded liar to pick up my paperwork for the random testing.

"I'm saying something to him Bert."

"No you're not, Sean," was Bert's response. He added, "If you want more trouble, be my guest. He could take you right back into court for not following court ordered directions."

I was annoyed, but knew he was right. You must pick your battles carefully, and that wasn't the time.

Bert asked Det. Smart to take me back to my vehicle at White Lake PD. I told Bert I wanted him to take me, but he said he was too busy. It would turn out that Bert would be busy often.

*

Smart smoked with me and talked more football on the ride back. He allowed me to sit in the front seat, without cuffs! I told him his car needed work. It sounded like a u-joint was going bad.

Smart smiled at me. "We have the best mechanics in town, so don't you worry about it."

"Fine," I said indifferently. "If you wipe out, don't say I didn't tell you."

He rolled his eyes. If I were a cop, I would want my vehicle running in the best shape possible. You never know when your car will really let you down in a tight spot. Apparently, he didn't care. *Someday he would.*

Upon dropping me off at my truck, he said, "See you in a month for the preliminary hearing."

I nodded and went home. That's enough for today. I was feeling drained and at a loss for words. I told Nikki how the white bearded man lied through his teeth and that I had to go to alcohol and drug testing weekly. She was as surprised as I was. Our experience thus far was minimal and we had plenty to learn. We would learn it fast. I had to call a special phone number every day to see if I was up for testing. It turned out to be two, sometimes three times a week for me. ($10-$15).

"The world is not fair, and often fools, cowards, liars and the selfish hide in high places."
-Bryant H. McGill

Strength through Strategy

It was time to put together a defense and chase away the bogus accusations. I would tend to get assertive when I was building my case, because I figured it couldn't be contradicted since I was telling the truth. The way my father raised me, the liars and crooks that got theirs; but I knew there were some innocent people who did too. That knowledge gnawed at the pit of my stomach. So many blameless men and women incarcerated in this country. It could happen to anyone at any time.

*

A police officer reared me, so bad people busted and jailed were the beliefs taught during my formative years. My dad meant well, but he was tough on me when teaching his way of thinking. If he thought you were lying, you were. There were no questions and no chance to state your case. A number of times I *did* lie to him, but I learned quickly that my fabrications would not work. However, if you were telling the truth, it didn't matter if you swore to your God in Heaven. Once he made up his mind that was it. This caused me to become cynical about law enforcement before I even became a teen-ager.

"Don't lie to me son," he would bellow. "I know what you're thinking before you think it."

My dad was also the type of man that finished your sentences for you.

"Dad, can I go to-- "NO!" My mouth was still open, but I was unable to utter another word.

"Dad, what if--" "I'll kick your ass, that's what'll happen."

I suppose this was from thinking ahead of the crooks he would question. My brother reached a point where he would clam up mid-question and let Dad do all the talking, which he preferred because of his controlling attitude. It was an alpha male issue for sure. I argued more than my brother would, but I was louder and more obnoxious. I knew I'd lose the argument, and probably get decked, but my mouth would "runneth over." Yes, my dad the cop: A hometown Waterford cop, no less.

*

Putting all the phony statements together thrilled me. I was extinguishing the lies being told.

About two weeks after my visit to the district court, I met with my lawyer to begin mounting our defense. We had two weeks in which to work before the preliminary hearing, so I wanted to be prepped and ready to roll. I met with Michael in his office and he told right away that the next hearing meant nothing except to face my accuser and hear the story she had to tell.

"Don't get any false hopes, Sean." He told me, "It's just a formality so you can face your accuser."

80

I was taken aback because I thought you hit them with the truth during this hearing and naturally, your charges would be dismissed; and then we'd all live "happily ever after."
My biggest mistakes were in trusting the courts and I still hadn't learned. I needed further beatings so I would get the picture.

*

I told Michael about the statistics and information I had put together so far and all he said was "Could you prove these things?"

Well, in fact, I could. By calling the church alarm company and gathering all the data sheets between August and June, I was able to document every instance of when and who alarmed the school or church to the precise time by reading the codes on the sheet. I could also account for every door I alarmed to the *exact* time. This is how I was able to figure out exactly how many times I had in-common work time with my accuser.

It wasn't good enough for Michael. He wanted someone who could vouch that they had seen me every minute of every day. That wasn't possible. I worked alone. I would run across people from time to time, but not *all the time*. Besides, why was I the one who had to come up with all the "proof?" The accuser only had her word. She isn't even sure what months these "events" occurred.

"Why was that good enough?" I often asked myself. It appeared that anything said to the authorities that was illegal sexually would hang the blamed out to dry. It turned out that most of my investigative work I had done was for naught, according to Michael. The one good thing was that I had my friend, Danny. He would testify to the fact that I didn't drink or possess alcohol in the garage during working hours. In fact, he would testify that he never saw alcohol in my possession on the job *ever*. Only at night *during* the fall fair did I drink. Mind you, Danny and I were best friends off the work site, but that wouldn't influence his potential testimony. He would tell the truth first. There was no way would he put himself on the line to protect anyone, including me, by lying. The alcohol story enhanced their case against me.

Speaking of alcohol during the fair, I was unofficially off the clock at those times. I was having fun like everyone else, but kept it to a minimum in case an emergency arose. I never once overdid it or offered it to anyone. I would drink in the beer tent with the crowd. Gail reminded me to stay sharp in case of a problem. I did as she told me.

Michael liked that aspect of Danny's testimony; along with Mr. Smart's statement at the end of the police report that said, "Sean appeared to be truthful." As far as my own investigating went, I kept trying. Soon I would receive the victim's statement from the Pontiac Care House interviews and I would go from there.

*

One minute everything can be so promising, than the next minute, you're floored again. I couldn't keep taking this up and down emotional roller coaster. Before the accusation, my blood pressure was normal, (120/75). Since, it had risen (150/90). That was no fluke; that was stress.

"It takes two to speak the truth: one to speak, and another to hear."

-Henry David Thoreau

Nauseated

The days nervously passed and finally I received the Pontiac Care House statement. I was excited because I wanted a closer look at what we faced. Who knew it would be this farfetched? I sat in my truck, read it and then vomited out of my open vehicle door. My stomach was in knots and my head ached. I've been sick to my stomach before, many times in fact, but this was the worst. The empty gut, head whirling, anxiety-ridden sick was what I felt. I didn't care who saw me, I just wanted it to stop. My heart palpitated with each wretch and I felt like I was suffocating. This went on for a half hour, and then finally mellowed. Looking in the mirror, I saw a ghostly white face.

I couldn't believe what I was reading. The report included some of the information that was in the original police report, such as the drinking, offering alcohol and the inappropriate touching. Along with this was the fact that Blair told her mom's boyfriend Carowitz about these incidents while they were *alone at their house*. How creepy was a teen-ager talking about sex with Mom's boyfriend?

At the beginning, it reeked of a set-up. Now it could be even worse. Maybe Carowitz was the guilty party. Perhaps he should've been investigated closer merely because he admitted to talking with Blair in a sexual manner. Maybe the conversation NEVER EVEN HAPPENED! It also smacked of me unfortunately placed in a child's disturbing fantasy. I couldn't begin to digest all the information. My body language was that of pure disgust.

My mind continued its uncontrollable racing and figuring. First, I was convinced that I might be a scapegoat for some sick perversion going on at Blair's home, or in her head. Then my thinking would shift to the "getting even with Sean" theory. Could it be that I was onto something? It didn't matter, because no proof meant no dice, unless you're the "victim," so I had to shift my thinking. Nobody who mattered legally would go for any of my facts unless I was the young innocent female who had claimed horrible abuse. Then, it seems, everyone would listen. Changing gears might've been a good idea for me. Perhaps I should look at things from a different perspective. I continued to dissect the statement and I came up with more tidbits.

*

Carowitz claimed that the family cleaned the church and school. They only cleaned the school and had no business cleaning the church. Another custodial group within the same company handled that. Carowitz also stated that the family would clean on Wednesday, Thursday and Friday with Blair present. The cleaning crew never showed up on any Fridays and I had the alarm records to prove it. The group would clean on Wednesday, Thursday and *Sunday night*. Blair continually referred to Carowitz as her stepfather. Carowitz was Mom's boyfriend. Blair claimed that she would come out to the garage to see my truck, because she likes pick-up trucks. She said I parked my personal vehicle *in the garage.* The company snowplow truck was parked in the left-side bay and my office was on the right. A single door separated the bays. My truck, the one she was supposedly interested in, would not fit into my office space even if I wanted it to. There wasn't enough room. My pick-up was always outside, never inside. Anybody who came out to the garage would testify to that. More importantly, Danny would testify to that per his statement to White Lake PD, even though it didn't show up on the report. Smart must have conveniently forgotten it.

*

Michelle Rollin's statement that Blair told her I touched her breasts was simply hearsay. She didn't add much, I thought, but how do you disprove gossip if it's entered into court as evidence? Michael said her testimony was good for their side because those two were best friends. My friend Danny's testimony, however, would be less convincing because we were best friends. It was funny to me how a female seems to have all the advantages over a male in a sex abuse case. It felt like gender bias.

I was battling against words. Everybody's words on their side, especially Blair's, were considered evidence. Words supporting my character or schedules were considered irrelevant. I would now wait for the preliminary hearing to do more comparison and continue to prove that these allegations were made up. I didn't know what could or couldn't be used in trial. This was why I'd hired Bert.

*

    I was more than frustrated at being told "no, your ideas won't work," repeatedly. It felt as if the system was sucking me in and a conviction was the only goal of the state. The prosecutor didn't really believe this, did he?

    It didn't matter. To hell with the facts, and to hell with the actual proof. This girl said something happened, so it did. In the meantime, I continued my court mandated drug and alcohol testing with no trouble at all. I continued to pass every time at five bucks ($) per test.

    "Any time I got in emotional turmoil, I felt sick all the time, like at any minute I would die."
                                -Skeet Ulrich

The "Save the Word" Vigilantes

The Pontiac Care House. The "save the world vigilantes" was my name for them. They'd find the underlying cause of *anything*. There always seemed to be at least one person working in these types of facilities who carries interviews too far. Crime programs have videotaped footage that featured young children interviewed by an adult. It was revolting to watch and see how the interviewer would lead these kids into saying what they wanted to hear.

"It was your dad who did it, wasn't it?" they'd ask with a put-on, sympathetic tone. "You can tell me, it's okay, don't be afraid, you can trust me."

They badgered some of these kids for hours. The results were often confessions that weren't true. I've seen these kids bawling their eyes out over the questioning. The interviewers sometimes acted worse than the perpetrator they were trying to bring down. They'd say they were simply following appropriate procedures to find the truth. I had seen more than one of these interviewers sued, fired or brought up on charges themselves. They looked so surprised when that happened. "We are only trying to protect these children."

How? By badgering them into psychotic frenzies?

This went for police interrogators as well. They pound and pound relentlessly until you either submit or admit to something that may not be true, break down in tears, or both. Conviction, not finding the truth, seemed to be their motivation.

The *actual* Kid' Haven statement:

The Pontiac Care House Interview
Radison, Blair
Pre-Interview

Victim disclosed to Mom's long-term partner, David Carowitz while talking about sex.

Victim talking with Step-Dad about sex?

Carowitz works w/ cleaning crew that cleans school attached w/ the church.

Suspect cleans church.

Allegations occurred Dec 04-Jan 05.

Victim went w/Carowitz to work day occurred.

Victim disclosed 2 1/2- 3 weeks ago.

Victim talking to Step-Dad alone.

Victim said that there are 2-3 things that she has done that said she didn't want people to know.

One thing she would never tell.

David got her to tell-took 3 hrs.

Victim's behavior appeared to have changed since victim disclosed alleged abuse.

Victim can't sleep alone.

Victim doesn't want to be alone at all.

Victim said that suspect keeps alcohol out in service garage.

He drank in front of victim.

Victim says suspect drinks a lot.

Carowitz claims suspect smells like alcohol when he gets to work @ 3 P.M.

Carowitz never reported to suspects supervisors?

<u>Hypothesis</u>

Nothing happened

Wrong suspect

Accident

Compliant

Interview

Victim met suspect when she started working @ church.

One year after working there victim started to talk to suspect.

Suspect made comments about victim's breasts.

Suspect then started asking to touch victim's breasts.

Victim told no for few months?

Victim let suspect touch breasts.

Rub w/ hands.

Over time progressed to shirt up & touch breasts.

Progressed to bra off.

Suspect would lick and suck nipples.

Suspect rubbed vagina over clothes.

Progressed to rub over panties.

Progressed to touch vagina under panties.

Sometime outside & sometimes inside vagina.

Fingers in private?

Progressed- suspect took out penis.

Suspect made victim rub penis w/ her hand.

91

Suspect told victim not to tell because he could go to jail.

Suspect told victim he loved her.

Suspect told victim he would stop smoking if he could touch her.

Victim didn't want suspect to smoke.

Victim & suspect talk about life?

Victim tells suspect about things happening w/ Brother & Dad.

Suspect touched only on day's victim was stressed out.

No touching?

Suggest interview w/case worker.

Police present.

Different suspect?

Interview complete

*

The one vital part of the interview that had me asking many questions was on the second page where a hypothesis was written.

Allow me to define "hypothesis"; *It is defined as a proposition or set of propositions set forth as an explanation for the occurrence of some specified group of phenomena, either inserted merely as a provisional conjecture to guide investigation or accepted as highly probable in the light of established facts.*

The hypothesis said; 1. Nothing happened. 2. Wrong suspect. 3. Accident and 4. Compliant.

It is important to know that the Pontiac Care House interviewers were trained to conduct forensic interviews with children that can be used in trials.

The part of the hypothesis describing having the wrong suspect is obviously true. It didn't matter what I thought or suspected, however, because the state was going after me regardless of the truth. It was easy to shoot and kill a tiger when you have it trapped in a cage sitting in front of you. The task becomes much more difficult when you try to find an uncaged tiger on neutral ground.

Even though *I know* that this is made up, it can still be used in court. Blair's words were considered the evidence. I wondered if Michael or Bert would exploit this "hypothesis" during the trial. I suppose I'd have to wait and see. I researched hypothetical conclusions, and it would appear, through what I'd found, that serious doubt lingered within the interviewer's mind. This doesn't necessarily mean they were dismissing her allegations. I wanted to know for sure. I explained to Michael that this needed to be asked of Pontiac Care House during trial.

The "Nothing happened" statement refers to the interviewer expressing doubt as to validity of the interviewee. The interviewer appeared to be unsure about Blair's story. The "wrong suspect" statement refers to the interviewer's suspicion that someone else was being protected from detection. "Accident" refers to possibly coming out with the story "on accident." This happens when younger people develop crushes and tend to make up stories about the "fantasy" relationship. "Compliant" describes interviewee's willingness to come forward.

93

Another part of the report included Carowitz himself. He claimed to have smelled alcohol on me when he would see me around 3:00 P.M. I was getting aggravated at his involvement in the case. He was always getting his nose in the middle of it. Was there something to hide? I guess we'll never know. I personally thought so. Call it an intuition. Talking about subjects of a sexual nature with a fifteen year-old was creepy. Being so closely involved in the attempted prosecution? He was probably angry because I snitched to his company, and I was going to pay for that.

I took it a step further; did Carowitz ever report the smell of alcohol to anyone in the School? No. Did anyone else ever testify to smelling alcohol on me during work? No. Only Carowitz did, and that was months later. A point that bothered me a great deal was Blair saying I *loved* her in the report. "LOVE?" How dare her. To me, love was a very special and sacred word that was to be used *only* when you feel that deep, close feeling for somebody else. Be it a family member or spouse. I didn't flagrantly toss that word around. Shame on her for saying that in her statement. Obviously, it was there to enhance their case.

"A biblical false prophet was a servant of the devil attempting to lead people away from the truth.
-Walter Martin

94

Sick (sic)

On October 14th, after a two-week delay, it was time for the preliminary hearing. I re-emphasize that my lawyers told me that this hearing would not result in a dismissal unless Blair had an "epiphany" and admitted to all of her lies. It was very unlikely. If Blair turned tail now, it could result in me possible filing charges for slander. That's what the prosecution told her. It was a strategy to keep Blair on the task.

*

I arrived at the courthouse with my family: Nikki, my mom, my brother Scooter, sister-in-law Liza and my dad. We waited outside the courthouse next to our vehicles when we noticed ten parking spaces to the right, Blair, Sara Joan and Carowitz were waiting in their van. Blair was crying loudly.

"Listen to her cry," Liza giggled. "She can't handle this pressure."

Blair continued weeping and we heard her say that she did not want to do this. If I were lying the way she was, I wouldn't either. She wanted out, but had no idea how to do that. Her mom was desperately trying to calm her while Carowitz sat serenely in the driver's seat smoking a cigarette. I imagined Blair wanted to bury her head in the deepest hole she could find. In my opinion, Blair and Carowitz brought it up, so they could deal with it. If Blair was any kind of decent person, she would've gone into court and admitted that her story was made up, thus ending it.

I even told Michael to let the prosecution know that if she would do that, we would walk away without suing her and her family.

"We can't do that," Michael told me in a sharp tone. "It's not how this system works."

I'll tell you how the "system" works. You're accused and you're guilty; end of story. You spend all of your own time and money trying to defend yourself, even when you've done nothing wrong. Worse, Blair's family was not out one dime. The state took care of everything financial on their end. If they had to pay, we wouldn't have been here.

*

Blair's mom gave us a series of scowls after she spotted us, but we ignored it and kept to ourselves. We didn't want to rock the boat any further. We had to chuckle once or twice because she looked ridiculous. She marched back and forth across the parking lot to talk to other people, grunting, sneering and stomping her feet all the while. She was acting like an overgrown, spoiled child. She appeared to have lost quite a bit of weight. Maybe the stress was wearing her out.

A few minutes later, we formed a circle, held hands and prayed, my father leading us, making sure they had to walk by us while we did it. After finishing, we entered the building for the hearing. We were steadfast in our belief that justice may

yet prevail. It was time to show them that despite all the
commotion surrounding the accusations, we were not afraid.

*

Michael arrived, so we sat and talked for about an hour
until it was our turn in the courtroom. Michael was given the
chance to get to know my family better. During our
discussions, he told me that Judge Dorothy Taylor would try
our case in circuit court.

I found this odd. "Why assign a judge before we even
know 100% that it's going that far?" I asked.

He countered, "I don't make the rules, Sean and I've told
you over and over that this is going to trial."

It was going to trial because Blair said I touched her.
Maybe it would eventually sink in. I needed to understand
that there was no escape from this, as much as I'd hoped there
was. In the preliminary hearing, we faced my accuser and
listened. It was a chance to hear the story right from the girl's
own mouth. We would see how she handled herself under the
extreme pressure that I hoped she was feeling. If she wasn't
feeling the strain, then she was a lot better as a liar than I
thought. I knew I couldn't go through something like this if I
wasn't telling the truth. I would fall apart.

The state tries these crimes with absolute, unrelenting
vigor. You may have read newspapers in your town and
noticed this. Here in the US, more than one person had been
acquitted, or had cases dismissed due to overzealous
prosecutions. For example, the Duke Lacrosse team case in
North Carolina comes to mind. An over the top, incumbent

prosecutor looking for votes combined with a weak, fabricated story by a girl. The men were finally exonerated after public pressure forced the dropping of the charges. The prosecutor ended up disbarred and jailed because of his obsession with that case. The men involved will always be stigmatized and traumatized. It'll never be forgotten. It would never go away for me either, whether I was acquitted or not. I would get to carry this cross around for the rest of my life.

*

As we stood next to the courtroom doors in the lobby, Blair strode past us surrounded with people who included her family and the prosecution team, along with a support person. It reminded me of a celebrity shielded from the paparazzi. They were intentionally trying to hide her from us. Liza sneered at her through this mob with as much nastiness as she could muster. If this were high school, she would've given Blair a good butt kicking. Blair's mom was sneering back at us with equal enthusiasm. Carowitz, with a grin on his face, mysteriously hung low and distanced. Blair looked nervous and skeptical. She entered the court with her people, and then Michael and I followed. My wife and family sat in the lobby with a combination of tension and hope; hope that it would be over today. Not likely, but one can always pray for a miracle. My brother stood with a blank face. It's hard to tell what he was thinking. That might be his secret to life. I knew he was rooting for us quietly. My mom sat and stewed, wondering what she could do to make it better. God bless Mothers.

Meanwhile, my dad seemed more interested in whether he knew any cops or deputies from his police days. He cared; but in a cop-like way. Stoic and hardened was how I would describe it.

The District Judge, Kim Kelpert, entered the court and ordered the room cleared except for council and Blair's Pontiac Care House representative. There was another case going on, but they stepped aside so we could get this over. I was nervous yet hopeful. If Blair acted in the court as she had outside, she may well give up the charade.

It was annoying to me that Blair could have her support and I could not. They gave all the advantages to my accuser, regardless of whether they're truthful or not. This is how the wheel turned, whether I liked it or not.

Judge Kelpert asked the prosecution to call their first witness and Blair took the stand.

Here is the complete, as written statement given by Blair at the preliminary hearing. She looked at me once during the entire hearing to identify me. It's all she had the guts for.

*

The Preliminary Hearing Statement

Friday, October 14, case called at 10:45 A.M.

The Clerk: Your Honor, calling the case People of the State versus Sean Albert West; 221-04630 AC. Today's the time and date set for Preliminary Exam.

99

Mr. Gardner: Ronald Gardner appearing on behalf of the People.

Mr. Casper: Good morning, Your Honor, may it please this Honorable Court, Michael Casper appearing on behalf of the Defendant, Sean West.

Mr. Gardner: Your Honor, the people are prepared to go forward with the Preliminary Examination. I would indicate to the Court that the People have provided Defense Counsel with a copy of, to date, discovery, which is, Judge, a 27-page packet of police reports and witness statements. Any further discovery that we receive, we will certainly pass along to Defense Counsel.

Mr. Casper: In response, that is correct, you're Honor. I have received 27 pages of documents from the Prosecuting Attorney. It is my understanding that, at this time, there is no further discovery.

As an initial point, I know there is a request to close the courtroom. There are two individuals who I don't recognize right now in the courtroom.

Mr. Gardner: That's correct, Your Honor, I filed notice with Defense Counsel as well as this Court to close the courtroom as well as have a support person in for the victim, which is allowed pursuant to statute and I would ask the Court to grant my request.

Mr. Casper: Again, I have no objection to the support person. It is my understanding; I just want to make the record clear, the support person, Tammy. It's my understanding she's present in the courtroom now. I just want to make sure that there's not going to be any possibility or chance that she, Tammy, will be called as a witness in this matter in any future proceedings. If that's correct, the stipulation- - then I have no objection to her being in the courtroom.

Mr. Gardner: I- - I would stipulate to that in so far as it's- -that's- -there's no allegation that Tammy has provided- -has told the victim what to say. If she has, then, I believe, I would be entitled to call Tammy to defend that but, with regards to the case in general, no.

Mr. Casper: Then I have no objection then, Your Honor.

The Court: Alright, with that stipulation, the court will grant your request.

Mr. Gardner: Thank you, Your Honor.

The Court: This courtroom is closed. Thank you.

Mr. Gardner: Thank you. May I call my first witness?

The Court: Yes, you may.

Mr. Gardner: My witness- -People call Blair Radison to the stand.

The Clerk: Please raise your right hand. Do you solemnly swear the testimony you're about to give this Court will be the truth, the whole truth and nothing but the truth, so help you God?

Ms. Radison: Yes.

The Clerk: Thank you. Please have a seat and watch your step.

Blair Radison called by the people at 10:48 A.M. and sworn by the court testified:

DIRECT EXAMINATION

BY MR. GARDNER:

Q: Would you tell us what your name is?

A: Blair Radison.

Q: Okay, Blair, you're kind of soft spoken, so it's important that you keep your voice up so the Judge can hear you, alright, and you have to say yes or no because they're recording everything, alright?

A: Okay. Sorry about that.

Q: Blair, would you spell your last name for us?

A: R-A-D-I-S-O-N

Q: And your first name, you said, is it spelled with an E at the end?

A: No.

Q: Blair, how old are you?

A: Fifteen- - sixteen.

Q: Okay, what's your date of birth?

A: 4-10-89

Q: And what grade in school are you?

A: Tenth grade. I'm a sophomore.

Q: You know somebody by the name of Sean West?

A: Yes.

Q: How do you know Sean West?

A: I worked with him.

Q: Okay, and where did you work with him?

A: At St. Pauls

Q: Alright, what is St. Pauls?

A: St. Paul.

Q: Do you know what city or township it's in?

A: Oakland County, I don't know what city or township it's in.

Q: Alright, if you saw Mr. West again, would you recognize him?

A: Yes. I would.

Q: Okay, do you see him in court today?

A: Yes, he's right there. (witness nods head towards me)

Q: Okay, could you tell me what he's wearing?

A: He's wearing a blue jacket, blue pants, white tie and a white shirt.

Q: Okay, is he seated closet to me or farthest from me?

A: Furthest from you. Over there. (witness points in my direction)

Mr. Gardner: May the record reflect identification of the Defendant.

The Court: So reflected.

Mr. Casper: No objection Your Honor.

The Court: Thank you. Ms. Radison, I'm gonna (sic) ask- -I know you're very soft spoken, but you can kind of hear some noise back there and it's very important that I hear everything you say-

The Witness: Okay. Sorry.

The Court: So if you can try real hard to just try talking a little bit louder than you think you're talking so I can hear your answers, okay?

The Witness: Okay. Sorry.

Mr. Gardner: I can- -let me move this way. Are you still getting me here so we can face the Judge so that you can direct your voice at her?

The Witness: Okay.-Okay.

Mr. Gardner: Is it okay if I stand here, Your Honor?

The Court: Yes. You may.

Mr. Gardner: Alright, thank you. May I continue Your Honor.

The Court: Please do. Thank you.

BY MR. GARDNER:

Q: How do you know- -you said you worked with Mr. West.
In what way did you work with him?

A: I was a janitor and he was a maintenance man.

Q: Okay, you were employed as a janitor or were you helping
out as a janitor?

A: I was helping my step-dad.

Q: Okay, what's your step-dad's name?

A: David.

Q: What's his last name?

A: Carowitz.

Q: Could you spell that last name for us?

A: No, I can't. He's asked me to spell that a million times, I
can't.

Q: Alright. is it- -begins with a "c", begins with a "k"?

A: C.

The Court: How- -could you repeat that name again? I did
not hear that.

The Witness: Carowitz, David

The Court: David Carowitz?

The Witness: Carowitz.

The Court: Carowitz, thank you. Please continue.

BY MR. GARDNER:

Q: How many days a week did you work as- -with your step-
dad at- -at St.Pauls?

A: Three nights a week. Sometimes four.

Q: How old were you when you first started doing this?

A: I was thirteen.

Q: And what were your jobs when you first started doing that?

A: I was- -I vacuumed.

Q: And- -

Mr. Casper: I'm sorry, your honor, I didn't hear the last part--the last- -part, she said what?

The Witness: I vacuumed.

BY MR. GARDNER:

Q: You said you worked there for three years, is that right?

A: Uh-hmm.

Q: Is that a yes?

A: Yes. Sorry.

Q: Okay, what was your job at the end of that time?

A: I trashed.

Q: Okay, what does "trashed" mean?

A: Like I would go around and collect all the trash from all the classrooms and I would take it out to the dumpster.

Q: When you were there- -when you're with your step-dad, how long would you be there for; how many hours?

A: It's very hard to tell because it- -it depended how bad the school was; if they had a party that day or- -it just depended.

Q: Would you be there 'till (sic) midnight? Or after?

A: No, it- -

Q: Okay.

A: - - was from- -we could go at like four or so and then we'd leave around seven, seven-thirty.

Q: So you worked- -you started when you were 13 and you stopped working- -how old were you when you- -you stopped working there?

A: Fifteen.

Q: You encountered Mr. West there? Would you describe for the Judge, please, what your- -the- -the first year when you were working there, what was your encounters with him like?

A: I really didn't know him all that well and I wasn't really sure how I felt about him. I didn't know if I liked him or not. So we really didn't talk all that much. He'd stop in and say hi and I'd say hi and that was pretty much the end of that- -I didn't like his tattoos.

Q: Okay.

A: - -the first year.

Q: Alright, and then the next year when you were fourteen years old, did it change at all?

A: Yeah (sic).

Q: How?

A: He came in more and talked more about our lives and stuff like that and got to know each other a little more.

Q: Okay, at what point when you were working at St.Pauls, was there any physical contact with you when you were fourteen?

A: No.

Q: Did you work during the summers at St.Pauls?

A: No.

Q: When you came back, when you were fifteen, did you work there?

A: Yes.

Q: Was that the year you were doing the trashing?

A: Yes.

Q: What grade were you in when you were fifteen?

A: I was a freshman, I was in ninth grade.

Q: Did you see Mr. West again that summer- -or that year when you started to work at St.Pauls?

A: Yes.

Q: When you were done- - withdraw the question. When you were vacuuming, would that occupy your time the entire time that you were at St.Pauls?

A: No.

Q: When you were trashing, what would you do after you were done picking up the trash?

A: If I had homework, I would stay in the school and finish that or go out in my car and finish it or I would go out to the playground and either talk to the kids that were there, or listen to music

or read a book. It was boring.

Q: Okay, did there come a time when you stopped going out to the playground or went and spent time in another part of the school?

A: Yes.

Q: Okay, and what part of the school was that?

A: His garage office area.

Q: When you say "his garage," who are you talking about?

A: Sean.

Q: Did Sean have any vehicles?

A: Yes.

Q: What kind of vehicles did he have?

A: He had a pick-up truck. He parked it in the garage.

107

Q: Alright, and when you would go back in the garage- -do you remember what time of year it was that you started to go back into his garage?

A: Around wintertime when it was getting colder and we- -we don't stand outside.

Q: Okay, so when you say around wintertime, was that before or after Halloween?

A: After Halloween.

Q: Okay, before or after Thanksgiving?

A: Before.

Q: Okay, when you went back into the, you said it was sort of the garage maintenance area, is that right?

A: Yes.

Q: Okay, what did you guys do back there when you first started going back- -going back there in November?

A: We would just talk about our lives. I would tell him about my problems with my family and he would tell me about his problems with his family and we had some things in common with our dads and stuff like that.

Q: Alright, did there come a time when you did more than just talk?

A: Yes.

Q: Okay, was - -how long after the- -the initial part when you went in November, how long did that- -was that after that? Let me ask- -that was a horrible question, I'm sorry. You started to go into the garage, I think you said, at the beginning of November, is that correct?

A: Yes.

Q: Okay, how long after the beginning of November did the relationship change?

108

A: Probably within two or three weeks.

Q: Was that still before Thanksgiving or was it after Thanksgiving now?

A: Before.

Q: How did the relationship change; what changed about it?

A: He would ask me more personal questions, as if- -like he could- -if he could touch this or if he could touch that.

Q: When you say "if he could touch this", did he describe what "this" was?

A: Yes.

Q: What did he say, what was "this"?

A: If he could touch my boobs.

Q: Okay, did he- -and, when if he said he could touch "that" what was "that"?

A: My vagina.

Q: Okay, and did you- - when he said that to you, did you let him do that?

A: I let him touch my breasts, yes.

Q: Okay, the first time that he asked you that, did you do that?

A: No.

Q: Okay, how long after when he first asked you to- -did he ask you again?

A: Maybe a week later.

Q: Alright, when he touched- -you said that he asked to touch "that" and you agreed; where on your body did he touch you?

A: Just around my breasts with my clothes on.

Q: Okay, was it over your clothes?

A: Yes.

Q: Alright, how did his- -how were his hands acting? Were they still or were they moving around?

A: They were moving. Kind of a circular motion.

Q: And when he touched you on your body- -on your breasts, what part of your breasts did he touch; anywhere in particular?

A: No.

Q: Okay, did he touch your nipples?

A: Oh. Yes.

Q: How old were you at the time?

A: Fifteen.

Q: How old was the Defendant, if you know?

A: He was in his thirties, I'm not sure of the exact age.

Q: Okay, did you tell the Defendant how old you were?

A: I told him I was fifteen.

Q: Did it eventually change where he touched you on your chest in a different way?

A: Yes.

Q: How did it change?

A: He would put his mouth on my nipples. He would lick and suck them.

Q: Okay, was that over your clothes or under your clothes?

A: Under.

Q: Was that the same day he first touched your breasts?

A: No.

Q; Okay, how long after, after that did it- -did it change to where he put his mouth on your breast?

A: Maybe a month later, three- -three- -four weeks.

Q: So, if it were in November when it first started- -

Mr. Casper: I'm sorry- -I'm sorry, I didn't hear the last part, did she say a month later?

Mr. Gardner: Yes.

The Witness: Yes.

BY MR. GARDNER:

Q: And if it was a month after November, what month would that have been?

A: January- -

Q: Okay.

A: January.

Q: Alright, what- -when he put his mouth on your breast, were your clothes on or were they off?

A: They were on.

Q: Okay, what would your clothes be like when he'd put his mouth on your breast?

A: It would be pulled up around my shoulders.

Q: Alright, alright, and did you have anything under- -under your shirt?

A: No.

Q: Did you wear a bra?

A: Yes.

Q: Okay, what was your bra like when he was doing this?

A: It was undone.

Q: When he would put his mouth on your breast, what part of your breast would he touch?

A: My nipples and all around.

Q: Okay, so he went from the one time in November to second time in about January and between there- -

A: In between there- -

Q: Go ahead.

A: - -he did.

111

Q: How many times?

A: I don't know.

Q: Would it happen every time you went to the- -you went to the school to clean?

A: No.

Q: Alright, would it happen once a week, twice- -twice a week, once every two weeks?

A: At least once a week.

Q: And would he always only touch you over the top of your shirt?

A: No.

Q: Okay, how- -how did that change?

A: He asked me if he could remove my bra and touch me under- -underneath. Touch my nipples.

Q: Okay, so he would just go from touching over your shirt and he- -and he eventually worked through touching you with his hands on your breasts and nipples?

A: Uh-hmm.

Q: Is that a yes?

A: Yes. Sorry.

Q: After he- -he touched you, did he say anything about what he had done?

A: Not- -he just said that he liked it and that it was- -just that I was beautiful.

Q: Did he talk to you about not telling anyone?

A: Yes.

Q: What did he say?

A: He told me that if I'd ever told anyone, he would go to prison.

Q: Did he tell you that every time he did it?

A: Yes. I think so.

Q: Now were in January and he's- -he's putting his mouth (sic) on your breasts and nipples- -mouth on your breast and nipples, did that behavior- -how long did that continue for; how many months did that continue for?

A: I don't know, for about maybe two months.

Q: Okay, and did it- -did it eventually change where he started to touch you somewhere else?

A: Yes.

Q: Okay, where is that?

A: He would touch my vagina.

Q: I'm sorry you're gonna (sic) have to keep your voice up, I know it's tough. Where on your body did he touch you?

A: He would touch my vagina.

Q: Okay, was that over your clothes or under your clothes?

A: At first it was over my clothes.

Q: When- -do you remember what month it was when he first started to touch you- -you over your clothes?

A: No.

Q: Okay, the last time that- -that anything happened between you and him, what month was it?

A: April.

Q: And how many months do you think that he spent putting his hands on your vagina?

A: Maybe one or two.

Q: Okay.

Mr. Casper: Did she say one or two?

The Witness: Yes.

BY MR. GARDNER:

113

Q: Would he always touch you over your clothes?

A: No.

Q: How many times did he touch you in another manner on your vagina?

A: Four or five times maybe.

Q: Okay, so he touched you on your vagina four or five times?

A: Without the clothes, yes.

Q: Okay, and when he touched you without your clothes, were your- -were your pants up or were
they down?

A: They were up.

Q: Was your underwear up or was it down?

A: It was up.

Q: Okay, how was he able to touch you on your vagina if your pants and underwear were up?

A: My pants were unbuckled and he would just slip his hand in, through- -over- -under my
underwear.

Q: Okay, when he did that and he touched your vagina, did he touch the outside of your vagina or the inside?

A: Both. He rubbed my pubic hair and then stuck his hand down further.

Q: Okay, how many times did he touch inside your vagina?

A: Once. I think. I'm not sure.

Q: And what he did he use to touch the inside of your vagina?

A: His finger.

Q: When he touched you with his finger, how far inside of you did his finger go?

A: Not very far at all. I couldn't really tell.

Q: Okay, if you were- -describe it on your hand how far, if you can give the Judge an idea, how many- -how far down on your finger?

A: To- -

Q: Okay, where are you pointing to?

A: To his knuckle.

Q: Okay, is that the first knuckle on his finger or the second?

A: The first.

Q: Okay, thank you. When he had his finger in there, did it move or was it still?

A: It was still.

Q: And- -and when he did that, how did you react?

A: I was kind of scared.

Q: Okay.

A: And I was confused.

Q: So what did you do?

A: I told him that I didn't like it.

Q: Okay, did you do anything with your body to indicate that?

A: I backed away.

Q: Did- -was this- -this the last time that he touched you when he did this?

A: No.

Q: Where were you when these incidents happened?

A: In his garage office.

Q: Okay, at- -at what building?

A: At St. Paul.

Q: Every time at St. Paul?

A: Yes.

Q: When you were in there and- -in the garage, were there any doors to the garage?

A: Yes.

Q: Okay, when- -when he was doing these things, was- -was the garage doors open or were they closed?

A: Closed.

Q: And once again, when he would touch you on your vagina, would that happen every time you saw him or would it happen once a week, twice a week, once every two weeks?

A: It didn't happen every time. It was every now and again.

Q: Did you ever kiss him?

A: Yes.

Q: Where did you kiss him?

A: On his lips and on his penis once.

Q: Okay, you put your mouth on his penis? Is that a yes?

A: Yes.

Q: Okay, did- -when you kissed his penis, did his penis go inside of your mouth or did it stay outside?

A: It stayed outside. I kissed the side of it.

Q: Do you remember when that was, what month it was?

A: No.

Q: Was that the only time you saw his penis?

A: No. I saw his penis a few times.

Q: Was that the only time you touched his penis.

A: No.

Q: How many times did you touch his penis with your mouth?

A: Oh, once.

Q: Alright, and what part of your body touched his penis if your- -if your mouth only touched it once?

A: My hand.

Q: How many times do you think you touched his penis with your hand?

A: I don't know. A couple I guess.

Q: When you put your hand- -well, let me ask you this question; did you- -did you put his- -your hand on his penis or did he put your hand on his penis?

A: He put my hand on his penis. He forced me.

Q: Okay, was that over the clothes or under the clothes?

A: Both.

Q: Alright, the times when it was under the clothes, were his pants up or were they down.

A: They were up.

Q: Were they all the way up or were they pulled down partial?

A: They were pulled down partially.

Q: Okay, were they pulled down to the knees, thighs, how far down were they?

A: Thighs.

Q: And were his- -was his underwear off or was it down?

A: It was down.

Mr. Casper: I didn't hear the last answer.

The Witness: It was down.

Mr. Casper: The underwear was down?

BY MR. GARDNER:

Q: When he put your hand on his penis, what did you do?

A: Sometimes I'd go along with him and other times I would back away.

Q: Okay, when you said you went along with it, what does that mean?

A: I'd just, I didn't know what to do. I just stood there and let him do whatever he was gonna (sic) do with my hand 'cuz (sic) I had- -I had no control over my hand. I just- -rubbed his penis.

Q: Okay, who was controlling your hand?

A: Sean was.

Q: Okay, and what would he do with your hand?

A: Move it up and down on his penis.

Q: Okay, on what?

A: On his penis.

Q: Alright, did you ever see anything come out of his penis?

A: Yes.

Q: Okay, and what did it look like?

A: It was clear looking fluid. I think it was sperm.

Q: Okay. and what- -when you touched his penis, was it hard or soft?

A: I'm not sure. I think it was hard.

Q: When- -the first time you put your- -your hand or he put your hand on his penis, how long was that in relation to the first time he put his hand on your vagina?

A: Maybe a week later.

Q: Okay, so he put his hand on your vagina first and a week later put your hand on his penis?

A: Yes.

Q: Did he ever discuss his feelings for you?

A: Yes.

Q: Okay, did you ever discuss your feelings for him?

A: Yes,

Q: What did he say to you?

Mr. Casper: Objection, relevance, Your Honor.

Mr. Gardner: Your Honor, I need to show that these things were done for a sexual purpose and the fact that his feelings towards her certainly goes towards that.

The Court: Objection, overruled.

Mr. Gardner: Thank you, Your Honor.

BY MR. GARDNER:

Q: What did he say to you about his feelings for you?

A: He said that he was my friend and that he loved me and that I could trust him no matter what and he wouldn't do anything to hurt me. I think he wanted to be my boyfriend.

Q: Alright, did you have a crush on him?

A: Yes. He was cute.

Q: Did you like these things that he was doing to you?

A: Not all the time.

Q: Okay, sometimes you did?

A: Sometimes I did. It depended.

Q: If you didn't like what he was doing to you, why would you- -why'd you go back there?

A: 'cuz (sic) I was looking for love and I thought he was giving it to me. I wanted to be his girlfriend, I think.

Q: Alright, did you ever talk to him about his smoking?

A: Yes.

Q: Okay, what did he say to you about his smoking?

A: He said that he would quit if I would do some of the things I did for him.

Q: Did he ever have alcohol back there?

A: Yes.

Q: What kind of alcohol?

A: Beer.

119

Q: Okay, did you ever drink beer with him?

A: No.

Q: Did he ever offer you any beer?

A: No- -yes. I think so.

Q: Okay, how many times?

A: Just once.

Q: How do you feel about being here today?

A: Scared and nervous.

Q: Who was the first person you told about this?

A: My best friend, Michelle.

Q: Did you tell- -when did you tell her?

A: I told her in February or March.

Q: While it was still going on?

A: Yes.

Q: Who's the next person you told about this?

A: My step-dad. We were listening to music and sharing stories one night and I told him.

Q: Was that after it stopped happening or before it stopped?

A: No, it was after.

Q: So it was after April?

A: Yes.

Mr. Gardner: One moment, You're Honor.

BY MR. GARDNER:

Q: You said the doors were closed, were there any locks on those doors?

A: Yes.

Q: Okay, and when he closed the doors, were- -were the doors locked or were they unlocked?

A: They were locked.

Mr. Gardner: Nothing further.

The Court: Alright, any Cross- Examination?

Mr. Casper: Yes, You're Honor.

CROSS-EXAMINATION

BY MR. CASPER:

Q: Every time that you had contact with him, did that always occur inside of his garage office?

A: Um, what do you mean like- -inside?

Q: Physically, like did it happen- -did it ever happen outside the garage or- -

A: No.

Q: - -in his truck- -

A: No.

Q: - - or in the school, or was it always inside the garage office?

A: It was always inside the garage office.

Q: And when you would go to the garage, approximately how long did you stay there with him in the garage?

A: About ten to twenty minutes.

Q: Ten or- -did you ever stay longer than ten or twenty minutes or was it always about ten or twenty minutes?

A: It was always, pretty much, about ten or twenty minutes.

Q: Would it always be around the same time of the day?

A: Yes.

Q: And what time was it?

A: Around 4:40 p.m.

Q: In the afternoon?

A: Yes.

Q: You- -you testified earlier that you worked with him; was he your supervisor?

A: No.

Q: Did he have any type of control over you in terms of did he ever tell you to do certain things like you have to clean this room or you have to clean that room?

A: No.

Q: Were you employed by St. Paul- -St.Pauls, the school?

A: No.

Q: Did they ever issue you a paycheck or pay you any funds directly?

A: No.

Q: And in your last year, is the only duties you had there was collecting trash?

A: Yes.

Q: You said you- -you guys would talk about- -you had things in common with your- -both your dads; what was the thing you had in common with both your dads?

A: That, pretty much, that his was a- -his dad was a jerk to him when he was a kid and he finally gave up on him and that I was getting to the point where I was giving up on my dad because he was a jerk to me.

Q: And you said that, at least some of the time, that you guys had physical contact, that you consented to that; that you were okay with that, is that correct?

A: Yes.

Q: And you said when he took your hand, he was controlling your hand and your hand went limp, I believe; did he do something that prevented you from pulling your hand back?

A: He held onto it. It was frozen.

Q: So did he have such a tight grip that you were incapable of pulling it back?

A: I probably could of (sic) pulled it back but I didn't.

Q: When you were placing his hand on your penis or he was touching your (sic) vagina, were you, also at the same time, kissing each other?

A: No.

Q: Were you doing anything like talking to each other, or what were you doing when you had the other type of contact other than kissing?

A: We were just talking.

Q: You said he pulled his pants down to his thighs, if I was to display right now- -if my pants were down to, say, approximately here, right- -just above the knee, is that how far down his pants would go?

A: Yes.

Q: And then his underwear would go down that far?

A: I guess so.

Q: And you said the first person you told about this was Michelle in February or March of 2005, is that correct?

A: Yes.

Q: And the second person you told was Mr. Carowitz in- - after this was all over in April of 2005, is that correct?

A: I didn't tell him in April but I- -I told him aft- -after it was all over, yes.

Q: Do you remember when you told him?

A: The end of July.

Q: And he's your step-father, is that correct?

A: Yes.

Q: Do you know how long he's been married to your mom for?

A: They're not married. I consider him my father because he is a father figure to me. They are not married but have been together three years. I trust him a lot. I consider him my father figure.

Q: But they- -they've never gotten legally married, is that correct?

A: Yes.

Q: So you call him your step-dad but he's not legally your step-dad, is that correct?

A: Yes. but he's like a dad to me.

Mr. Casper: Can I have a moment Your Honor? (Michael looks over my notes)

The Court: Yes, you may.

BY MR. CASPER:

Q: When you had the interview in August at Pontiac Care House, do you remember that?

A: Yes.

Q: Did you take any notes during that interview?

A: No.

Q: Did you see anyone else taking notes during the interview?

A: Yes.

Q: Who did you see taking notes?

A: Um, the lady that was talking to me, I do not know- -

Q: Ginny (sic)?

A: I do not remember her name.

Q: You don't remember? Haley (sic) maybe?

A: I'm not- -I'm not sure. I don't know.

Q: You can't remember? Was there only one person you saw taking notes when you were talking?

A: Yes.

Q: Who was in the room with you at the time?

A: Just one lady- -the Pontiac Care House, I don't remember.

Q: One lady was in the room with you and she was the one who's taking notes?

A: Yes.

Q: Do you have any idea if they videotaped or audio taped that- -your interview; if you know?

A: They might have, I'm not sure.

Q: Did anyone tell you that they videotaped it or audio taped it or no?

A: She said that there were people watching us through the- -through the mirrors but I could not
see them and I don't know if they were or not.

Q: And you didn't see like a video camera or something?

A: No.

Q: You didn't see like a little tape recorder- -

A: No. nothing like that.

Q: - -or anything that would give you a reason to believe that? Other than Michelle and your step-father, did you tell anyone else about this?

A: I ended up telling my mom.

Q: Anyone else you tell?

A: No, she- -my mom told my dad about it- -my real dad.

Q: So the only people you've talked to about this was Michelle, your mom's boyfriend, and your mom, is that correct?

A: Yes.

Q: You haven't told anyone else about this?

A: Not- -not anyone else who's here, no.

Q: I'm sorry?

A: Not anyone else who's here; no one knows anything about it, they just know I'm in court for something.

Q: But you- -just to clarify because maybe I- -Michelle, your mom's boyfriend, and your mom

are the only people you told about what happened with this, is that correct?

A: Yes.

Q: And the- -the last question, you talked about how you think his finger went inside, are you 100% sure that it went inside or did it maybe stay on the outside of your vagina?

A: No, I think it went inside.

Q: And you said it was inside as far as his first knuckle, is that correct?

A: I think so. I really couldn't tell.

Q: And that happened on one occasion, is that correct?

A: Yes.

Mr. Casper: I have no further questions, Your Honor.

The Court: Alright, thank you. Any Redirect?

Mr. Gardner: Just very briefly, You're Honor.

REDIRECT EXAMINATION

BY MR. GARDNER:

Q: You- -you also told the woman at Pontiac Care House what happened to, didn't you?

A: Oh, yes.

Q: Okay, and you talked to me about what happened also, correct?

A: Yes.

Q: Okay.

Mr. Gardner: Nothing further.

The Court: Alright, Blair, I have just a couple simple questions. You- -you kept talking about working at St. Paul's and I just wanted to make sure were talking about the same pla- -the same place. Is that St. Paul Church and/or School?

The Witness: Yes.

The Court: Alright, is that right across the street from a senior center which is a- -which is a home for- -our senior citizen center, it's a white building?

The Witness: Yes, there is a white building, I'm not sure.

The Court: Would that be White Lake Township, do you know?

The Witness: I'm not sure.

The Court: You don't know for sure, but it is St. Paul school and church.

The Witness: Yes.

The Court: - -is that correct? I just want to make sure were talking about the same place.

Mr. Gardner: One moment, please.

You're Honor, Defense Counsel will stipulate to venue and I appreciate that for the purpose of preliminary examination only that St.Pauls is in White Lake Township.

The Court: Great, thank you.

Mr. Casper: Stipulate, Your honor.

The Court: Alright, thank you.

Mr. Gardner: I have no further questions. I don't know if defense Counsel has any other questions?

Mr. Casper: Yes, very, very briefly.

RECROSS-EXAMINATION

BY MR. CASPER:

Q: So in response to opposing counsels- -you also talked with him about this and the woman from Pontiac Care House, is that all- -is that the only people you've about this, no other friends or family members?

A: Yes. No, Yes.

Q: Yes, you've told the- -like- -

A: No, I haven't told anybody else?

Q: The only friend you've told this about- -

A: Is Michelle.

Q: Is Michelle, and the only family members you've talked to this about is your mother, your mother's boyfriend who you consider your step-father and that's it, is that correct?

A: Yes.

The Court: Alright, thank you. Blair, you may step down. Watch your step on your way down because I've had people trip. Thank you.

(At 11:19 A.M. the witness was excused)

Mr. Gardner: Your honor, that would conclude the witnesses that the People have for this hearing.

The Court: Alright. Defense, any witnesses? Any witnesses?

Mr. Casper: No witnesses, Your honor.

The Court: Alright, closing arguments?

Mr. Gardner: Your Honor, I believe that the testimony as provided by Blair establishes to a preponderance of the- -I'm sorry, a probable cause level that the acts of Count I, Count II and Count III were committed on her between October and April in the Township of White Lake.

The Court: Alright, thank you. Defense?

Mr. Casper: Your honor, specifically the count CSC 3, I'll respectfully submit and request this Honorable Court to dismiss that charge. I don't believe they've met the burden on the CSC 3 count. Blair indicates that she "thinks" his finger went inside of her vagina, but she's not really sure. No further comment on the other charges, Your honor.

Mr. Gardner: The- -the testimony was very clear from her that his- -his finger went inside of her vagina and I think that that is sufficient to bind the matter over.

The Court: Alright, thank you. The Court has had an opportunity to hear the testimony in this matter and the evidence presented. The Court does note this is a probable cause hearing. The Court is satisfied that the Prosecution has met it's burden by probable cause based upon the evidence presented today as to each- -as to Count I. Counts II and Counts III. Therefore, the Court will bind this matter over as to all three counts.

Mr. Gardner: Thank you, Your honor.

The Court: Anything regarding bond?

Mr. Casper: Your Honor, we would just request bond be continued.

Mr. Gardner: Nothing from the People.

The Court: Bond is continued.

Mr. Gardner: Thank you, your honor.

The Court: Thank you. You should be able to get that bind over information at the front desk.

Mr. Gardner: Thank you. Have a good weekend, Your Honor.

The Court: Thank you.

(At 11:31 A.M., the matter was concluded)

*

In less than thirty minutes, it was laid out for us to see and hear. My inquisitiveness was piqued and I couldn't wait to get a copy of the hearing to compare to the police report and Pontiac Care House statements. Timelines, consistency and whatever else I could exploit were my goals. So far, I'd had no trouble finding her "brain lapses." This girl couldn't tell the truth if her life was on the line. I would take great joy in turning Blair into nothing more than the sniveling, lying, spoiled child that she was.

*

Judge Kelpert wasn't thinking about dismissing any charges whatsoever. She shifted the responsibility. It was going to trial on all counts, a trial that, in my eyes, I had a good chance of winning. I continued to believe that justice would prevail, despite what I'd learned thus far.

I was disappointed that she allowed the 3rd degree, felony "finger to vagina" count to stand. Blair was very apprehensive about that point. She continuously stated that she really couldn't tell if a finger "entered" her vagina. I'm not a female, but it would seem to me that you would be able to tell if someone's finger was in your vagina. I would like to know, out of curiosity, what exactly warrants a "finger in vagina" charge in the first place. Is it the action of the touch of the vaginal area? At what point does your finger "enter?" Along those lines, if you touch a woman's breast, but don't touch the nipple, is it still illegal? The same question applies to using the mouth. If you lick or kiss the breast but not the nipple, is it the same as licking or kissing someone's hand, foot or elbow? Blair stated that she kissed my penis, but no other charges were brought against me. If she said she had put it in her mouth, would it then have been considered illegal and warranted further charges?

All good questions in my book.

*

Exiting into the lobby, I met my family. I told Nikki that I was extremely confident in the fact that Blair had hurt her case.

"I really think we have a good chance," I told her. "She can't keep anything straight."

Nikki seemed happy about this news.

"I know we'll be okay," she said.

Liza, in the meantime, was showing her utmost concern while at the same time looking for Blair so she could toss another nasty glare her way.

Scooter clapped me on the back, "It'll be okay," he quietly told me.

My dad was speaking with some of the deputies he had met. No surprise there, as he seemed more concerned with the police uniform then he was about the case at hand.

"C'mon Dad," I urged. "Let's go home now."

Another matter of point that concerned me; was Gardner sucking up to the judge? It sure seemed like it. My lawyer seemed to be doing just that. Your chances for winning in trial are definitely related to who can put on the best show, land the hardest punches or have the most convincing performance. It's not a great deal different from competing in a boxing match for the World's Championship. Gardner vs. Casper is what it was blossoming into, and I was the stakes. We should have had a weigh-in before the trial started.

My views? I found Gardner to be stuttery and shaky in his questioning. He repeated himself quite often, as his inquiries always seemed to start with okay or all right.

"Okay, umm, alright, let's see, okay."

I was having little trouble sizing him up.

Mr. Casper, on the other hand, *seemed* confident. He told me it would be tough to convince all twelve jurors that this occurred. He also told me not to talk to the press. I was to steer them his way if there were questions. Why? So he could look like a hero and stick up for me? At forty bucks ($$) an hour, it had better be the latter.

Please keep an open mind and let me have my day in court.

-Michael Jackson

132

No Consistency

The case would not reach trial until December, so I had a couple of months to work. Clarity and consistency were the ties that bound all of my points together. I had to spend all my time looking for "proof" that these actions *did not* occur. I had a truckload of good information to refute Blair's claims. All I could do was present them to Michael for final judgment on their worth. I knew how that would probably turn out.

I knew what he would say before he said it.

"Sean, I don't know. We don't want to take any dumb chances. Trust me; I have your back. We'd better not."

Blair had that bothersome habit of referring to Carowitz as her stepfather. Michael successfully cleared that up in court. He asked her under oath if Carowitz was, in fact, her stepfather.

She said "yes." The answer was "YES."

He then asked "So he and your mom are married legally?"

Blair backtracked, "He's not really my stepdad but I think of him as such." The answer now was "NO."

This may not seem like much, but every non-truth was vital when approaching that type of delicate situation. It showed that someone couldn't be trusted with even the smallest detail. It also bodes better for the prosecution if he was a "Father" rather than "Mom's Boyfriend." It was a trick to show family unity. If Carowitz is a "Step-Dad," it somehow justified in their minds her talking about subjects of a sexual nature with him. Blair didn't trust her mom, was fooling around with Carowitz or someone else, or, sat down with both to assist in making this story up. If, for some reason, Blair did not want Mom to know, then I would think that she was fooling around with Carowitz. If it was I she was messing around with, why try to hide it from Mom? My final conclusion continued to be that it was revenge for snitching Carowitz out on the stealing issue. What better way to get rid of someone than to say I was molesting their daughter, especially working in a Catholic Church and school.

I could almost hear their conversation in my mind.

"What can we do to teach that Sean a lesson?" Carowitz would scheme.

"I know!" Says Sara Joan. "Let's screw his whole world by saying he molested Blair. What do you think, Blair?"

"Definitely," Blair would say. "I always thought he was strange anyway."

Thus a scam of the worst proportions is born. Even if I were right about this theory, it would take the family months to work up the courage to go through with it. I was sure a lot of planning, rehearsing and detailing goes into something so contrived.

*

Blair mentioned early on that we would meet up and "talk about our lives." If "how are you," and exchanging pleasantries was talking about our "lives," than I had a lot to learn. The only subject that slightly broached "life" talk was the short conversation we had about her biological father. I thought I had defused that rather quickly.

Asking about school, music and sports constitutes courtesy talk; being nice even if you were not overly concerned. I chatted with kids from kindergarten to eighth grade at the school; not to be personal, but to be polite and build a link. When the kids liked you, it significantly lowered the chances of having to clean up huge messes during the year. Cleaning peanut butter or spit wads off the restroom ceilings were not exactly my idea of "efficient" work. Pulling rubber balls or whatever other objects out of the toilet were not what I referred to as "fun" jobs. The worst, however, had to be cleaning up urine or feces that were deposited *outside the bowl.*

My technique also helped me because kids would rat each other out if I asked for names. It may sound mean, but it was simply to help my job run smoothly. I cared about these kids. In the nine years I worked at St. Paul, I never had one problem or complaint from the kids or parents. In fact, some parents complimented me on helping their kids build confidence. Often, I would use boys from the Catholic high school to do community service around the church. I was able to help them develop some responsibility and work ethic. This, I hoped, would help at trial. These same kids were 100% behind me, as were their parents. They were willing to testify as to my character and personal ethic.

*

If you read the reports carefully, you will see that Blair stated in the pre-lim that the "request for, and touching," started before Thanksgiving. She said two or three weeks after the beginning of November. In the police statement she said it was a little before Christmas. Why was it so difficult for her to keep timelines straight if the abuse really happened? It was as plain as day to me. Because she didn't tell the truth, she couldn't keep the facts in order, yet I must prove my behavior beyond a reasonable doubt. I scratched my head and exhaled sighs of air as I continued my investigation. I was stubborn though, which came in handy in these instances. Obsessiveness was an ally for me when studying the facts.

Next, we have the shirt issue. In the pre-lim, she stated that her shirt was *pulled up around her shoulders*, and her bra was "undone". In the police report, she said I *removed* her shirt after begging her to remove it. The Pontiac Care House reports say's shirt up, *bra off*. We had three different versions there, all from the same girl. You couldn't tell me that you don't remember or know in what position your shirt was during intimate moments. If you are being friendly with your significant other, you knew if your pants were off, down to your ankles, or below your waist. They were either up, down or off. The same went with your bra: Off, partly off, or on? You must know. Wouldn't somebody feel a rush of air on their naked torso? I know I would.

Moving on, Blair stated in court that the touching went on from the first time in November to a time in January and "In between." This put us from *Thanksgiving until after the New Year*. We had no in-common work time from 12-17 thru 1-3. In the police report, she stated that the touching advanced to

136

nipple licking *and* my hands underneath her clothes *"A little before Christmas."* How long was a little before Christmas? The Pontiac Care House report simply reads, *"Progressed."* Which means what? I assume it means progressed to happening. I had no way of knowing for sure, because I couldn't read people's minds. The Pontiac Care House notes differ dramatically from the police report version of the *same interview*. My point was that she couldn't seem to pinpoint times or occurrences. It sounded very cut and dried to me. Why was it not to them? Court documents show that Blair mentioned the touching under the shirt happened for the first time *after the New Year*. The police report says *a little before Christmas*. Again, it was like beating a dead horse. The stories changed repeatedly. I suppose they needed a little more time to rehearse their side because Blair kept messing it up.

Let's continue on to the "alleged" touching of her vagina. Pre-Lim hearing: The vaginal touching *occurred/started in March*. Police report: *End of January or beginning of February*. Notice in the Pre-Lim that Blair said the vaginal touching began two months after the breast touching, but a mere nine lines later, could not say what month it was. She goes on to say that the intimacy ended in *April*, but that I had spent one or two months touching her vagina. Now we are back to *February or March*. That was still not the end of January or beginning of February. The more I read, the angrier I became.

Don't try to tell me that the shock of it all makes you forget. If you truly like someone, as Blair said she did about me, you know exactly when, where, what and by whom. I remembered my first experience, which was *twenty-five years* earlier. You don't forget those things. They stay with you all your life.

Pre-lim report: She stated that I touched her vagina without clothes *four or five times*. The police report said *Twice*. The pre-lim said finger inside vagina *once*. Police report? *Twice*. She also stated during the court hearing that my finger entered to the first knuckle, then stayed *still*. In the Pontiac Care House report, I *rubbed* around when entering. Reviewing the conflicting allegations was revolting and very hard to stomach.

We do have one more issue to discuss regarding the allegations against me. This would be my alleged forcing of her to touch my penis.

During the preliminary exam, Blair said she I forced her to put her hand on my penis. When questioned by Gardner, she stated that I pulled my pants and underwear down to my *thighs*. In the police report, she stated that my pants were down *"a little."* On Michael's cross, she agreed that my pants were *below my thighs*. When Michael demonstrated to her in court, he put his hand down to the top of his knee. She agreed with him. She also testified to kissing my penis. That was the first such testimony of that kind. I hadn't heard one word about that until the pre-lim.

In her closing remarks with the prosecutor, Blair claimed I told her I loved her and would quit smoking if I could touch her. One time during the school year while passing by her in the hallway, she must have smelled cigarettes on me and asked me if I smoked. At first, I thought she was going to ask me for a cigarette. I said yes and she told me I should quit. I told her to mind her business.

"That's not your issue, Blair," was what I said with a frown. I continued down the hall without looking back.

I wasn't happy that she felt the urge to tell me what I needed to do. Blair didn't even know me. During testimony, she mentioned the alcohol, which would turn out to be a zero issue in Circuit Court because of Danny. When Michael crossed, he wasn't going to give away our defense strategies. All in all, I think it was effective questioning and pulled out many of the irregularities I was sure were going to be there. Although I was feeling more comfortable, I knew deep down that a jury could still throw me in prison. I tried very hard not to think in those terms because it did much more harm than good.

"When a man's knowledge is not in order, the more of it he has, the greater will be his confusion."
-Herbert Spencer

Shaun Webb

Patience really is a Virtue

Do you know that feeling you get when you screech on the brakes to avoid a huge car wreck? That was the feeling I kept getting whenever I thought about the case, which was twenty-three and a half hours a day. The pressure included tension, nervousness, nausea, heart palpitations, and difficulty concentrating and breathing. The underlying fear ate away at my insides. It was like a worm tunneling through my soul.

*

I continued my studies into the case and went over it a thousand times before trial. There wasn't much to add because there was nothing more to refute. There had been no written communication between us, no phone calls, no fingerprints found in the garage, and no internet connections. It was the state's responsibility to prove their case. I had to continue going over everything with Michael and try to trust him. The opportunity to argue my side would come in court.

I kept wishing this nightmare would go away. I didn't want to deal with it for another second. Depression was creeping in. Sleep seemed to be the only time I could escape. When I was awake, the hauntings continued.

Staying busy was important for my mental health. Having too much time on my hands would be counterproductive. I had worked all of my life, so I was accustomed to a routine. Wake up every day around four in the morning, drink my coffee, read the paper, go to my job, do my work and come home. I was, up until now, leading a very quiet life, but now it became altered. I needed to fill my time with positives so I decided that all the unfinished repairs around the house would merit my attention.

*

There was a short period of calm after the initial accusation. As I considered the lack of evidence and all the contradicting statements, I hoped justice would prevail and my name be cleared. It was only a short time before the trial, so I stayed as busy and involved as I could. It was a good thing, because doing the chores distracted me from my "too much thinking" routine. I painted, repaired, cleaned, laundered, painted some more, cleaned some more etc. To my mounting frustration, it only distracted me minimally.

Despite my best efforts, my thoughts continued to run through every moment, every action and every word, searching for the "whys," and "what ifs." Why are these people lying about me, and what if a jury believed them? That was too much to imagine. I seriously wished it would stop.

*

In retrospect, I may have been doing some nesting for my wife. I didn't think for one second that this would be an open and shut case. The realization of going to prison for a very long time was nerve-wracking. This made me think about my daughter, who was ten at the time. Perhaps I wouldn't see her go through her teens, find and lose boyfriends, graduate high school, go to college, get married and have a family of her own. Twenty or so years in prison would put her at thirty-plus years old upon my release, causing me to miss much, if not all, of those wonderful things she would experience in life. Thinking that way only accomplished making me angrier. The stress was intense, but I had to keep my wits about me. My daughter was a good girl. The situation would leave a scar, though. She can deny it all she wants, but the effects are long lasting and painful. Imagine your father going through a sexual misconduct case. How would that make you feel as a son or daughter? I would be heartbroken and angry. I believed she was. Paying attention to her was very important. We did as much as we could together before the trial. I never went into detail with her, but I think she knew. Her mom had heard about it earlier through the Child Protection Agency before I even had a chance to mention it. I was sure she had at least talked about it with our daughter. Surprisingly, I was wrong. My ex-wife didn't want to upset our child, so she kept it quiet, which was fine. We'd wait and see if I was found guilty before talking with her. My next task was to explain to the ex-wife what was going on. After talking about everything with her and fielding her questions, she seemed content that I was *not* guilty. She had been married to me for five years, so

143

she had a good idea about how I acted around children. She
told me she would back me up, if needed.

*

I began thinking irrational thoughts such as murder and
suicide, which frightened me to my core. I would call and talk
to Fr. Patrick and he managed to calm me down. Did the
people who brought this awfulness against me realize the
stakes? I don't think they cared. Did they deserve to die? Of
course not. Besides the fact that I was no murderer, that
would put a wrench in my defense machine. I can definitely
understand some innocent people going to jail, getting out, and
then evening the score. Imagine being in prison for any length
of time, let alone twenty or thirty years, for something you
didn't do. The mere thought gave me the shivers; but murder?
That would solve nothing and complicate everything. I
needed to put my trust in God and pray often. My spirituality
was key in helping to alleviate the stress that had built up
inside of me.

*

Michael told me that allegations of sex assault happened all
the time. Really? Why? If I knew that answer, I would've
been better off. However, I didn't and it goes on right under
our noses. This was why I say, "You could be next." You
really could. I'm nobody special in this world. I'm simply a
person trying to make a decent, honest living. Look what
happened to me…in a day!

*

Suicide crossed my mind, even though I didn't have the guts for it. I had to ask myself a few good questions first; would killing myself be a viable alternative? Would it relieve my wife and the rest of the clan of this burden? How would it affect my daughter? Am I acting out in a quest for sympathy and attention?

I knew it didn't only affect me, but many other people whom I loved. It even affected people who know you more casually from work, the corner store or your neighborhood. I ultimately decided that suicide wasn't a reasonable solution. I now had an idea of what severely depressed people go through. You feel such desperation in dark times. You sense the rope of reality slipping through your hands. I had to continue the fight with the ammunition I had and hope twelve of my peers would agree with me. I would continue to believe that the "system" would come through.

"There is but one truly serious philosophical problem and that is suicide."

-Albert Camus

Shhhh, Be Very Quiet

My employer chose not to share this situation with the school parents. I understood. They didn't want a panic situation breaking out, which the overzealous prosecutors and mass media have already caused in our society. Sex crimes are worse than murder. They also bring more attention than arson, home invasion or armed robbery. I feel it is by far the nastiest crime of which you can be accused. It's a crime that inspires the greatest fear, terror and hysterical reactions from the public, the lawmakers and your neighbors. You're suspected of violating a child.

"How dare you," society says, and with good reason.

Nobody wants their children violated. I know that even with a full acquittal, there will be doubters, and the stigma will live with me for the rest of my life. A guilty verdict on any count and the stigma doubles, even triples.

Our country is leaning towards very conservative thinking. You can't discuss anything of a sexual nature. Nudity and sexuality are taboo. A woman's nipple was shown for $1/16^{th}$ of a second on television and the entire country loses its collective mind. I know men and women from European countries that are shocked more by our tepidness than anything else. Nude beaches are the norm overseas, while we hide ours behind the tallest fences we can find. We are a tight,

147

tense and anxious society. Until that changes, every little complaint or falsehood will be treated with the upmost fear mongering. We will flail our arms and demand justice. We will light our torches and track those perverts down. Anything less than that is not satisfactory. We must find the perpetrators and punish. Until all these diseased people are behind bars, we cannot rest. The ones who aren't in jail will be placed on a list so they cannot work or be functioning members of the country. That will surely solve the problem. As laws are needed, we will pass them.

"No parks, no bus stops, no ice cream parlors. In fact, nowhere if kids are present. No social media, schools or ball fields."

It is the ultimate goal of some, namely John Walsh and Mark Lunsford, to rid our world of this "illness."

*

Despite not telling the parental population at St. Paul, the word did eventually buzz in a quiet, deep and resonating way around the campus. The vast majority of the school people were on our side. There were some who raised their eyebrows or distanced themselves from the problem altogether, but very few thought I was actually guilty of the crimes. I have never been on the other side of the issue with a friend or acquaintance being accused, so it was tough for me to gauge the fear level. The support we did receive, however, was amazing and magical. We literally had parents offering *their own children* to testify on my behalf, saying that I was upstanding, kind and would never touch or hurt them. Parents expressed trust in me, saying that I could be relied upon *alone* with their children. Some wanted to go right up to the police station and complain about why the case was continuing. Other parents wanted an announcement in the school so they could rustle up more support for me. I was very apprehensive about that, though, because it could open a huge swath of anger and fear. Father Patrick wanted it kept quiet.

The support was so amazing. It brought tears to my eyes. This was another reason I continued to fight. My wife and I had worked together in this facility for years and never once have we heard so much as a whimper suggesting I was some kind of pervert or predator. People had faith in me, and with good reason.

I continued to do everything asked of me by the "system." I also continued my drug and alcohol random testing ($). There were no positives. Clean as a whistle. I met with Michael a couple of times during this stretch, and when December began and we inched closer to the trial, our meetings intensified.

"Truth stands, even if there be no public support. It is self-sustained."
  -Ghandi

149

Shaun Webb

He Said, She Said

The trial was scheduled for early December, so it was time for Michael to interview all the character witnesses suggested by me. I had submitted to him a list of at least fifty men, women and children who were willing to do what they could to help. This list included my ex-wife, neighbors and friends who had small children, along with workmates from the job. My physician and many school parents also wanted testify on my behalf. Michael scheduled the witness meetings in very early December, so he could have his roster together for the pre-trial hearing, which would be December 5th.

The meetings lasted two days and covered over ten hours. Michael met with all the witnesses I had submitted and chose only four possibilities for trial. He chose Danny, my buddy/workmate, a private investigator that we had hired to look into Blair's life, and he reluctantly chose the facility secretary, who could "possibly" attest to me being in the front office and ready to go home no later than 5:05 p.m. *every day*. Michael was leery of her though, because she could not definitely say I was there every single day by 5:05. She took days off and had vacations.

I was told my ex-wife would be good as a character witness. However, Michael was reluctant to use her because

151

she was my ex-wife and would be considered less believable to a jury. This had changed since our original meetings.

We already knew that Danny would refute the drinking on the job because he was there nearly every day before and during the time of October-April.

The only weak spot, Michael told me, was that nobody was there every minute to watch me. Who would be? What human being can verify every moment of every day from months earlier? Who could say *anything* with 100% accuracy? Blair appeared to be the only one. Nobody could keep a twenty-four/seven check on me. I was far too busy. I hadn't had to answer to anybody since I was a kid, but at thirty-nine years old, I'm trying to validate my whereabouts for every single minute and hour of each day that this accusation covers. Did that mean I would go in with no witnesses? I think that sometimes you can be too cautious.

*

The secretary could've been used to verify my presence in the front office every day at 5:05 p.m. only on the days she was present. She could not testify that I was there on the days she was not. It wasn't as if I completely changed my schedule only on the days she wasn't in the front office. Someone was always there when it was time to go home. She'd eventually be dropped from consideration due to Michael's apprehension. In combination with all the front office people, we could have verified each day.

The Private Investigator we hired was more complicated. Michael decided we needed a window into Blair's life, I

152

agreed and we hired Sam, a retired police officer, to shed some light on the case. Sam's job was to contact Blair and her friend Michelle so he could interview them himself. According to Michael, he was an expert in interviewing children and finding out if they were lying. This was a good strategy, because he could expose the discrepancies and fabrications through live testimony in court.

Sam called Blair's house and Sara Joan answered. She wouldn't allow Sam to interview her daughter until she spoke with her state supplied attorney. She also said something very interesting. Sara Joan stated that she had hired a litigating attorney for a civil lawsuit against my employers and me. Before the trial? It continued to sound planned-out and scripted. Maybe they were broke and needed easy money. Some interesting testimony would come out in trial involving that situation, with Carowitz being the leader of the pack.

My suspicion of David Carowitz was now growing from a raised eyebrow to out and out vehemence. I believed he was masterminding and perpetrating the whole problem. He's the person that seemed involved in every single aspect of the drama. From the original police report, to the Pontiac Care House interview, to the pre-lim hearing, Blair told Carowitz after he badgered her. Carowitz was Blair's step-dad. Carowitz this, Carowitz that. I would've loved to expose him as the fraud I believed him to be. Unfortunately, there was no way to prove anything. It was a pure guess on my part.

Later, after contacting her lawyer, Sara Joan called Sam back and told him that Blair wouldn't be available for questioning. Michelle's mom followed suit, so there would be no inquisitorial of either girl. Were they afraid they'd be

caught in their own game? Prosecutor Gardner had even
given Sara Joan the green light to allow the interview! Mom
was worried that her daughter would be exposed, thus
implicating her and Carowitz as the masterminds behind this
fraudulent scandal. What was good though was that Sam
would testify as to what Sara Joan had told him pertaining to
hiring a lawyer before the trial. He would also testify as to his
expertise in interviewing kids and weeding out truth from
fiction.

*

I would go to court with three witnesses: Nikki, Sam and
Danny. Michael told me it was simply a "he said, she said"
case, so the lack of witnesses was a normal circumstance. I
asked him about character witnesses and he told me the judge
wouldn't allow it. If that was the case, then why was Nikki on
the list? When I watch Court TV, everyone has at least one
character witness. You can't tell me that having a lineup of
about twenty eighth-grade children ready to testify on my
behalf doesn't help. Even if the judge says no, it would still
be a fact that the jury couldn't ignore.

My ex-wife, who probably isn't very crazy about me, was
willing to testify on my behalf. Why not let her? It could only
help.

"The judge won't allow it, Sean," is all Michael kept
saying about any character witnesses I brought up. We were
told in the initial meetings with our lawyers that the ex-wife
would be good, because she has no reason to defend me. I'm
not an attorney; I paid one to represent me. I didn't know

what was right or wrong, but it was too late to change, as much as I was thinking about doing just that. I'd like to know, besides the Judge saying no, why I'm consistently shot down on the character witnesses. Straight answer never came. I finally let it go, but not without resistance. I was going in with both feet to the fire. If Michael were making the wrong choices, I would pay. Even when our potential witnesses were crossed by the state, it wouldn't matter, because we were hiding nothing. Frankly, I was tired of keeping my mouth shut.

*

Why couldn't I stand up and scream "WHAT THE HELL-IS-GOING-ON!" as loud as I wanted? Why couldn't I stand up and say, "She's a liar?" Why did she get all the trust and the "you poor baby sympathy?" Was it because I was forty and she was' sixteen? Teen-agers *can* and *do* lie. Michael had to settle me down. He told me that everything had a process and we must follow it to the T. He explained that he was a great arguer who loved confrontation. So far, I had only seen a tiny bit of that. Why be so nervous about witnesses? Let them talk. We had our bases covered.

I was losing my grip and needed to stop, focus and stay together for the good of our defense. It was a tough thing to do. I felt as though Michael doubted my word. I asked him about it and he insisted that he believed everything I'd said to him. It sure didn't feel like it.

155

"Any perjury case is a tough case. You just don't go on 'he said-she said.' You have to find corroborating evidence."

-Victoria Toensing

Detecting Hope

"Sean, I have an idea." Michael suggested, "Were going to have you take a lie detector test."

I heard him out and countered, "Ok, but lie detectors are inadmissible in court."

The debate continued, "Yes, but if you pass it with flying colors, I can show prosecution and *maybe* they'll drop the case."

I mulled this over for a few minutes and told Michael that it sounded all right, but I didn't like the word "Maybe." What was maybe? Maybe meant "not for sure." Did I honestly think the state would drop the case because I pass a lie detector test? I was apprehensive and highly skeptical, but my lawyer was finally able to talk me into it. What was there to lose, besides another five hundred bucks ($$$)? Money doesn't mean anything unless you're short of it.

Michael set me up with a man named Peter, known throughout the state as a lie detector expert. I called this man to make an appointment.

I told him I was a client for Michael Casper.

"Oh sure, Mike Casper, one of my best buddies. He told me you'd be coming. Your name is Shane, right?"

I told him my name was Sean.

"You get down here Saturday and we'll get you all taken care of."

I told Peter I was taking Xanax and a couple other medications that may affect the test's accuracy.

"Don't you worry about that Shane, my test is foolproof. I've been doing this for twenty years and I've caught a lot of crooks, no worries."

I interjected, "Peter, my name is Sean, not Shane, and secondly, I read on-line that the test can be flawed by medication."

"No chance, Shane, you just get down here and you'll see its all good."

I didn't care much for him, but I shrugged my shoulders and went, along with it.

I arrived at Peter's house early Saturday morning for the test. He met me at the door and welcomed me in.

"Why you must be Shane, come in, please."

"Sir," I corrected, "It's Sean, not Shane."

"Oh yeah, sorry."

Peter was a little man with this HUGE smile on his face. He looked happy. I was reminded of a morning TV game show host.

As I walked through his living area, he had at least fifty pictures on the wall with him accepting awards from local police agencies. It seemed as if he was darned proud of himself. I was feeling very lackluster towards this whole thing. It didn't feel right. I don't have faith in these things. How can a machine tell if you're lying or not? A magic eight ball seemed more reliable. "Magic eight ball, will I be acquitted?" TRY AGAIN LATER.

"Come over here and have a seat on my 'truth chair.'" Peter asked while grinning ear to ear. "If you're telling the truth, this will prove it."

I told him again that I was skeptical about my medications mixing with the test.

"Nonsense, don't worry about it. If you're honest, it will show, Shane."

I sat on the "truth" chair and was hooked up with a blood pressure cuff along with some little cloth finger cuffs that looked like they'd been through a war. The material on these little gadgets were torn and discolored. I asked him how old the equipment was.

"It's not old, Shane, its state-of-the -art stuff. Relax and we'll get underway."

"Fine, and its Sean, sir."

"Oh yes, of course."

Peter told me he had to calibrate the machine, so he gave me a choice of ten cards with the numbers one through ten on them. I selected card number four. He asked me one thru ten if I had that card, and told me to say no to each number.

"Did you have card number one?"

"No."

"Did you have card number two?"

"No."

He finishes all the numbers and says to me, "You had card number two."

I corrected him, "No, Peter, I had card number four."

"Okay," he says, "let's do it again."

We did it three more times before he picked the right card. He beamed, "See Shane, it works."

I was unimpressed. Now we had to select ten questions which he would ask me in descending order, ascending order and at random.

He began asking me these questions in these three different orders. I answered them honestly. I sat back quietly in the chair as we were doing this. I shut my eyes and relaxed the best I could. Peter asked me on two occasions if I was trying to cheat the test.

"How do you cheat a lie detector test?" I asked with anger in my voice,

"You seem to be breathing funny, Shane."

I was breathing as I always breathed and told him so. I then called for a time out during the test.

"Look, Peter, I don't believe in this test and I don't really care how the results turn out. Moreover, my name is SEAN, not Shane. C'mon."

His smile disappeared. We had to stop for twenty minutes because he said my hissy fit was a hindrance to the integrity of the test. I figured my skepticism, along with the anti-anxiety medication I was taking were more of a hindrance than anything else. A few minutes later, we finished and I was unhooked from this contraption.

"I'll get the results back to your attorney," he said, obviously dejected by my difficulty.

I asked him why he could not give them to me now. He calibrated his machine, after all, so he should know the results. He said he had to go over all the results carefully before he could make a determination. I think it was so I wouldn't laugh in his face. My sarcasm was turning the room red.

*

A couple of days later, Michael called me into his office. He had the results. They were even funnier than I originally thought they'd be. Peter claimed that the test was "inconclusive" because of my attitude. Here are the results. Judge for yourself:

1. Are you in my office?
1. I answered yes, and the test said I was lying.

2. Did you put your finger in Blair's vagina?
2. I answered no, and the test said I was telling the truth.

3. Are you wearing a hat?
3. I answered no and the test said I was lying.

4. Is your wife's name Nikki?
4. I answered yes, and the test said I was lying.

5. Did you touch Blair's breasts?
5. I answered no, and the test said I was telling the truth.

6. Is my name Peter?
6. I answered yes, and the test said I was lying.

7. Are we on planet earth?
7. I answered yes, and the test said I was lying.

8. Did you put your mouth on Blair's nipples?

8. I answered no, and the test said I was telling the truth.

9. Is Michael your lawyer?

9. I answered yes, and the test said I was telling the truth.

10. Did Blair kiss your penis?

10. I answered no, and the test said I was lying.

I told Michael this was a huge waste of time and money. He told me that Gardner wasn't going to let me use a perfect test anyway.

"I told you, that, Mike. Whose money are we spending here?"

I felt like a guinea pig for Michael's experiments. The state wanted a conviction, to hell with the truth. Besides, Mike just made five hundred bucks ($$$) for his friend.

Admittedly, my attitude was not ideal for the test, but how can you do it when you don't believe in it? This exercise in futility could not determine anything about my emotional state.

I called Peter, but he didn't want to talk to me. Why not? Because your formula doesn't work? His secretary told me he didn't want to talk to a test "cheater."

"Fine, but I didn't cheat on his ignorant test, it doesn't work," I said. "Oh, and tell him my damn name is Sean, will ya."

> ***"All the truth in the world adds up to one big lie."*** *-Bob Dylan*

No Discovery

On December 5th, I arrived at the Oakland County 6th Circuit Court for the pre-trial hearing. It was an icy winter day and driving on slick highways added to my already tattered nerves. Traffic was slow and jammed. My urge was to pass on the curb, but that would bring more trouble, so patience would be my friend. It took much longer to reach the courthouse than I expected, but I did so safely.

*

I met Michael in the hallway outside of our courtroom. This was when he informed me that he was going to attempt to subpoena Blair's school records.

"We probably won't win, but I have to try," Michael informed me.

Nikki had done some computer "investigating" and found that Blair attended an alternative high school. A prerequisite of admission was an interview with a staff psychologist. We could find out if she had been a problem in school. We could also find out if she had seen a counselor, or if Carowitz was her only "counselor." It was one of the few times Michael took our advice.

Michael was going to ask for an "in-camera" inspection of the records. This means that the court would look over the records and decide if there was anything useful for the defense. Michael would argue that this constitutes discovery on our part, and that we were entitled to it. He again told me it was a pure shot in the dark, and he would probably be denied, but what was there to lose? If you can help yourself, please do. I wasn't crazy about his "probably won't work" attitude. I wanted a confident, arrogant lawyer who was afraid of nothing. We all would if in a situation like this.

*

Upon entering the court and waiting for our names to be called, I was shocked at the large amount of people present for a various myriad of crimes. It was a potpourri of criminals and lawyers. They had a large blackboard near the Judge's bench where the defense and prosecuting attorneys would write their name when present. As soon as they would leave the room, they would erase it so the court clerk would know they were not in the room. The judge was due on the bench at 8:30 a.m., but did not arrive until closer to 10:00. Why? Because a judge can do whatever they like. They're like a five thousand pound gorilla, and who is going to stop that? Finally, she showed up.

"ALL RISE!"

We stood up as the Honorable Dorothy Taylor took her seat. I could see already that she felt like she was above all the riff-raff. After all, her rich father financed her entire run for the bench. She spent what turned out to be a record

164

amount of funds on her campaign. She had a scowl on her face and her eyes were beady and cold. She appeared angry even when she smiled, which was rare. Taylor ripped apart every attorney that approached her.

A prisoner in for sentencing tried to fire his lawyer, but she wouldn't allow it.

"But it's my motherfucking life, Judge"

That was the wrong thing to say. She had him removed from the court and mentioned that this outburst would be taken into account when he returned for sentencing. She had an ominous reputation within the legal community for being degrading and belittling. It took me all of fifteen seconds to see that. I could tell this was making Michael nervous. I asked him about it and he said, "You have to have a thick skin to be in this business."

I would find out later that this judge was not all she was cracked up to be. It seemed she liked to play hooky.

Finally, after what seemed like hours, I heard it.

"Case # so and so, People vs. Sean West. Please come forward."

"Right here," Michael said, and we both approached the bench.

The Judge stared me down like the dog she thought I was. She didn't like me from first sight, and I'm sure it was because of my charges. I smiled at her only to be given an extra scowl. Michael then asked for a motion allowing the release of Blair's school records.

"DENIED," Taylor barked.

It was that quick.

She also said, "Nice try counselor," with a smirk.

Geez, she couldn't listen to the argument? She ran that courtroom like it was her own personal circus. The clerks were her clowns, the attorneys her feeble hoop jumpers. She was the ringmaster.

"I set trial for December fourteenth at 8:30 a.m."

The funniest part of it all was that trial was originally set for December 10th after the preliminary hearing; however, the Radisons and Carowitz were on a cruise ship in the South Seas and were granted a delay. Trial would be a few days later.

It must be nice. They were working on their tans while I stewed in our cold state of flux.

Blair, supposedly so traumatized that she could hardly go through with the trial, took a nice trip to the Caribbean to help that. There was no stress for these folks, even though they were deliberately trying to ruin my life. What could I say or do? I could tell Michael, but he wouldn't be able to do much, not that he would even try. I begrudgingly went with the flow; a flow that felt like I was swimming straight up a waterfall.

In twenty minutes, we were on our way out of the courtroom when Prosecutor Gardner stopped Michael in the hallway. They chatted out of my earshot, and then laughed with each other aloud. I was mad. You can't be friends with the enemy. After their giggle fest, Gardner headed down the hallway. He stopped, turned back, gave me a sarcastic grin and then continued his walk. I returned him only a glare. I chewed Michael up and down on our way out.

He said, "You need to have a little respect for opposing council."

166

"Respect?" I shrieked, "These people are trying to destroy me. The respect I want is for them to notice all the misstatements and lies and dismiss this thing."

That would never happen. The predators need to be put away where they belong. Did they really commit the crime? Who cares? It was a prosecutor's job to prosecute and they would stop at nothing to get that coveted conviction.

*

Michael told me to be at his office at nine the next morning for trial preparation. I told him I'd be there early because we had so much work to do. On my way home, I was calling my mother on the phone when my truck slipped on ice, spun around and smashed a tree. I didn't hang up; I just tossed my phone to the side while I struggled to retain control. My entire profanity filled tirade ended up recorded on her answering machine. They would save it because it was hilarious. Listening to it later was funny, but it was still injury to insult. My truck had a busted tailgate, but it was quite drivable. I threw my hands up in a truce. When it rains, it pours.

"Credulity is belief in slight evidence, with no evidence, or against evidence."
        -Tryon Edwards

Shaun Webb

The Final Preparation

The next morning, I headed to Michael's office to begin my intense trial rehearsals. I was going to be questioned extensively by Michael and Bert so that when I took the stand I would know how to answer and what my manner should be.

I argued this. "Why do I need rehearsals to tell the truth? It's easy to talk when you don't have to remember your lies."

Michael explained to me, "This is the most vital part of your defense, and I need to make sure you have it down."

I scoffed. "Go ahead and ask your questions, this'll be easy."

I would be in for a shock because Michael and Bert mixed up my words and attacked me verbally and emotionally during this exercise.

"Did you say Blair looked provocative? Did you tell Detective Smart that Blair had a crush on you? How do you explain this? **ANSWER THE QUESTIONS, SIR!**"

I was flabbergasted. They came after me with anger and scowls. I couldn't get one question answered before another one was slung at me. "Wait a minute, That's not true," I'd say. "Give me a second guys, good Lord."

"ANSWER THE QUESTION, MR. WEST!"

They explained that this was how the questioning could go. "It could get a little hairy up there," Bert said. "You'll be better off after this exercise, trust me"

Lawyers have a way of making you crack. After two hours, I needed a break. I was given an hour to go have some lunch and a smoke or two.

*

I sat down at a local pizza joint and mulled over what I had just experienced, and what my fate could hold. I could go to prison as early as the next day. It could really happen. Do I have all of my affairs in order? Do I need to get anything else done? Do I have time left? I don't know. Besides dying young, I can't give these feelings a proper comparison. It feels like you're sinking and out of control. I smoked a cigarette, ate a half slice of pizza and continued my thinking.

I was relying on a jury of my peers to make the right decision, but what if they didn't? What if they were so dead-set against child sex crimes that they didn't focus on the testimony or the facts? My lawyers had told me that while this sort of accusation happens every day, not all get convicted. I had heard on the news of a Principal at a local high school acquitted on four counts of CSC because there was no evidence. It turned out that some school kids were upset about his discipline and wanted revenge. I should point out that there were no penalties against these kids for the false allegations. Michael told me that turning around and charging them would send a "chilling message." What chilling message? That if you're lying you will be penalized? Perhaps that was needed to slow down what I believe to be the heavy rash of accusations against adults.

I do think a higher percentage of the accused are guilty, but some aren't, and they're penalized equally. The sentences for sex crimes are greater than others. Even after your sentence is completed, your name and photo are on a sex registry that affects where you live, if you can find work, and where you can travel for the rest of your life.

Michael did say a couple of things that gave me hope. He said the state must convince all twelve jurors that I'm guilty. By contrast, if only one juror says "not guilty," the very worst result would be a mistrial. I say worst with tongue firmly planted in cheek. A mistrial would mean a completely new waiting period if the state decided to continue its pursuit of the case. The other thing he said was that a jury would much rather set a guilty man free than send an innocent one to jail. I hope my jury saw the light and acquits on all counts, as they should.

"Courage is being scared to death... and saddling up anyway."
-John Wayne

Shaun Webb

Playing the Game

I returned to Michael's office at noon to continue my grilling and decided this was the right time to share my "Ace in the hole." Thankfully, I had a large, brightly colored tattoo on my upper left thigh. It measured six inches from top to bottom, and four inches in width. I'm glad I'd had this work done and I couldn't believe how handy it would come in now.

I went back to the tattoo parlor where I'd had it applied and spoke with the man who did the work. He gave me a receipt stating that it was inked in *1999* and told me he would testify if needed. This assured me that the prosecution could not come back with the "He just had it done" card. There's a huge difference between a new tattoo and a healed one.

The night before my meeting with Michael, I had my wife take pictures of the tattoo. She took a picture with my jeans down to hips, waist and knees; all these areas because we didn't know what Blair would say. So far, she had said my pants were down to my hips, knees and thighs. Nikki also snapped pictures with my underwear up and down. There's no way that Blair "kissed" my penis and didn't see this work. There is also no way that Blair saw me with my pants to my knees and didn't see this work. In one statement Blair had said that she didn't look at my penis, but in another statement, she said she saw "clear" fluid exiting. Either way, we had the

173

girl backed into a corner and she didn't know it. Her smug "victim" attitude was to be put to the test. My wife was giddy with excitement, as we both thought this was our saving grace. The work was multi-colored, bright and unmistakable. It could be we were naive, but to me, it was solid evidence to prove that Blair was a liar.

Michael was not 100% amused. He asked me, "Are you sure you want to use this?"

"Hell yeah, I'm sure. She can't describe it," I barked.

"Is there a chance she ever saw it?" He inquired.

"Are you kidding me, Michael? The only way she saw it was if I had my pants pulled down in front of her and I didn't; so no, she didn't see it."

Michael continued to argue, "Is there a chance you told her about it?"

I began to get aggravated. I had the straw that would break the camel's back sitting right in front of him, and he was acting like a complete coward about it. It was as if he didn't want such strong evidence. I was puzzled.

"Do you doubt me, Mike? If you don't believe me then tell me now so I can try to get another lawyer."

"No." Michael said, "I believe you. You don't need another lawyer."

I tried to reassure him. "Stop being so scared of every idea I get. This is foolproof."

"Well," he countered, "I hope she doesn't guess what it is."

"If she guessed what it was, that would make her either the luckiest person on earth, or a fortune teller."

I was getting exhausted going over it with him, so I ordered him to go with the tattoo and that was an order. Michael explained to me that he had to give the prosecutor the word because it is added discovery.

"Why?" I inquired. "They wouldn't give us any access to discovery, such as school records. The only discovery they had was her word and nothing else."

Michael ignored me and phoned Prosecutor Gardner. He told him I had a distinguished mark in my groin area that he was submitting as evidence. Michael also explained to him that we had photos, but would not share them until trial. Apparently, Gardner called Blair quickly. Within an hour, Michael told me that Blair could not remember what was on or around my groin area, but she was sure there was a tattoo.

"Of course she was. She saw the tattoos on my arms and wrists at work. It was a logical guess to make. If she really saw it, she would remember it."

Gardner wanted the photos now, but Michael surprisingly denied him. Obviously, Gardner wanted to show Blair the pictures so she could testify accurately in court.

"Don't make me petition the court for the release of these pics," Gardner threatened.

Michael told him to go ahead, but he would be denied access. At least he hoped so, but with Judge Taylor in charge, who knew for sure. Gardner didn't move to get the photos, so I figured he was relying on the fact that Blair was being truthful. Besides, she wore a WWJD (What Would Jesus Do) bracelet, so she must've been telling the truth. For once, I felt as though I'd gotten the upper hand. Incidentally, I was confident that what she was been doing is NOT what Jesus would do.

*

It was during a court rehearsal that I found out Bert was not going to be at the trial. I was angry yet again.

"I wanted two lawyers by my side for this," I complained. "You guys keep changing the rules on me."

"Bert has a busy schedule," Michael expounded, "so it'll be you and me. You'll be fine, don't worry."

I couldn't do anything about it, though. I was going in with Michael alone. I felt shortchanged. It would've been nice to know this a few weeks earlier. This is how the lawyers get you. They were saving a ton of money and time by having Michael, and only Michael, working with me. This freed up Bert to make more money on other cases. (Bait and switch?)

"Trust us Sean; we know what we are doing."

Perhaps I should have had a court appointed attorney. I wasn't so sure they could do any worse.

We finished our daylong meeting ($5,000) and I went home to be with my family and do a lot of praying. I'm not the most religious man on the planet, but it is amazing how close you get to God when the fire is on your tail.

"A common mistake that people make when trying to design something completely foolproof is to underestimate the ingenuity of complete fools."
-Douglas Adams

The Trial

I woke up on the morning of the trial after a restless two hours and twenty minutes of sleep, and felt both a knot of dread in my stomach combined with a guarded feeling of confidence. If you'd ever been in the type of a situation I found myself in and really cared about your existence, you knew exactly what I meant. I might come home a free man. I might go to jail, or prison. Everything I'd worked for was on the line; my job, my future, my wife, my daughter and my family. This was as real as it could get.

We had a small breakfast as a family and then headed to the courthouse. I was able to eat today, but it didn't taste very good. I figured that if I walked out of court a free man, I would regain my appetite.

*

The trial was scheduled to begin at 8:30, but as was with the pre-trial hearing, it would begin when Judge Taylor decided it would begin. She was arrogant, pompous and entitled. All of those words crossed through my mind when describing her. It was bad enough that I was facing the most critical part of my life without having a judge with an attitude and propensity to show up whenever she felt like it. Did she

care? Did she have the best interests of the parties in mind? I
didn't think so. The only thing this woman appeared to have
in mind was Dorothy Taylor. I wasn't railing on the woman
because she was my judge; I was on her because of her
obvious lack of responsibility.

*

"ALL RISE!'

It was finally time to begin at 10:15. Her Honorable Judge
took her place on her pulpit, scowl present, and called for jury
selection to begin.

"Let's get a jury in here," She ordered.

Judge Taylor had her clerk usher in forty-five potential
jurors. They filed in and sat behind us in the gallery. The
selection process, I might add, was a very interesting study.
Out of these forty-five or so citizens, twelve jurors and one
alternate would be selected for the trial.

As the jury shuffled into the room, Taylor started what
would turn out to be continuing antics, shouting, **"WHO'S
SITTING IN THOSE SPOTS?"** She pointed frantically at
the pews behind the defense table. Her voice sounded like
fingernails dragged across a chalkboard.

 It was my family and friends, there for the trial.

"MOVE OVER THERE!" she scolded. She dramatically
waved her arm to the right.

My supporters, with surprised and confused looks on their
faces, moved to the right, behind the prosecution table. After
the selection, they would move back to my side.

178

"When you judge another, you do not define them, you define yourself."

-*Wayne Dyer*

The Trial; Voir Dire

The jury selection started with the court clerk naming thirteen people to come forward and sit in the box reserved for the final chosen jurors. Michael and Mr. Gardner were both given a diagram of the twelve jury seats and the names and occupations of the first potential jurors occupying those chairs. Prosecution and defense are allowed to dismiss six potential jurors each. The process was called Voir Dire. When Voir Dire was complete, the jury was considered final and on to the trial you go.

The judge read off all the jury rules and expectations in a monotone voice, and at such a rapid rate that it was clear that she was disinterested in the outcome and anxious to get the trial finished. Her focus seemed to be on clearing her docket quickly, not searching for justice. She asked the jurors as a group if they had prejudices or personal matters that would affect how they deliberated. Taylor asked them if anybody had a history of sexual assaults, personally or within their family. She also asked if they had a problem with the way I looked, or any general problems or circumstances that would be a hindrance to their serving.

You would be shocked at the whining some of these people did.

"I don't feel good, my knees hurt, and I can't sit through this, I have to work.

You don't feel good? Try it from this side of the room. I'll bet sitting in my chair would send some to the hospital, maybe even the morgue. Taylor was very reluctant to dismiss jurors herself. She wanted us to use up our six choices quickly, thus rushing things along. Most judges will dismiss complaining jurors themselves. Not this judge; she would dismiss only one by her own hand.

The selection process started with each lawyer removing someone and having them replaced at random. The attorney's removal process is, I believe, 60% age and 30% appearance. The other 10% is how they answer the questions. I wanted a middle-aged jury, which would be more advantageous for us because they were not as likely to be misled by a teen-ager. They could also be a more understanding about my situation. I could be wrong. The prosecution, however, wanted a younger, female jury. This would give them a better chance of conviction because women may be more compassionate towards another female. In the end, it was all about the conviction. A prosecutor with a good record would get more prestigious cases. They would be more likely to have a successful personal practice, thus collecting more money in their pockets. Guilty or innocent? Who cared? As long as they get that coveted conviction. This is another part of the game that's played every day and in every court around the US.

We haggled with the process for a while longer. Anybody in the maintenance field or over forty years old were eliminated by the state, while anyone younger or angrier looking was excused by Michael.

One prospective juror was someone I knew from childhood. I mentioned this aloud and was quickly reprimanded by Judge Taylor.

"YOUR CLIENT CAN'T SPEAK IN THIS COURT!" She barked.

I didn't know. I felt like someone dropped a snowball in my underpants. It would've been nice if my attorney had mentioned this beforehand.

"I'm sorry your honor," Michael told her. "He knows that gentleman right there."

"DISMISSED!" Taylor croaked. Afraid that he might side with me, she took care of it herself. This was the only time she would personally dismiss a potential juror.

Both lawyers exhausted the six eliminations they were given and we had the final jury. I hoped Michael had made good choices, but I didn't have any idea one way or the other. Juror's moods, habits, upbringing and other intangibles made all the difference. I could conceivably be convicted because someone didn't like the way I looked or carried myself. If all were to go according to the law, I'd be acquitted because I was innocent.

*

The final jury consisted of seven women and five men, with one female alternate. Of the seven women, four were middle-aged (40-50) and three were younger. By younger I mean mid-twenties. The alternate was a middle-aged female.

Out of eight women total, seven were white and one was Asian. The men were as follows; three middle-aged (40-50) and two older (60's). Four were white and one was black. I liked our selections. One girl had tattoos, which I thought would help me significantly. One woman was a temporary worker at the Waterford Police Department. How could that hurt? Maybe she knew my dad. Not likely, but was worth the shot. What would be bad was if she knew him, but didn't like him. There was also a couple of average looking men.

I would notice during the trial that one woman in particular looked like she was going to burst into tears at any moment. This made me nervous.

"Who was she sad for?" I wondered, "Me or Blair? Was she even sad at all? Maybe this is just how she looked."

I didn't notice this during selection, but what was done was done, so on we'd go. These people held my life in their hands.

*

Michael sent Nikki, our private investigator Sam, and Danny into the hallway because they were potential witnesses and could not listen to the testimony. What a waste of time this would turn out to be. The state's witnesses were sequestered in a room somewhere near or inside the jury deliberation room. I'm sure they had been giving Blair and her family their final coaching instructions on how to best make me look like a pedophile. It had taken about forty-five minutes to select and seat the jury. Judge Taylor hastily re-read what was to be expected, and at 11:20, it was time for the prosecution to state their case.

The opening statements were short (five minutes) and not so sweet. The prosecution stated that I committed the crimes.

"Blair's words will convince you. You must convict him."

Michael stated that I hadn't done this, and the case was short on evidence.

"She's a liar. You must acquit him."

The entire opening by both sides was as pointless as a busted pencil.

"A jury consists of twelve persons chosen to decide who has the better lawyer."

-Robert Frost

The Trial: Prosecution's Case

David Carowitz led off for the State. He was looking more tanned than the last time I'd seen him. As you know, we had to delay the trial for a few days so this "family" could get their Caribbean cruise out of the way. He walked up to the stand acting arrogant and cocky.

During the state's examination, Carowitz generally echoed the same statements he had given in the police and Pontiac Care House reports. This time, however, he mentioned how I had spoken with him about the development of Blair's breasts. This was brand new. I hadn't heard or read anything about this subject up until that moment. He also mentioned that he'd called a litigating attorney for advice after Blair had informed him of the alleged touching.

"It was a friend," Carowitz reasoned.

Michael, I hoped, would attack the testimony when it was his turn to ask questions. Carowitz continued to be smug. He smirked continuously. On cross, Michael was able to pull out a couple crucial bits of information. Carowitz stated that after Blair had told him about the alleged assaults, he had indeed called a litigating attorney who specialized in civil moneymaking cases.

"Why didn't you talk to Sara Joan first?" Michael asked.

"She wasn't home yet," Carowitz replied. "I needed to take some action.

It made sense that it was looking more like a set-up due to the new allegations that were coming forth. I continued to find it strange that Carowitz and Blair were talking about sex together, by themselves, while listening to music. She would speak to Carowitz before talking to her own mother? Michael asked about this.

Carowitz replied, "I know Blair well, we can talk about anything. Nothing is off limits."

*

I had a pen and paper so I could take notes and slide them toward Michael during the trial. I knew better than to open my mouth again. That judge would've wrung my neck if I'd made the same mistake twice. The notepad wouldn't matter, though, because Michael wasn't going to listen to my advice. I would write my notes and show him when I felt the need. I had written a few tidbits during Carowitz's testimony. Michael ignored them with a wave off. I returned him a look of discontent.

Michael finished his cross with Carowitz by asking him a few more key questions. "Did you think Sean was carrying on a relationship with Blair?"

He answered that he thought it *might* be happening.

"Did you alert the school? The parish? Anyone?"

"No, just the police," Carowitz answered with a blank look.

"Did you alert Sean's bosses?"

"No sir. I did not."

Carowitz also re-testified to Michael that I had mentioned Blair's rapid development into a woman by mentioning her "growing" breasts.

"Did you mention that to anyone, David? Did you mention it to the police?"

"No," was his answer.

These were odd answers by Carowitz. Michael was somewhat aggressive, but not overly so.

*

I had worked with kids from kindergarten thru eighth grade. I wasn't sexually interested in the schoolchildren in any way. It didn't appeal to me and frankly, I never thought about it before this case became known. Wouldn't any parent inform someone in authority if they thought their child was being abused or if some man in his thirties was mentioning their breast development?

Michael finished questioning Carowitz and now it was Sara Joan's turn to take the stand. She entered the courtroom every bit as tanned as her boyfriend, but had one important addition; she was wearing a diamond on her ring finger. Did they think that made it okay for Blair to call Carowitz her stepfather? Were they trying to look like the perfect family? My eyes were rolling as I endured this nonsense.

The secret for the state is that the jury doesn't know the story either way. They were not at the pre-lim and had not yet had a chance to look over any reports. I fully expected Michael to expose the "Brand new" wedding ring during his cross. I wasn't against people getting engaged or married, but it struck me funny that they were going for the theatrics, and were being dishonest about it. This also went for the prosecution. None of the testimony, reports or statements up that point was the truth. It seemed like the most impressive *actor* would win the case. If I were the loser, I'd go to jail. They would simply walk away if I were acquitted, so it was no harm and no foul for them. The truth seemed to be an afterthought.

I can picture the meeting in the back room involving those people and the prosecutor.

"OK, what can we do to enhance our case?" The family would ask, "Let's do whatever we can to show the jury that you're a legitimate couple. Let's make a huge spectacle out of it so these jurors will think you're the modern happy family."

That was what I thought. My mind continued to paint vivid pictures of the situations and conversations I figured were happening. My thinking was suddenly and rudely interrupted.

"WHAT'S THE HOLD-UP?" Taylor said loudly and angrily. **"I THOUGHT BOTH COUNCILS SAID THIS WOULD TAKE ONE DAY, TOPS!"**

I was flabbergasted, and it continued, **"WE'RE SUPPOSED TO GET TWELVE INCHES OF SNOW AND IT'S CLOSE TO CHRISTMAS. THIS JURY WANTS TO GET FINISHED. LET'S MOVE IT ALONG!"**

This was from a judge who showed up late for the start of the trial. Who did she think she was? This was my life on the line. I wrote a note to Michael asking him to delay the rest of the trial until after Christmas. He shook his head no. I tried to reason to myself that he knew best, although that was getting harder to do. I didn't want this rushed. The jury was right there to hear her outburst. Maybe that was a good thing.

None of Judge Taylor's remarks would show up on the trial transcript. When it came to a possible appeal, her tirades, which would've come in handy, wouldn't be recorded. Taylor would continue her outbursts throughout the day.

*

The state asked Sara Joan the same questions they asked Carowitz. She insisted that she believed I touched Blair inappropriately, and that she suspected I was a pedophile. She also mentioned my referring to Blair's growth habits in exactly the same words as Carowitz had used. Her brows were furrowed and she was scowling. She looked as angry as she could.

As you could see from the statements, it was never certain whom Blair told first. Was it her friend Michelle? Was it Carowitz? Did Carowitz go to Sara Joan, or was it Blair that told her mom? In the police report, it read that a phone call was overheard by Blair's mom, who then questioned Blair about it. If that's not true, why did Detective Smart lie to me? The truth was that Sara Joan said that she'd heard it from Carowitz after Blair told him.

"David told me as soon as I got home," Sara Joan admitted. "I wasn't a part of the conversation."

So Smart *did* lie to me. Why? Was he trying to implicate me before listening to my side of the story? I'll never know the whole truth, but I still can't get a grip on why a detective would lie. It made me feel like it was a flat-out headhunt. I wept for our "system" of justice.

*

It was Michael's turn to cross, and he asked her the same questions he had asked Carowitz.

"Did you report your suspicions to anybody at all?"

"The police," she answered.

She, like Carowitz, testified about me not only mentioning Blair's development, but also that I had put my cupped hands in front of my chest and said to her, "Man, your daughter sure has some big, full breasts."

That was an out-and-out lie! She looked at me with a scowl as she testified to that. My reaction was complete disbelief. I would never make that type of comment to *anyone,* let alone, a parent. As with Carowitz, She told *nobody* in the school, church or law enforcement about that statement.

"Why?" Michael asked.

"I don't know, but I should have," she muttered.

In fact, neither she nor Carowitz mentioned this in any police or Pontiac Care House reports after the allegation. It was made up to enhance the case.

As the questioning continued, she was asked by Michael how long she had worked for the cleaning company.

"I was never employed by them," she innocently replied, "I was simply helping David for free."

Her angry snarl was turning into a shrugging of her shoulders and a puzzled, wide-eyed look. It turns out that neither Sara Joan, Blair nor Bonnie worked for Tornado clean. Only Carowitz did. He brought them in to help. I was hoping the jury saw the insanity in this testimony. To my continued surprise, Michael never seemed intent on trying to cross up either Carowitz or Sara Joan.

He was straightforward with the last of his questions.

"Do you think you should have told someone? Are you telling the truth?" was Michael's line of inquiry.

"Yes. Yes." were her robotic responses. I think Michael should have mentioned the fact that a lot of her testimony was missing from any reports and statements. I asked him to try to confuse them so they would impeach themselves, but he told me to trust him. I had no choice. It was too far along now. Between Carowitz and Sara Joan, the questioning by the state and defense took all of forty-five minutes to complete. It was time for the states next witness. It would be Blair's friend Michelle.

*

That girl was a train wreck. She sounded like a cross between Cheech and Chong on helium and an old southern belle.

Please state your name: "Aye, I'ym Meechelle. I'm heyere too teystify for Blayer. Myyy beyst frieynd."

Michelle's hair appeared disheveled and she was dressed in white t-shirt and jeans. I kid you not; there were stains on the tee. She was very unkempt. I wasn't complaining. It certainly didn't hurt to have a sloppy, slurring state witness.

All of Gardner's questions centered on Blair, and what the relationship between them was like.

"We spent nights at each other's houses and did things together with each other's families," she answered tentatively.

It came down to a couple pieces of testimony. First, she said that Blair had told her I had "Felt her up" and second, Michelle claimed she was raped in the past. Her testimony quickly ended and it was Michael's turn.

"LET'S GET THIS THING MOVING!" Taylor sharply piped in. **"IT'S ALMOST LUNCHTIME AND I WANT THIS FINISHED TODAY!"**

We were moving as fast as we could. When I looked up at her, I was met with another glare. She was eyeballing me, and I shrunk down in my chair. It wasn't my job to stand up to her; that was for Michael. So far, he had done a less than stellar job of it and was very intimidated

*

Michael questioned Michelle on the two items I previously mentioned. Michelle's testimony that Blair had told her I "felt her up" was hearsay, although Michael didn't object to this. I suspected her testimony might hurt my case if the jury looked past her appearance. The second question was much more interesting. Michael expressed his heartfelt sorrow that Michelle was raped, then asked her when this happened. She couldn't remember.

"I guess a couple years ago," she slurred

"You guess? You can't remember when you were raped?" Michael asked.

"Nope," she repeated, shoulders shrugged.

"Okay, where were you treated?"

"Oh, I didn't go to a doctor or report it, I just told my mom and we tried to forget about it."

It was a blatant attempt to hit the jury with the sympathy card. I cannot emphasize enough that *she did not report it*. Maybe it happened and maybe not. I hoped the jury would take this as relevant testimony, even if it didn't matter in this case, because it tested her credibility. Michael didn't pursue it any further. He handed her a copy of the police report to refresh her memory on the "feeling her up" testimony she had given the police. It said nothing about this statement in the report.

"But I told the detective; he just didn't write it down," she reasoned.

It was another in a series of lies. Michael relied on the jury seeing through the rubbish. "Nothing further, your honor."

Michelle stepped down and it was Blair the state called next.

*

Blair was sworn in around 11:30 and the state started their examination. I had spent a great deal of time watching the jury, as per Michael's instructions, and the woman in the front row third seat still looked like she was going to cry at any moment. It was very unsettling and made me nervous. I continued to hope that the jury saw the light, even with Michael's half-hearted defense.

Blair seemed calm, maybe even too calm. She had a glassy look in her eyes that made me think she was either really tired or over medicated. Her speaking was slow and careful, not indicative of the couple of times I had spoken with her. It wasn't a surprise, because this would be her fourth time going over the story. I suspected she was probably nervous coming into this situation and was given a sedative to calm her. Blair was dressed in a blue turtleneck and blue jeans. She looked far neater than her friend, who had just finished. Her hair was brushed and she had no stains on her clothes. I still couldn't get over that spacy, stoned look she had. This would be a subject of conversation among my family members at the end of the day.

*

Prosecutor Gardner, as was his strategy throughout, asked her most of the same questions that he did at the pre-lim exam and she didn't answer them much differently. The current questions centered more on her accusations, and her relationship with her friend. There were no inquiries, however, involving Carowitz. They skipped straight to her accusations.

This time around, she had to answer a question that she knew nothing about; Gardner asked her about the "distinguishing mark" Michael had so dumbly mentioned.

"Does Mr. West have a mark or tattoo in his groin area?"

She stated that I had a tattoo *on my penis*: Not around my penis, not on my leg, but *ON MY PENIS*. This was the most obvious lie yet. It was the break I was looking for. I turned

196

around and gave my family a huge grin and they gave me smiles and a thumb's up in return. As you remember, in the pre-lim hearing she mentioned "kissing" my penis, while also mentioning that she saw clear fluid exiting my penis. That meant that she had allegedly looked at my private area. I felt that there was no way the jury could miss this one. She had perjured herself. It would be up to Michael to take advantage of this and keep the momentum we had gained. After answering a couple minor questions about her friend Michelle, Gardner closed, "No more questions."

Judge Taylor then broke for lunch. It was 12:00 noon and we had to return at 2:00.

"I WANT THIS TRIAL CONCLUDED TODAY!" Taylor sneered. **"YOU PROMISED A ONE DAY TRIAL AND I'M HOLDING YOU TO IT!" "COURT IS ADJOURNED UNTIL 2:00!"**

She instructed the jury to keep from talking about the case and off to lunch we went. Michael instructed me to stick with him. I wanted to have lunch with Nikki, but I couldn't because she may be testifying on my behalf. Upon exiting the courtroom, I did give her a blown kiss and an A-OK sign. I sense she appreciated that.

*

Michael took me to a local restaurant just down the road from the courthouse, and it was here where things became tense between us. I wanted to smoke and he didn't want to let me. He was afraid a juror might see me.

197

"So what?" I barked at him, "I'm a grown man and can smoke if I want to. If that made the difference in this trial, then the "system" was even more warped than I originally thought. Let the jurors see me how I am, not how you think I should be."

Michael had me go outside behind a dumpster to smoke so I was out of sight, which is probably worse than standing on the sidewalk. If a juror saw me behind a garbage can sneaking a cigarette, it could be a disaster. After I finished, I went inside and grabbed a seat with Michael. He bought me a sandwich, but I wasn't hungry.

The next thing he said was the scariest part of this whole day.

"So, Sean, how am I doing?"

Shocked, I replied, "What? Are you kidding me? How are you doing? You tell me how the hell you're doing?" My eyes were bulging out of my skull.

If I had the guts, I would have fired him on the spot. I couldn't go back to court, though, and face that witch of a judge without him. She would have probably popped a head gasket and thrown me in jail just for the sport of it. No, I had to follow this through. By the way, I thought he was below average as a counselor. He could have tied Blair's parents in knots, but didn't. He could have given Michelle more trouble, and mentioned hearsay or irrelevance, but he didn't. It wasn't even his doing that Blair perjured herself. It was my idea. This goes all the way back to my arrest when I didn't disclose "the tattoo" to the police. I kept this secret "under my belt" because I knew she would not be able to identify it. Yes, I told him all these things over lunch.

198

I also asked Michael to attack her for perjuring herself. He said he couldn't because Taylor would say she was terrorized and didn't remember clearly. What kind of a "system" is this? If you lie that's it, you're done. I thought the point of a trial was to decipher truth from fiction. How can lies be justified? It suddenly occurred to me that Michael was afraid of Taylor. He didn't want to upset her and be sent to jail for contempt. He also wanted a nice, smooth transition to the end of the trial. Michael's thinking was that they had done enough damage to themselves for a complete acquittal. He also mentioned possibly not having me testify. He was afraid that I would have to answer hard questions when called to the stand, and it may tie me up.

"I'll answer any question, Michael. I have nothing to hide and I'm not intimidated by Gardner."

When you tell the truth, it's simple. Keep your answers short and don't argue. We finished lunch and headed back to court. Very few words were exchanged between us en route. Michael did remind me to answer yes or no only to the prosecutor's questions. He said he would clear everything up on cross exam. *Of course he would.*

*

At 2:00, Taylor re-entered her domain and the trial resumed. Blair was Michael's witness.

"Don't screw it up Mike," I said. "You have her by the tail."

Michael meant to be gentle with Blair. He did not want to upset the jury into thinking we were monsters on the attack. I could agree with that to some extent. I found myself wishing that I'd hired a female attorney. My philosophy was that a woman might better understand what I faced plus be a little tougher on Blair and get away with it. I could be wrong though. Blair appeared to be in the same mellow mood she was in during the state's exam. Michael started her off with informal questions and progressed to the more difficult ones as he went on.

Michael then asked questions that were more personal.

"Blair, did you testify that you kissed Sean's private area, but his penis did not enter your mouth?"

"Yes," she answered.

"Did you also testify that you saw clear fluid exit his penis?"

"Yes."

"Just before lunch, you also testified that Sean had a tattoo on his penis. Is this correct."

"Well," Blair added, "I don't really remember if I saw it or not. I think Sean might have told me about it."

She was hedging. According to the reports, Blair stated that she saw fluid exit my penis. Michael referred her to the spot in the pre-lim hearing transcript where she testified to this. He handed her the document and asked her to read the lines where this testimony occurred. As Blair was reading, Taylor piped in loudly and rudely,

"I THOUGHT WE AGREED TO HURRY THIS THING ALONG; SHE'S HAD ENOUGH TIME TO READ IT, CONTINUE WITH YOUR QUESTIONS COUNCIL!"

Michael looked startled. "Yes, your Honor," he said, very softly.

We had every right to defend ourselves in whatever timetable it took and Michael should have told her that. He didn't and continued his cross.

"Now you testify that what you read is true, Blair?"

"I guess," she lazily stated. "But I looked all around the area when I was down there and when I was holding it. I never really looked straight at his private area for more than a second."

"So you looked all around instead of directly at his private area? Then you surely saw the very large, very colorful tattoo on his upper left thigh, not his penis" Michael had her on the run.

"I don't remember, I don't know for sure. I was traumatized."

She was cracking and trying to cover her steps. The sleepiness appeared to be wearing off, replaced by alarm. I'm sure she was coached extensively during lunch as to how she should answer Michael's questions, but she was choking. It was time for Michael to go in for the kill. Yet, for reasons unknown, he moved on to other, simpler questions. I was astonished. He had her on the edge of admitting her lies, or better yet, breaking down in tears and looking like a fool on the stand. He took his foot off the accelerator and slowed the pace. The only thing I could figure is that he didn't want to appear too aggressive with her, for fear of upsetting the jury.

The remainder of the questioning was uneventful and Michael ended his cross. I thought he should have compared her statements from the police report, Pontiac Care House report, and the pre-lim hearing, but he didn't. Upon returning to the table, I asked him why. He told me he had done enough to sway the jury and didn't want to look like he was being nasty to her. I thought you go for the win at all costs. Was this guy really on my side?

The state rested and it was time to mount our defense. Michael had me, the PI Sam, my wife and Danny. Michael no longer needed Danny, he said, because the alcohol accusations never came up. The state knew we had that covered because of Danny's testimony in the police report. Michael dismissed him. I still think Danny should have been called as at least a character witness. A very important point needs to be made here; The Pontiac Care House interviewer, who was considered a forensic expert in questioning children, was not called by the state. I think it's because they would testify to serious doubt about Blair's testimony.

"Now that I have called you on your false allegation, you are using additional smear tactics."
                                        -George Soros

The Trial: Defense's Case

Michael started our defense by calling Sam. He was the Private Investigator we hired to look into Blair's life. Testimony was disturbingly quick. Michael asked Sam what he found out when he called Sara Joan to interview Blair. He testified that Sara Joan told him that a litigating attorney had been hired and she was suing the church and me. He also testified to being turned down by Sara Joan to interview Blair and being denied an interview with Michelle by her mother. There were no more questions by Michael. He should've asked more about his professional ability to interview kids and find out if they're truthful or not.

Mr. Gardner crossed by simply asking Sam if he were a former police officer. Sam answered that he was. Gardner than asked if he was a licensed private investigator. Sam said he was and that was the end of it. It took all of ten minutes to direct and cross this man? What did I spend five hundred bucks ($$$) for? Incidentally, that day in court was the first and last time I actually met him.

*

It was apparent that both lawyers were shook up by Taylor and that they were hurrying along. I'm sure Michael was because this was his first experience with her. Gardner, being a county prosecutor, had more court time with Taylor. I also noticed during Sam's testimony that Taylor was nodding off. Her head was back and her eyes shut. What a slap in the face. I felt like I was in the middle of a cruel practical joke. She was making a further mockery of her own courtroom. How can you sleep when you're responsible for justice being served? I wanted to slap this woman awake and tell her to buck up and pay attention. Sure, she's the boss and can do what she wants, but she didn't need to be blatant about it. If I slept on my job, I would be dismissed on the spot. I needed to re-focus on the case and not her. Since it was my turn to take the stand, she decided to come around. Perhaps I wouldn't be as boring to her as the rest of the proceedings. Now it was my chance to make a good impression with the jurors, despite the judge's behavior.

*

"Defense calls Sean West."

I took my seat next to Judge Taylor. I looked at her and received another cold, calculating stare. It made my skin crawl. I decided to try to avoid eye contact.

It was time to pay very close attention to the questions. I felt like I was on stage in front of a huge crowd, reciting a speech. I knew I could do well under the pressure.

Michael began the questioning by asking me about my relationship with Blair. I explained that I knew her at the school and that I was simply cordial with her, nothing more or less. I made sure to meet eyes with the jurors, as Michael instructed me to, so they could see that my face told the truth. Michael continued with the preliminary questions, than reached the good ones, which we hoped would destroy the prosecution's case.

"Do you have a tattoo on your penis, Mr. West?"

"NO," I proudly stated while still looking at the jurors.

"So Blair did not, in fact, see a tattoo on your penis? Is that what you're telling me?"

"Yes. I have a tattoo on my left thigh, not my penis."

I knew I had a satisfied smile on my face, but I couldn't help it. I had damaged her entire testimony. Michael entered the picture of the tattoo into evidence. It was unmistakable. The picture Michael entered was the one with my underwear on, and my jeans pulled down below my knees so there wouldn't be any question whatsoever about the placement of my pants. Judge Taylor was the first to receive the photo. She looked at it, then looked at me and smirked. Apparently, she was unimpressed with my underwear choice of tighty-whiteys. Maybe the tattoo frightened her. Perhaps she knew as well as I did that I had just disintegrated Blair's case. I didn't know and I didn't care. I was glowing because I felt that this had broken the prosecution's back. When Mr. Gardner looked at the pic, he tossed it to the side on his table. Detective Smart, who was sitting next to him, picked up the photo and studied it, then looked at me with a straight face. I sensed an undercurrent of anger as he put the picture down next to him. They both knew it was a killer. I could see it in their expressions. Gardner had his head propped up on his fist as he swept his hair off his forehead. Smart continued to look puzzled. I felt like he had a touch of sympathy. Did he finally see his mistakes in pushing the matter. Michael asked me a few more questions, which included whether or not I mentioned Blair's breasts to her mom and Carowitz.

"I did not!"

Michael had done something right. It was Mr. Gardner's turn. I had been very confident, yet fidgety on the stand. I hated the suit I was wearing. It was uncomfortable and heavy. The tie felt as though it was nearly strangling me. I had been scared to death, but Michael's questions relaxed me immensely.

Gardner began his cross.

"Mr. West, I'm not going to double talk you or try to confuse you. I'm just going to ask you my questions straightforward."

The introduction was a scare tactic, but he had no choice but to be straightforward with me. If he tried to use tricks, I wouldn't argue and I couldn't be had. Yes or no answers only. I had truth on my side and he knew it. He did the best he could.

"Did you sexually assault Blair Radison?"

"No."

Gardner went on, "Did you touch Blair's breasts, nipples or vagina?"

"Absolutely not," I said confidently while looking over the jury as I responded.

Carowitz was sitting in the third row behind the prosecutors table. I happened to look that way when I was answering a question, and he was making very subtle slashing gestures across his neck while defiantly smiling ear to ear. I should have said something. I tried to ignore him, but it was

206

tough. By the way, where was Taylor's screaming we had come to expect? I looked up at her and she was nodding off again. She had no idea what was going on in her courtroom. I continued answering the questions despite Carowitz making another mockery of this trial.

Gardner shifted his strategy, "Is it true that you told Detective Smart that Blair was 'Dressing provocatively?'"

I answered simply; "That was Mr. Smart's quote, not mine."

Gardner asked me if my daughter ever dressed provocatively.

"Not in a church, and besides, she's ten".

If you look back at the police report, I was looking for the word to describe the way Blair sometimes dressed at work, but Smart found it himself. I simply agreed. It was still his word. I was given a copy of the report and asked again. I answered the same. Now he asked me if I was calling Smart a liar.

"No, I'm just telling you that he said it. I think half-shirts and belly exposing clothes were inappropriate for the facility we worked in."

I was giving too much information, I thought.

The questions continued, "But they work in the school at night after the kids are gone, right?"

I countered, "This facility is holy, from the school to the church to the offices."

What could he say? It was true. I wasn't trying to fool anyone. He moved on.

Gardner asked me about the vacuum incidents. "Did you pull the plug on Blair's vacuum? Were you flirting with Blair?"

"I pulled the plug on Carowitz's vacuum, Sara Joan's vacuum and Bonnie's vacuum too," I stated. "It certainly didn't mean that I wanted to be sexual with them, nor was it perceived as such."

Gardner again brought my daughter into it.

"Did you joke around with Blair like you would with your daughter?"

"No. I joked around with Blair, Carowitz and the rest of them like they were workmates."

I really don't know what the relevance was with my ten year old. They were strange questions if you asked me. Michael should have objected on the grounds of irrelevance. Gardner was trying to paint me as a pervert with my own daughter. I must emphasize that I never told Smart that Blair and I had "tickle fights." He included that quote in the report himself without my knowledge.

I asked for water and Gardner gave me some. Gardner then asked me if Blair came to the garage.

"Yes," I answered.

He asked if she entered the garage.

"Yes." *(Always with the door open and she did not come inside, my brain was screaming.)*

Michael had instructed me to answer only yes or no. I knew he would clear things up on re-cross. The next series of questions mainly centered on Blair's home life, of which I had no idea.

"Do you think Blair has a good home life?"

"OBJECTION!" Michael screamed. "How could Mr. West possibly know about Blair's home life?"

208

OVERRULED!" Taylor screeched, **"HE CAN ANSWER THE QUESTION."**

Michael tried to object one more time, but Taylor denied him loudly. She then looked to me and shouted, **"ANSWER THE QUESTION!"**

"I guess okay, but I don't know for sure."

Gardner would tell the jury in closing arguments that I said her home life was okay. The jury heard my answer. I didn't even know how this mattered, but I had to respond. Hindsight being 20/20, I wish I would have said her home life must be terrible, that was why we were here. Let it be known that I *never* talked with Blair out of work. I *never* wrote her, telephoned her or e-mailed her. I *never* gave her gifts or notes of any kind. These were additional questions Michael should have asked me, but didn't. Gardner didn't ask either.

"No more questions, your Honor."

Taylor then asked, "Re-cross counsel?"

I looked at Michael thinking he was going to re-cross, but he sat there looking at paperwork.

"Nothing further, Your Honor."

"WHAT? YOU DIRTY SON OF A BITCH!" Was exactly what I was thinking. "You hung me out to dry."

Gardner opened the knee-high door where I was sitting and I stomped back to my seat next to Michael. I glared at him, and then violently wrote down on my pad WHY DID YOU NOT RE-CROSS? He waved me off. What a jerk. My testimony was over, and the jury only knew half of the story. What could I do at that point? We had only one more witness, Nikki. She would be the character witness I would need. He'd better do well with her.

Michael stood up and inexplicably said, "Defense rests, your Honor."

I looked daggers at Michael and I violently scrawled on my tablet again. CALL NIKKI! My blood pressure had to be dangerously high at that point. If I had been using a pencil, I would have busted it in half.

He shook his head no, "were okay," he whispered, "we have enough."

It was too late. Once you rested, you were done. I could have punched Michael right in his nose. What in the hell was the guy thinking? Was he thinking at all? The jury had *half* of the story. I wrote "ASSHOLE" on my tablet. He ripped it away from me and put it in his briefcase. He snatched my pen from my hand as well.

> *"A trial without witnesses, when it involves a criminal accusation, a criminal matter, is not a true trial.*
> *-Bill McCollum*

The Trial: Closing Statements

Judge Taylor called for Gardner's closing statement. He wagged his finger at me and called me a rapist and a pedophile.

"This man raped a teenage girl!" He insisted.

He talked about the fact that there was no evidence in this case, but said, "A woman's vagina was a wonderful and amazing organ that can be stretched out and go back to its original form."

He also said it could "accommodate much more than a finger. So Mr. West could have put his finger in and it would not show any signs of stress." He went on, "It would show no evidence of penetration, even if she was checked within twenty-four hours of the alleged touching. Nobody would be able to tell. Not even a professional gynecologist."

Gardner rambled on. He had the audacity to say that Blair was so traumatized that even if she did look at my private area, which she testified that she did *and* didn't, she wouldn't see details on my penis or legs.

"Can you imagine if it were you? Wouldn't you look right through any details?" Gardner asked the jury. "That was what happened to Blair. She was so shook up; she saw nothing except blank space."

211

That's contrary to everything I've heard about trauma victims. According to the "experts," the details of the experience should be forever etched in their minds. It was an attempt to justify another in a long list of lies.

The prosecutor called me a rapist a few more times and told the jury that I groomed, pursued and conquered Blair. He never explained how. There were no gifts, phone calls or letters. Michael should have made that a major point.

He also mentioned what a litigating attorney does and how they do it, thus embellishing the Carowitz testimony.

He also talked about Blair's mom. "She would never hurt her child by putting her through this just for money."

Again, he was embellishing testimony. A prosecutor is not allowed to add to a witnesses' testimony. These instances should have been objected to, but Michael was frozen in fear. He sat beside me with not a thread of emotion. Gardner never looked me in the eyes.

*

It was Michael's turn to speak. I was burning hot inside. I was also surprised, angry and scared. Michael took all of fifteen minutes to present my closing.

"Sean is innocent, Sean did not do this, Sean has too much to lose and Blair saw the tattoo and lied about it. Thank you for hearing our side."

It was not a good job. I rubbed my eyes, trying valiantly but with no success to ward off the oncoming freight train called a migraine headache.

Gardner finished with one important point during his second closing. (Prosecution is allowed closing and rebuttal, defense only closing.)

"Mr. West's wife didn't even come up to testify. She wasn't even in the room."

I sneered at Michael again, knowing he had left my wife, my strongest supporter, out in the hallway throughout the entire trial. Michael said nothing. Gardner called me a rapist one last time for good measure

It was now 4:00. The entire trial, which included seating a jury, took four hours and forty minutes. One hundred and twenty minutes were taken for lunch, so that knocked it down to two hours and forty minutes of actual trial time. We were done in a dramatically short time. I supposed Judge Taylor had successfully made sure her docket stayed clean.

*

I thought Taylor's antics would bode well for an appeal, if we needed to file one, but her **"HURRY IT UP!"** comments were mysteriously stricken from the record. We were in the United States of America, and I was at a loss for words at how blatantly corrupt our court system was.

Taylor spoke to the jury again. "Don't talk about this case with anyone; we will start deliberations at 8:30 a.m. tomorrow."

The way I saw it, this court should run until 5:00 p.m., like everyone else's courtrooms. This would give the jury about forty-five minutes to get started and discuss it while it was fresh in their minds. As it stood now, they could go home and think about it all night. That didn't sit well with me. They were twelve different people with twelve entirely different lives. I figured they would probably talk to their spouses or friends about it. That was human nature. I didn't fault them; I only wished they had had a few minutes to discuss it together before leaving. It may have given them a truer glimpse of how they really felt.

*

My family, along with Michael left the court. I told him everything I felt.

"Bert should have been here," I told him. I also criticized his fear of the judge.

Michael angrily countered, "Hey, I'm not going to be jailed on a contempt charge!"

"Really? What's the matter, are you afraid of a few hours in a cell that would mean nothing in the long run? Even if she found you in contempt in the first place, which was unlikely."

"You're a spineless, gutless attorney." Now I was really rolling, "You even left Nikki in the hallway the entire trial! You are a sad excuse for a lawyer." I continued my rant, "You gave her no chance to vouch for me and you left that door wide open for the state to tell the jury how she was not even there for me." I was shouting, **"Not to mention leaving the jury with only half a story by not re-crossing me."**

Michael shouted back, **"This conversation is hereby terminated!"**

He went his way and I went mine. If he'd used a bit of that tenacity in court, we would have stood a better chance of winning. I was starting to think that he thought I was guilty. I told my wife that no matter how this turns out, we were filing a grievance against this firm. She agreed. We entered in the truck and went home. I fumed.

"The prosecutor, who is supposed to carry the burden of the proof, really is an author."
                                                        -Scott Turow

The Last Supper?

On our way home, we stopped and picked up food for everyone. Call it my version of a possible "Last supper." My wife, Mom, Brother and his wife were all with me at the house. We would eat like kings, and then discuss what had happened in court.

I think my brother's wife, Liza, was the most vocal of all. She sat in the courtroom with her arms angrily crossed over her chest for the entire trial, and could not believe her eyes or ears. She said that Michael talked about nothing of any consequence except the tattoo story. He cross examined everyone and seemed to be getting them to break, but then would let up off the gas. He was afraid of Taylor.

My mom agreed. "Your lawyer was as disappointing as I've ever seen in any court, EVER; on television or in real life."

My mom was such a good person. I had always gotten along with her well since I can remember. She was always supportive and loving, and had gone to bat for me. She even made calls to Michael expressing her opinion on how we should proceed.

"You fight hard for him, Mike," she would tell him.

This is my family and they were biased toward me. They still questioned me extensively leading up to the trial and told me if they would have had doubts or thought I'd committed a crime, they would say so and tell me I deserved my punishment. My quiet brother grilled me more than anyone else, excluding Nikki. He had asked me pointed questions,

"Why do you say this, why does she say that? Tell me everything from the beginning."

I answered all his inquiries the best I could. After reading the conflicting statements and hearing my answers, he was on my side for good. My entire family also said they would have been there for support either way. My mom and step-dad believed me from the get-go, knowing this was not in my nature. Reading the police report convinced them. The same went for Liza. If she didn't believe me or had doubts, she would've said so loudly.

My wife was a little different. She would have dumped me fast if she thought this nonsense was true. I would have found my belongings on the front lawn. She didn't though, because she read everything and questioned me closer than anyone else. My family all saw and heard Blair's testimony. Everyone except Nikki heard Blair lie on the stand. She was convinced of my innocence.

We talked for a few more minutes, and then it was time for everyone to go their separate ways and sleep on it. Nikki and I went to bed, hugged each other as tightly as we could and tried to fall asleep. Nikki cried. She put her face in my shoulder and let it out. I could feel the emotion inside her soul. Would it be our last night in the same bed for *twenty* years? I hoped and prayed that it wouldn't turn out that way. If it was going to, I wanted us to be as close as possible beforehand.

"I get nervous, irritated, very tense or stressed, but never bored."

-Catherine Deneuve

Shaun Webb

The Trial: Deliberation

I woke up at 6:00 a.m. and was glad that I'd slept in my own bed. I was surprisingly well rested considering what could face us today. We would be in court at 8:30 again, but this time it was for jury deliberations that could last for who knew how long. As was the case before the opening day of the trial, I showered and shaved, and we went out for a nice breakfast before going to the courthouse.

*

As a family, we had a general feeling of confidence. I thought I would almost certainly be acquitted on all counts because I knew deep down that the jury heard and listened to the testimony closely, even though they only received half of the information. My only worry was Michael's failure to re-cross after Gardner had finished. That caused an underlying current of tension. What if the jurors stewed all night and decided that I was guilty? What if I was headed to prison? So many thoughts and so many prayers. I've never been in a situation even closely resembling this kind of unbearable tension. Falling off my bike when I was a kid or hitting my head was about the only thing in which to compare it. The panicky feeling you get when you see the blood on your

221

hands. I had to keep my wits about me. As much as I could have freaked out, it would not help the situation. I felt like I'd been holding my breath for twenty-four straight hours. I wanted to exhale.

*

After we finished breakfast, we had a group prayer and headed to Oakland County Circuit Court for what we hoped to be a not guilty verdict and a joyous trip home. We arrived around 8:00, just in time for the doors to be opened. Upon arriving at the courtroom, we saw Sara Joan's sister Bonnie sitting in the hallway by herself. I could have cut the tension with a knife. She hated me. She was convinced that I had abused her niece, and nothing was going to change her mind. You could see it in her face. She had an absolute scowl of loathing. That didn't surprise me though, because she was standing up for her family. Perhaps she hadn't heard or listened to the testimony. Maybe she didn't want to.

We sat a good distance away from her, but two minutes later, she left. I thought she was staying for the deliberations, but then I figured she showed up to give me a moment of discomfort. At 8:15, the jurors themselves came walking down the hall right past us. I smiled at them as they passed us, and received one smile in return. It was from one of the middle-aged women. This helped to calm my nerves. The rest of the jurors looked straight ahead. At about 8:25, the courtroom doors opened and we filed in.

Oakland County Court starts at 8:30 in the morning and runs until 5:00. All except for this particular court. Judge

Taylor finally arrived at about 9:20. She with her arrogant stature and manipulating glares. She was a tiny woman, standing no more than 5'2" and weighing in at one hundred pounds soaking wet. She had a lot of nastiness in a little package. I figured she was the princess of the family or the apple of Daddy's eye. Anything you want or need Dorothy, and I'll get it for you.

"I want to be a judge!" She'd order,

"Yes Dorothy, anything for you. A judge is what you'll be."

I couldn't stand this woman because of her attitude of arrogance and entitlement. I can safely say I have never met or been associated with someone who was so rude and callous to others.

*

"ALL RISE!"

The jury filed in, Taylor took her throne and it was on.

"The jury will now go back and deliberate," Taylor said.

She didn't go over jury instructions again. She gave me another look of contempt, gave my family the same look and ordered me to stay on court grounds. The wait started. I wasn't sure if it would be twenty minutes or two days. Nobody knew.

Liza and I went back and forth outdoors to smoke. One hour, two hours, two and a half hours. I swear I smoked half a pack of cigarettes in that short time. Maybe I was trying to commit slow suicide.

Liza kept assuring me that I would be okay. "I'm telling you Sean, they won't convict with no evidence."

She really wanted that so badly, as did I. She was as supportive as she could be.

"We are going home together today," she said.

We talked about what Nikki and I were going to do next summer. Both of us wished the accusations had never happened. After an interminable two hours and forty-five minutes, the jury announced it had reached a verdict. The hand wringing and waiting was to end.

I would find out later that after two hours and fifteen minutes, the jury had requested some additional information. Taylor was contacted for this, and not fifteen minutes later the verdict was actually reached. I'll never know for sure, but maybe Taylor said something to the jurors. That's highly illegal. Some parties within the court believed that was the case. None of the people who said this would get involved, though. They wanted no part of that woman.

It was time to hold our collective breaths. I thought my heart would beat out of my chest and onto the floor.

"Money will determine whether the accused goes to prison or walks out of the courtroom a free man."
-Johnnie Cochrane

The Trial: the Verdict

"ALL RISE" Taylor arrogantly marched her way up onto her royal throne.

"I understand the jury has reached a verdict,"

"Yes, Your Honor." Gardner chimed in quickly, wanting to impress the judge.

Taylor growled out her next order, "Bring the jury in."

She perused her courtroom with the contempt of a spoiled adult. It was her domain, her sanctuary and her amusement park.

The jury filed in. I couldn't read their faces. I only hoped they had it right. I had a cross in my hand and rubbed it frantically, thinking it would make a difference. Neither the Radisons nor Carowitz were there for the verdict. Bonnie had darted off earlier. Why she showed up but didn't stay, I'll never know, but I think the fact that my family was here and hers weren't scared her away. Smart wasn't present either. Only Prosecutor Gardner attended for the state.

My family waited behind me in utter silence. A few of my closest workmates were also present. This included my boss Gail, along with workmates Jillian and Diana. My neighbor also showed up. I could almost hear them breathing. The air in the room could be cut with a knife. Michael whispered to me, "Stop fidgeting in that chair."

225

"Screw you, Michael," I cursed, "I'll fidget all I want. I'm the one with my life on the line here."

I turned around and looked at my family. I never saw so much tension and worry in my entire life. I asked Michael if I was going to jail if any guilty verdicts were reached.

"Yes, Sean, they'll take you immediately if even one count is guilty."

That made me even more fidgety. I had Michael take Nikki my wedding ring, just in case. I did not want it on my finger in the event I was taken away.

Taylor screeched, "Has the jury reached a verdict?"

"Yes, your Honor, we have," The foreman announced.

"Would the clerk please retrieve the jury forms and bring them to me."

Taylor looked at the folded piece of paper and put it down next to her. She looked at me, but her face showed zero emotion. I held my cross tightly. I believe I rubbed the shine off it.

"Would the jury foreman please rise and read the verdict."

"Please, please, please Lord." I begged

"Your honor, we find the defendant "not guilty" of the crime of Criminal Sexual Conduct, 3rd degree (finger to vagina)."

A huge breath could be heard from behind me. They had that right. This was the most severe charge, and held the most jail time. However, if I were found guilty on both of the next two counts, it would be considered the equivalent of one third degree count, as far as sentencing went. The tension continued.

"How does the jury find as to count II, CSC 4th degree (hand to breast)?"

I rubbed the chrome clean off that cross.

"We find the defendant "GUILTY AS CHARGED!"

"Ohhh nooo!" There was an audible "GASP!" behind me. I heard Liza specifically.

"Oh my God, no." My stomach tightened and my tears began to flow.

Taylor, smiling for the first time, happily piped in again, "As to Count III, CSC 4th degree (mouth to breast)? How does the jury find?"

"Not guilty, your honor."

*

I didn't hear the third count decision due to the excessive wailing, pouting, crying and gasping over count II. Mr. Gardner stood up and called for bond to be revoked. The Judge happily agreed. **"BOND IS REVOKED,"** she shrieked. **"TAKE THIS MAN AWAY!"**

A then sympathetic deputy who whispered in my ear, "I'm sorry, I have to cuff you, just relax", cuffed me.

His sympathy would turn into venom very soon.

Two deputies led me out of the courtroom and directly into hell. I told my wife I loved her while being led away. She wept uncontrollably.

My mother was hysterical. She shouted at the jury, **"HE DIDN'T DO THIS, HOW CAN YOU POSSIBLY SAY HE DID?"** They looked at her, unfazed.

Taylor sent her out of the court. **"GET THAT WOMAN OUT OF MY COURT!"**

They did. I was afraid they might arrest her too. I hoped not.

I heard Liza saying, "I'll go out with Mom."

It was complete pandemonium. I was weeping hysterically.

As I passed the jurors, I looked right at them and said, "You were wrong, you were so wrong, I didn't do this."

They stared at me with blank faces. Did they realize what they had done? They were basing their decision on half of the story. The whole story would have freed me.

*

A new way of living waited; no Nikki to hold me, and none of the little extras in life that I'd come to enjoy. All of the freedoms I took for granted were stripped away from me. I would no longer be Sean. I would be inmate # 885398. My new career would be as an inmate, not a trusted maintenance man that served nearly ten honest years at St. Paul. My retirement plan, insurance and all that goes with it was gone forever, all because of the lies of a single person. There was no evidence, only a kid's word, and half a story. I already knew that whatever my sentence would be, I'd be forced to start completely from scratch when free again.

The Sex Offender Registry awaited my name and photo. My only constants were my wife and family. Thank God for them. Some people don't even have that much to fall back on. This is not all about me. It is also about everyone close to me, and some not so close. The worst was yet to come. I had no idea how bad this would get. I knew nothing about jail. I knew nothing about this life. What was going to happen to me? Would I die here? Please help me somebody. This is only a dream. I'm going to wake up soon and everything will be okay. Please, please. Oh no, this is **NOT** real.

"There is no such thing as justice - in or out of court."

-Clarence Darrow

II.

Shaun Webb

232

Welcome To Hell

After the verdict reading, everyone in the courtroom was stunned. A deputy for Oakland County came up behind me and told me in a very gentle voice, "I have to cuff you now."

I was weeping and disagreeing with the verdict as he led me out of the courtroom. This time I was leaving through the wrong door. I was delving deeper into the building. As soon as we went through this door and it shut behind us, he yelled, **"SHUT THE FUCK UP BOY!"**

Whoa, that was unnecessary. He didn't need to scream at me. I was a human being, not a dog. All of a sudden, here came Judge Taylor bursting through the door behind us. **"I AM IN DANGER IN THAT COURTROOM,"** she hollered. **"I HAVE NO SECURITY."**

In danger of what? My mom was led to the courtroom hallway while the people who were still inside sat speechless. Liza went out to rescue Mom from the *five* huge deputies that were surrounding the tiny woman. The deputy told Taylor to hold on and a guard would be there soon.

"THERE HAD BETTER BE." She threatened.

She had that perpetual scowl permanently etched on her face. The guard laughed aloud and continued leading me along.

233

He looked at the other deputy on my left, "What a fucking bitch, huh?" he said.

"Yeah, she's a real cunt alright." They agreed.

We entered an elevator and went downward to a basement. My head was pressed against the back cushioned wall of the elevator.

"Don't turn around on me or I'll hit you," is the threat the deputy gave me.

I was going straight to hell, I thought. My emotions were jumping out of my skin. I was visibly upset and the guards knew it, but didn't care.

*

They took me out of the elevator and into a small room where a guard was waiting for me.

"Name," They asked. I didn't answer fast enough.

"WHAT'S YOUR FUCKING NAME?"

"AH, SEAN, Sean West," I weakly uttered.

"Well Mr. West, I can tell you one thing right now; you will either cooperate with us or you will be dealt with severely."

I knew they weren't kidding, so I got a grip on myself and continued answering the questions. When my initial interview was over, they led me into another small tiled room that looked like a shower.

I was ordered by a male deputy to; "Take all your clothes off and turn in a circle with your arms over your head."

I was looked over thoroughly. The guard instructed me to bend over and cough. I did so with much embarrassment.

The deputy stuck a gloved finger into my rectum and moved it in a circular motion. I had to lift my penis and testicles so he could see underneath them. My clothes were given back to me except for my tie, belt and suspenders. These items were placed in a bag and marked with my name.

"You'll get this back when you leave jail," he told me.

*

The guard led me down a long corridor of jail cells and placed me in one. I was alone in this cell with a wooden bench and a toilet. It was 1:00 p.m. or so. I had no idea what to do next, so I cried. I sobbed until 4:00 when two other men entered the cell with me. They were also dressed in their nice suits, sans the ties or belts. They tried to talk to me, but I was in no mood. I just sat with my legs tucked into my body and I was as close to the corner of the wall as I could get. I continued to sob quietly.

After about thirty minutes, one of the guys walked over to me and spoke, "You better get used to it dude. Crying will get you nothing except black eyes and an ass kicking."

I stopped the sobbing, but stayed quiet. I didn't want to talk, so I stayed silent.

*

After another hour or so, around 5:00, two guards came down the hall with four prisoners shackled by their hands and feet. You could hear them coming. The chains rattled with each step they took. They opened our gate, summoned us out, and we were shackled with them. Six of us, all hooked together like a chain gang. We were heading for the long walk through the underground tunnel and into the main jail area. It would easily be the most forgettable march of my life. I felt as though I was headed to my execution.

It was cold in the tunnel. The lights were dim and it was eerie. You could see your breath in the air with each exhale.

One of the guys said something, and our chain gang was stopped in the tunnel while he was chewed out.

"NO FUCKING TALKING," the guard screamed. **"THE NEXT GUY WHO MAKES A SOUND IS GOING TO THE HOLE AFTER I HIT YOU IN THE MOUTH."**

I figured the hole was bad, so my mouth would stay shut, as it already was. It took fifteen minutes to walk the length of the tunnel and up a series of stairs. We finally reached a large steel door. One of our guards rang a bell of some sort and the door clicked open. My next sight was of the main jail facility and all that it encompassed.

*

To my left was a row of four small white rooms with steel barred doors at the entrances. Two of those rooms were occupied. To my right was a "Booking" room, which looked to be where the inmates had their pictures taken and some sort of wristband placed on their arms. The lineup was out the door at this room. Straight ahead stood four very large jail cells so over-filled with people that they had to stand up to occupy it. In the center of all this were a series of orange, grey, blue and pink benches. I could already see three women sitting at the pink benches, so apparently, those were for female inmates. The other benches had men dressed in jumpsuits that were the corresponding bench color. Men in oranges were on orange benches, blues on blue benches, etc.

After being released from our shackles, we stopped by the jail clothing area, where we traded our street clothes for our colored jumper, and were led to the blue benches. I would find out that orange wearing prisoners were felony criminals with violent crimes and headed to prison. Greys were medium security, some going to prison and some not, while blues were minimum security. A few blues were headed to prison, but not too many. I figured this would bode well for me, even though I had not yet been sentenced. A guard with a large German Shepherd K-9 unit patrolled the entire room amidst the chaos. I say chaos because it was very loud in there. An inmate sitting near me was muttering something about kicking that dog's ass. Guards yelling, inmates screaming and arguing, and a general hum of activity combined with tension.

While waiting on my bench for whatever was to happen next, the kitchen help, with green jumpers that read "Trusty" on the back, were handing out bag lunches. I found out that a "trusty" was just that, a trusted inmate allowed to work. The bags they handed out contained two mushy, warm bologna sandwiches, an apple and a few cookies. I wasn't hungry at the time, so I held onto mine. The emotion and fear coursing through my veins would have led to a stomachache had I eaten.

*

A few hours later, a guard called me into that small booking room about twenty feet away from where I sat. My rear end felt like a board from sitting there, and my back cried out in pain. It was in this room that I had my picture taken and had a wristband with my name and jail ID number placed around my left wrist.

The guard told me that if I removed this ID band, I'd be charged with destruction of jail property.

"Don't remove the wristband, or your ass is grass."

A deputy told me I was a felon. I told him my crime was a misdemeanor. **"It's a fucking felony."** The deputy screamed. I stayed quiet.

Following the booking, they led me back across the large room to an office where a young black woman was sitting behind a keyboard.

"Have a seat. What's your name?" She politely asked.

I sat down in front of her and she asked me how I was doing. This was my first chance to talk to someone of whom I felt mattered and may listen to me.

"I'm doing crappy," I said. "I shouldn't be here and I'm pissed about it."

The woman asked me to continue.

"I would rather be dead than be here."

Whoops; that would be my very first of many stupid things I would say during my stay here at the counties version of fancy lodgings.

"Don't worry," she said. "I'll make sure you get a nice place to stay until you're ready to join the others."

That sounded OK, I guess. I was wrong. She was being sarcastic.

*

I was led back to the booking room, had my wristband clipped off, and was taken to a small white room on the left. Over the door, it read "SUICIDE WATCH" and I knew I had stuck my foot firmly in my mouth. The guard told me to strip naked, which I did in front of everybody, male *and* female, and sent me into this room with a tiny hospital rice paper gown and an even tinier blanket. The gown would cover my private area and backside while the blanket was big enough to put over my chest.

"My God I'm in suicide watch. I didn't really intend to kill myself."

The Point is, watch what you say in jail because you'll definitely be rewarded for it. What was funny though, was that they let me have my glasses in the room.

My next sixteen to twenty hours passed in this cell. I had only an exposed toilet and a small stainless steel bed. I lay on it, tried to cover myself the best I could, and longed for my family. I cried for my wife, my mom, my daughter and even my dog

"Please let this be a dream, I didn't do this, please help me someone."

Here I am crying out for something that was not going to change. I was awake. There were no miracles in there. I was stuck. It was also freezing in this room, because they keep the temperature so low. It made it very hard to sleep or even relax. The stainless steel bed felt like an ice covered pond. I thought that telling the woman I was suicidal would get me a better place to stay.

*

What a horrible place to be. This would be the longest sixteen hours of my life.

"My occupation now, I suppose, is jail inmate."
-Theodore Kaczynski

God Help Me

I think I fell asleep for a while, but I wasn't sure. My glasses were in the corner, bent up and useless. I rolled over them, I suppose. Now I couldn't see, but that was a blessing in disguise. Who really wanted to see any of this?

The next thing I remembered was being rousted by a half pint carton of milk that was thrown at me. I looked up and saw a guard standing over my head with a huge smile on his face. I saw two other guards at the entrance, one male, and one female.

"You alive, boy?" One asked. "If you are, you need to eat your breakfast."

I saw a tray of what looked like white mush and bread sitting in my cell. I would find out through my stay that the food here was usually unrecognizable.

"I'm not hungry," was all I could muster.

"Fine then, we'll give it to someone who is."

"Good. It looks like shit anyways," my smart mouth uttered.

I really wanted these creeps to go away, but they couldn't help themselves.

"Are you trying to starve yourself to death, son? You know that's a form of attempted suicide," the guard threatened. "I could report this and you may never get out of here."

The two other guards who were standing by laughed heartily at this and finally, after getting their fill of the funny naked guy, they left.

It was big joke. The guy lying half-nude in the suicide room catching the humor of masochistic guards, but it wasn't funny. Did they really think it was comical to see people hurting? I didn't want to imagine how nasty these guards could get. Human suffering was their stimulation; their pleasure. They could get away with anything they wanted. Who would believe any of us? We were here because we were all common criminals. I suppose they could beat you and get away with it. They could also prey on the females, housed on the opposite side of the building. The way they were acting made me think it was possible.

*

It was depressing when my thoughts traveled in strange directions. I wanted to go home. I wanted my wife and bed. I wanted my freedom. I could only imagine how the "evil" family was taking full joy in my misfortune. They probably had a huge dinner party and relished their "victory" in court. All these images went through my mind. If you wanted to search what was inside your psyche, go to jail. It brought out my innermost thoughts and feelings. My thoughts were not pretty. I allowed my imagination to wander until I dozed.

*

Later in the day, I was standing in my cell looking out into the jail area. My rice-paper suit was falling apart and I hung it over the back of my neck so I would not have to keep pulling it up. All of a sudden, the doors burst open and three guards piled in and ripped the suit off me. Now I'm completely naked again.

"Are you trying to kill yourself?" One of them asked. "That rice suit was wrapped around your neck."

I had to explain that I was simply trying to keep it pulled up to keep me covered. This suit was barely clinging to me. It wasn't "wrapped" around my neck, as they so dramatically stated. I guess I convinced them, because they finally left me alone. A guard gave me a new rice suit. Incidentally, one of the guards was female, and she stared at my penis the entire time. I didn't care, though. I figured this would be the norm. There was no modesty in that place. It was perverted and corrupt.

*

Sometime around lunchtime, I was awakened again. This time, a man stood at the door with a notepad and pencil. He was a tall figure with a short brown haircut and glasses. This wasn't a guard, however. He wasn't wearing a uniform. It was some man that had come to speak with me.

"Good morning, Sean," he gently spoke, "do you have a few minutes to talk?"

Was he kidding? I had many minutes. Minutes here and minutes there; minutes everywhere. I was loaded with minutes.

"Sure," I said, "let's talk."

This man introduced himself and told me he was a psychological specialist for the jail. He said that he wanted to see where I was mentally. He asked how I was. I surely wasn't going to make the same mistake twice.

"I really am fine," I promised. "I never meant to give the impression that I was suicidal." He told me he knew that.

Then God suddenly spoke through this man; "Have you accepted Jesus Christ as your personal lord and savior?"

I knew right then that I'd been granted a personal visit from the Lord himself, or at least one of the Holy Trinity. Perhaps he was an angel sent from heaven. I listened carefully.

"If you die today, will you go to heaven?"

I knew what he was doing, but I had to amuse him or I wouldn't get out of this room.

"Yes!" I told him, "I've accepted the Lord. I am a Christian. I'm saved. Am I getting out of here soon?"

"Good, okay, great, and yes" were his responses.

He made it clear that any more instances of suicide talk would banish me to this cell for a very long time: Maybe months. He stated that the jailers diagnosed me as a "bi-polar alcoholic" on my jail chart. *A bi-polar alcoholic?*

"The woman whom I'd talked to for thirty seconds came to that conclusion?" I inquired.

"Yep! She sure did," the man said confidently. "She's a smart woman."

244

This woman's diagnosis would haunt me during my incarceration.

"Your faith will get you through this" the man said, "God never gives you more than you can handle."

Ok, but in my mind, God had nothing at all to do with it. What was happening to me was a direct result of man and his crookedness. Corruption and injustice at its finest.

He placed his hands on my head and prayed. "Look after this young man and see him through this bump in life. Help him see the way of his actions and repent. Amen."

"I'll repent for my sins, but not for this," I thought. "I didn't do this."

As quickly as he came, he left me. I figured out that it wasn't a visit from God, Jesus or an angel. The visit had been by one of the many jail psychiatric specialists who doubled as an over-the-top Baptist ministering to his flock. I figured he was trying to earn some points for Heaven. There's nothing wrong with that. I had to shake my head because this was the last type of person I thought I'd meet in this joint. Were Jehovah's Witnesses next? He was one of those people who show up at your doorstep in your neighborhood.

This was a "sort" of neighborhood. The cells were houses, only in a more non-privatized way. Your home could be invaded at any moment and for any reason. This neighborhood was also a little rougher than what I had ever experienced. Maybe this was what it was like in a third world country. I had to get used to it and fast. In about two hours or so, I would leave this cell from Hell and upgrade to purgatory. The man did leave me with pencils and paper, though, because

I was no longer a suicide threat. I could write. Now that deserves an amen!

*

Daily Log 12-14-2005: Fear, crying, waiting. Put in Bam-Bam (suicide) room because I was interpreted as suicidal. Long night with no sleep. Clothes taken. Given small blanket and small 4x4 rice paper gown. Horrifying.

Dream Log 12-14-2005: No dreams. Hell, no sleep.

"It doesn't help to fight crime when you put people in jail who are innocent."
-Stephen Brayer

Purgatory

It was about two hours after my visit from the holy man that I was summoned out of the suicide cell by the guards and led back into the area where all the colored jumpers were kept. The guards re-issued my blues and told to put them on right there. I was naked again. I was starting to think that they enjoyed it. I haven't been this nude, this often, in my entire life.

After getting dressed, they led me back to the booking area. My wristband was re-issued with my inmate number, name and picture. The guard re-issued his warning about the repercussions of removing it. Two *nasty* fire blankets were handed to me and I was led into the "tanks," or general population.

The tanks are where you're lodged until a smaller, "living" cell opened up. The holding area was split into quarters; four cells in one very large square separated by plexiglass. Obviously, you're arranged by color. The fourth cell was reserved for the men who fought in the other three. It was the guard's favorite place to hang out and watch fights while snickering. There's nothing quite like putting all the violent men together in one cell. We could watch them fight and argue through the glass.

The tank areas measured about 20'x20' each. They all had one toilet out in the open and one telephone. No sinks, though, so you had to be careful not to mess yourself when using the "facility." A couple of other inmates showed me how to maneuver the blanket so you could have a little privacy when relieving yourself.

These cells accommodated about ten to fifteen prisoners, twenty tops. With the major overflow of prisoners lodged in the jail, there had to be at least fifty men per area. We were squashed in like sardines. If you didn't like human contact, you were in the wrong place. If you were claustrophobic, you would have a real problem, because this was what you were going to deal with. I saw guys trying to sleep standing up. The smell was repugnant: Horrible bad breath, body odor, feces, urine and old food all in one scent. It was like camping at a rubbish dump.

The worst smell, though, was that of a male. Testosterone, if you will. Some of these men had to "mark" their territory by acting tough. Pushing, shoving and fighting were the entertainment of the day. I was in this area for only two days, and I must have seen anywhere from twenty to thirty fights. Sometimes the fighters were moved, while other times, the guards watched the antics with that devilish grin on their faces. I kept my mouth shut and went with the flow.

Territorial and racial disputes were rampant in those cells. An older black man had taken a seat on a younger white man's blankets.

"What the fuck are you doin', old-timer?" The white man angrily asked. "Get off my fuckin' blankets you dirty son-of-a-bitch."

There was instant racial tension. One of the younger black men went toe to toe with the white man.

"You pickin' on an old black man, huh? I'll kick yo fuckin' ass."

"Bring it punk. You can suck my big white dick."

The punches were about to fly when two of the larger, tougher looking guards entered the cell and quickly removed both younger men. They were separated into single cells for a couple of hours while they cooled off, and then placed back into the tanks. The black man (wearing blues) went into the grey's cell, while the white man (also in blues) went to the orange's cell. After the white man was called out of the tanks to be moved to his "home" cell, the black man was returned to our tank. A day in the life of jail; I hoped everyone here was color coordinated.

My size definitely helped me. I was about six foot one and a half and pushed two hundred and forty pounds when I weighed in upon entrance to jail. I was thick and brawny so I thought that the mean guys would think twice before tangling with me. Trust me when I say that some of these men were mean and didn't feel pain, physically or mentally. They wouldn't have thought twice about crushing my skull. I stayed as far away from them as I could. I also remained quiet and observant.

There was a camera pointed into each cell, but I didn't think it mattered because the inmates would duck down to smoke or do whatever it was they were doing.

"How did they get tobacco or pot in here when they were strip searched on the way in?" I asked myself. I didn't like the answer.

They shoved the contraband as far up their rear ends as they could. Sometimes, if they were to report to jail on a certain day, they would swallow the stuff in balloons and wait for nature to take its course. One person went to the toilet and came out with a lighter and enough tobacco and papers to last him a few days. All this contraband came out of one person. Even though I was a smoker, I figured I would rather wait until I was free again. I wasn't touching anything deposited out of someone else's rectum.

It was also important that I didn't tell the guys that I was in for a sex offense. You cannot explain to some of those men what your situation was. They hear sex crime and they attack, period. Make up a crime and go with it. That way you'll have a better chance of survival. A guard once put a prisoner in the tanks and *told* all the inmates that he raped a child. He then stood and watched as another inmate beat him bloody before finally removing him. It was a sick sight. It scared the hell out of me. This warped guard was laughing! Nice "system" we had in place. It didn't get much better either.

*

Daily log 12-15-2005:   Removed from bam-bam (suicide) room by Baptist witnessing counselor. Given clothes and placed in holding cell with other prisoners. Slept on concrete, but was given two blankets. Kept quiet and watched.

Dream Log 12-15-2005: Dreamed of huge natural disaster somewhere. Many people hurt and screaming for help.

"One of the many lessons that one learns in prison is that things are what they are and will be what they'll be." -Oscar Wilde

Shaun Webb

]

Lost Time and No Space

I had completely lost track of time. There were no windows and no doors to see beyond the bricks of the old jail. All you saw were deputies shuffling inmates back and forth. I saw a man stripped and placed in suicide watch. He must be starting his own story.

"The "system" claims another victim," I thought.

I saw a person pushed from behind by a guard. "Don't turn around on me," the guard ordered.

This man stopped in his tracks, grunted loudly and literally defecated in his pants, and then laughed. The guard didn't get him new clothes. He shoved him in with the rest of us. We were stuck in the cell with him and were not too happy. We had the smell of raw human waste to deal with. Our protests were ignored. This place was for the birds. I can't sleep on the concrete and it stunk to high heaven. Hope was in the offing, though.

*

The state decided to do an inspection of the facility. The trusties brought out rows and rows of sleeping mats on rolling carts. The deputy on duty told us to come out single file and take a mat. I was very happy because concrete really hurts after just a few minutes of laying or sitting on it. We all took our mats and went back into the cells. Thirty minutes later, the state inspection officials came through and looked things over, pen and clipboard in hand. They looked in our cells from the outside and took notes. Men screamed to be heard but were ignored. Those people had a job to do and weren't going to be sidetracked. After about an hour or so, the officials left. I was then given another taste of the "system."

The deputies opened our cell doors and announced, "Return your mats to the rolling cart."

I was just getting comfortable. We all had to return our mats and go back to sleeping on concrete. Now I understood it better. It was a big show for the state honchos. Law required us to have those mats at all times. The mats only showed up when an inspection was forthcoming. When you are taken to your "home" cell, you will be given a mat for the duration of your stay.

*

I finally had the opportunity to call Nikki for the first time since being led out of court after the trial. The phone in the tank cell looked like a pay phone, but had instructions on how to call out. I would find out that the calls would cost about ten dollars (\$) for *every fifteen minutes*. Yet another way the county made a profit off the prisoners. The phone company gets their pay, but so do the jailers.

"If you're going to put these phones in our jail, it will cost you." The sheriff would say, "But let's compromise and make it so expensive that we both get our pockets lined."

254

No calls if you can't pay up. It didn't matter, because I needed to call Nikki and hear her voice. I needed to know she was unharmed.

Upon answering, she broke down in tears again. Poor girl, she's emotional without all the drama added to it. My mom, who thankfully did not end up in jail, was staying with her so she wouldn't have to be alone. It would turn into Mom staying with Nikki the entire time of my incarceration. Nikki told me she was crying steadily since I had left her in court. She also told me it had been two and a half days since seeing me. It felt more like two and a half weeks. She explained to me that she had called the jail to see how I was doing and they told her I was contemplating suicide. These people were bullies. Why would you tell someone that, especially when they're already hurting? It's the county way; no feelings for anyone else. I told her not to worry; I was not going to kill myself. It was a tough chat, because I was weeping and trying not to break down: Not only for her sanity, but also for my safety.

"YOU ARE SPEAKING TO AN OAKLAND COUNTY PRISONER! YOUR CALL MAY BE RECORDED!"

Every five minutes you're on the line, that was the announcement you heard to remind you of your predicament. It was hideous. With one minute left, you are told loudly, **"ONE MINUTE REMAINING!"**

I spoke with Nikki until the call terminated. I called her two times in a row after that. We had to stop, though. We

255

knew it was expensive, but when the bill came, it was worse than we thought ($$$). I would eventually speak with Nikki once per day for fifteen minutes. That alone is three hundred dollars a month. It sure felt better to talk with her, though. I was feeling more normal, and I had a renewed sense of time.

*

I was allowed out of the tank and into the shower area. I took advantage of that. I didn't care who was watching. I soaked for forty-five minutes. Feeling fresh and clean was better than I ever thought. The water was nice and hot. I felt like I was DE-fumigating. You get such a slimy feeling in this "rat trap." However, you have to go back to the smell of that cell.

After my long shower, dinner was being served. I was hungry. The guards dismissed each tank, one at a time, into the middle area of the room. Our wristbands were checked and we were given one tray of food and one warm cup of unsweetened fruit punch. I'm not sure what was on my tray. It looked like some kind of meat, but it had a greenish hue to it. I'm not kidding, a greenish color. I didn't care. I ate it all with my nose plugged and polished off my drink.

Men were trying to trade food for tobacco. "I'll give you my meat for a smoke."

The seller would make a counter-offer, "your meat AND your drink."

"Okay, it's a deal."

The smoke went fast, and the traders left themselves hungry. Some guys were picking scant leftovers off other men's trays. We finished our "meal" and stacked our trays outside the cell. I tried for some sleep; but it was very difficult on concrete. I would end up staying in this tank for another day or so. I again lost track of time.

"Men talk of killing time, while time quietly kills them."
-Dion Boucicault

Moving Day

"WEST!"

"Yeah, right here." I raised my hand.

"PACK YOUR SHIT; YOU'RE GOING TO A CELL."

Good news! I think I was getting the hang of this thing. That wasn't to say that it suddenly put me in a jovial mood. It was only a slight improvement. I packed my blankets along with my paper and pencils in my arms and off I went. I wasn't sure where I was going, but I seemed to be moving around quite a bit in my first few days here. Trust me, from the suicide room to the tanks to a cell was considered active. That would soon change.

The guard stayed behind me as we walked the jail hallways, telling me when and where to turn. After a walk that zigged and zagged deeper into who knew where, I had reached my destination. RI#2 was my new home. I was going to share a six-man cell with seven other men: Yes, eight men in a six-man area. I was happy to be going somewhere different.

*

When you walk in, the guys look at you like you're another unfortunate soul, and to see what ethnicity you are. I would

259

notice that the jail tried to keep it as close to fifty-fifty African-American/Caucasian as they could. That would prove tough, though, because there were so many more blacks lodged in jail. The percentage turned out to be more like seventy-thirty.

The cell entrance gate was automatic, so the guard would turn a key and the barred door would slide open. After you entered, the door slid shut. It banged steel on steel loudly upon closing. I would feel a shudder every time it would do this. It was exactly like the prison television shows.

There were four bunked beds: Two on each side of the cell, and two boats, or floor beds, for the two extra men. I took a top bunk on the left. It was the only vacancy. I now had two blankets, a sheet and a pad on which to lie. No pillow, however, they're not allowed. It wasn't comfortable, but it wasn't concrete either. I would use the sheet as my pad cover, and one blanket as my pillow.

This cell had a table in the middle, a shower, and a sink and toilet, all made of stainless steel. The big bonus, though, was that it had a TV situated outside the cell. Little did I know how many wars this would create among inmates. The cell was filthy. The floors were grimy and used up, while the walls were riddled with whatever people wiped or wrote on them. There was graffiti, too, usually mocking the Oakland County Jail.

I was exhausted and wanted sleep. I settled myself in my bunk, and burned out for the night.

*

Daily log 12-16-2005: Stayed in holding tank until 9 P.M. I was then taken to RI#2 in the main jail. Medium security. Seven other men in cell (six-man cell). I took a top bunk. Slept very hard. I was so glad to have a bunk of my own. I never realized how we take all the extras for granted.

Dream Log 12-17-2005:   Nikki and I were removing all the flowers from our front yard. One petal at a time until every flower was stripped completely bare.

"In jail I was just like everybody else. I was sitting there praying and feeling caged."

-Dennis Rodman

Shaun Webb

Critical Mass

It was bad enough being jailed and having to deal with that. It was rough on Nikki's side too. We were trying to get along as smoothly as possible until the sentencing. Nikki was working at the school when our local newspaper contacted her. We didn't want the story going public. It was already a nuisance without having the media spreading around their poison. No matter, though, because they were writing the article about the "Sex scandal at St. Paul." We could be interviewed by them or let it be written any way the newspaper saw fit. That was a dangerous gamble. Nikki decided that we should at least give our side. She checked with our attorney, Michael, who advised against any comments. Since we had lost everything following his past advice, she decided to follow her gut instincts and at least have our side heard. We were tired of listening to this man blow his hot air. Everything was a negative, no matter what we asked. This time we decided it would be a yes.

Nikki took a statement from me over the phone and said that the writers would see her the next day for the interview.

Unbelievably, the paper sent a parent of a former student who attended St. Paul. Her name was Karen. Nikki was pleasantly surprised. She knew Karen and knew she was a reporter, but didn't know it was for this newspaper. I didn't remember her from my time at St. Paul. Karen told Nikki that she was an independent journalist and had come across the story during her perusing of the cases in the circuit court files. She decided it was a good story and begged her superiors to let her write it. This involved her old parish, which made it even more interesting. It turned out that Karen herself helped push it. Nikki wasn't pleased about it, but what could she do? After all, the woman was simply doing her job. Karen did promise to be fair and told us up front she would take no favorites and needed to interview both sides. I was skeptical. You know how pedophiles are perceived in society. I would however, be pleasantly surprised at how this article turned out. It took Karen about three weeks to gather all her information and write the piece. Here is the actual article:

*

ST. PAUL WORKER JAILED FOR SEX CONVICTION
By Karen Kostic
Special Writer

The St. Paul Catholic Church and school community in White Lake has been rocked by news that long time school maintenance worker Sean West was recently convicted of fourth degree criminal sexual conduct with a 15-year-old girl.

West, who has no prior criminal record, denied the charges throughout the trial and wants the community to believe him when he says he did absolutely nothing wrong.

"While I will respectfully complete whatever sentencing requirements the court deems fit, I continue to maintain my innocence on all charges," he stated to the Oakland Times.

West, 40, will be sentenced on January fourth after being found guilty of developing a friendship with and fondling the girl repeatedly over a period of several months. The same jury found him not guilty of two more serious charges of sexual misconduct with the same girl, including a felony charge.

"Compromise verdict" is the term used to describe the jury finding West guilty on the lesser charge without being convinced of the girl's entire story beyond a reasonable doubt.

"The only evidence that the jury used to convict West was the girl's story, as well as the testimony of her best friend," said assistant Oakland Prosecutor Ronald Gardner.

The best friend was not a witness to any of the alleged activities. However, the accuser confided in her, and she testified as to her friend's emotional state, he said.

The prosecutor claims that the girl would have no reason to lie.

"The family seemed genuinely nice, and the girl was consistent with her story each time I talked with her," he explained. "They paid a very high price by coming forward and would have no ulterior motive for putting their girl through the trauma of trial."

Is there the possibility of the family filing a civil lawsuit against the church, or possibly filing a claim against the settlement fund for sex abuse victims maintained by the Catholic Archdiocese?

Gardner says that he does not know what the families' next step will be. "However, if the church had handled the situation differently, maybe there'd be no further action," he said. "The church personnel automatically discounted the girl's story as soon as she came forward."

He also noted that soon after the church found out about the situation, the family lost the contract they had to clean the church and school building.

West was suspended from his job when the charges first surfaced, and his employment was automatically terminated when the guilty verdict was reached.

Father Patrick, pastor of St. Paul, said he feels the church handled the situation the best they could.

"The parish cooperated fully with the investigation," he stated in a letter sent to all parents. "You should know that we always take these matters seriously. If there is ever a concern brought to your attention, don't hesitate to contact the school or parish."

Patrick also assured parents that no students were involved.

THE BEGINNING

It all started when the teenager was 13 and began vacuuming the school and taking out the trash to help her mother's new boyfriend with his job. They worked together from 4 to 7 P.M. about three nights per week during the school year.

Often the girl would finish early and hang out in the playground, do her homework or listen to music while waiting for her cleaning partner to finish his job.

During the first year the girl worked there, she knew West on a casual basis. He worked days as a maintenance man and did not have any supervision over her.

After that point, the stories of the man and girl differ completely.

"The entire trial was a 'he said, she said' contest," according to West's attorney, Michael Casper. "While I totally support and respect the jury and the jury process, I also support and stand by West and was surprised by the jury's decision."

Casper noted that West is well known as a responsible and dedicated family man with a long and perfect employee record at the school.

"Every school employee I talked to told me that he is a good person and full of integrity," he said.

HER SIDE OF THE STORY

According to the girl's testimony, she and West began talking more and getting to know each other her second year cleaning at the school. As the weather turned colder, the girl would go to the maintenance garage while she waited for her mother's boyfriend to finish his cleaning duties.

"I'd tell Sean about my problems with my family and he'd tell me about his problems, and we had something in common with our dads and stuff like that," she said. The girl explained that she had given up on her real father, and she considered her mom's boyfriend to be her step-dad.

Near Thanksgiving, the girl claimed that the relationship changed, and said that she and West had increasingly progressive and intense sexual contact about once per week until April.

"Yes, I had a crush on him," she told the court. "I was looking for love and thought he was giving it to me. He said he loved me and that I could trust him no matter what, and he wouldn't do anything to hurt me."

She said that every time her and West had an encounter, he warned her not to tell anyone or he would go to prison.

According to her testimony, in February or March, the girl told her best friend what was happening. She finally told her mom's boyfriend in April, after the relationship with West had stopped.

A VERY DIFFERENT VERSION

West, who testified on his own behalf, did not deny that he talked to the girl on a regular basis. She was a very troubled girl, and he said he felt bad for her. He did deny consistently throughout the trial that anything inappropriate happened between the two.

While only two people know for certain what really happened, West's family and friends continue to stand behind him and strongly proclaim his innocence.

Three years ago, West married a third grade teacher and drama coach at St. Paul. Both Nikki and Sean West have been very active at the parish for years. Parents often witnessed Sean helping Nikki with her school drama productions or afternoon parking lot duty.

For legal reasons, West's wife was unable to comment about the specifics of the charges, but did say the allegations were unfounded.

West's first wife also believes that he is innocent. She is the mother of West's 10 year-old daughter, and has known him since the seventh grade.

"Sean had visitation rights with our daughter right up until he went to jail and will absolutely have visitation rights after he is released," she said. "He is a great person and a wonderful parent." She gladly pays for the collect calls that come from the jail regularly for her daughter.

"Sean's biggest fault may be that he is a good listener and always tries to help others," she said. "He really cares about people. In this case, that may have worked against him. Maybe he should not have talked to this girl and referred her to a professional counselor when she started telling him all her troubles."

The archdiocese has set up a special fund to cover various settlements and counseling costs for victims of sexual assault in the church.

For the past few years, all the employees and volunteers of St. Paul and other catholic schools have been required to attend a seminar called "Protecting the Lord's Kids." These sessions provide child sexual abuse awareness for adults who care for children.

West attended and completed his training seminars.

West sits in Oakland County jail awaiting sentencing. Whatever it is, it will include a requirement to register on the state's sex offender registry.

*

I had some questions after I read the article. Was Mr. Gardner talking about the same case that I was involved in? He was the prosecutor representing Blair, or at least I thought he was. Did he actually have the audacity to say that Blair's testimony never changed? He honestly believed that Michelle's testimony was credible? Really, what could he say? "My client was a liar?" He wouldn't, especially since prosecuting attorneys hate admitting when they're wrong. That didn't make it any easier to swallow. Interesting how Karen also noted the inconsistency in Blair's testimony: Good for her to point everything out.

I asked Nikki for Karen's address so I could write to her and thank her for being fair in her article. She wrote me back soon after and explained to me how she was suspicious of the family's story and believed the jury was wrong. She also told me that Gardner was not up front with her about Blair's relationship with Carowitz. She said she kept getting a story from Gardner that Carowitz was Blair's step-dad. Carowitz and Sara Joan are boyfriend and girlfriend, and that was it. Nothing had changed. There was no wedding.

Karen told me to hang in there and that I could contact her any time after my release from jail. It was very nice for her to write me. She certainly didn't have to. I have not seen her since my release. She travels all over the state looking for new stories. I did stop by the local newspaper headquarters and left a note for her. I wondered if she ever received it.

Thankfully, this media coverage came and went with no other articles written. I was worried about the negative effects the publicity would have on my wife and ten year-old daughter. It was bad enough being on that damaging registry. As far as I was concerned, that alone was enough coverage. I also didn't want other greedy or fearful parents or kids jumping on the "Sean did it to me too" bandwagon. I had seen firsthand how far false allegations could go. I couldn't take another "surprise."

"The first duty of a newspaper is to be accurate. If it be accurate, it follows that it be fair."
-Herbert Bayard Swope

Shaun Webb

272

My Nikki

This wasn't all about me. This involved family and everyone who was close to me, especially Nikki. She was the strongest person I'd ever met. I prayed that the allegations would not ruin our marriage. Thankfully, they didn't. It actually seemed to make her stronger. This was one of the advantages of being married to a mature, confident woman. Being a teacher has also strengthened her as a person. She loved kids, as did I, and would never hurt them. I think this drew us together. Trust me, I was a huge challenge for her but nothing compared to what we went through. The love this woman continued to express and share astounded me.

*

Nikki had to inform the entire teaching staff at St. Paul when school started up in August. She let them know that I had been charged with a heinous crime, but that she was committed to me as wife and supporter, and she hoped others would follow her lead. The tears flowed among the teachers and staff at that meeting. There were many hugs and words of support. Father Patrick and Gail attended so the process was easier for Nikki. It was a tough task to carry out.

273

The questions about me had already begun when the teachers had started filing into the building in mid-August. Nikki fielded the questions the best she could by saying I was taking a little extra time off, but she wouldn't divulge too much of the matter until the staff meeting. Some teachers thought I was ill, while others thought I was changing jobs. We hoped the charges would be dropped before school started and life would be back to normal so we wouldn't have to deal with the matter any further. If that happened, Nikki would not have to partake in further meetings or announcements. Unfortunately, as you know, that wasn't the case.

I was usually there to help the teachers and staff with whatever set-up and preparation they needed assistance with in their classrooms in anticipation of the beginning of the school year. This included moving desks, cleaning chalkboards or repairing broken pencil sharpeners. I did whatever I could to help.

Not that year.

We had a long arduous task that we were undertaking and Nikki had to keep her chin up.

The staff, some of whom I would consider very close friends, continued to support her and were there for whatever she may have needed. A class act, if you ask me. I felt that there were factions who weren't sure. You aren't going to convince every person of your innocence, no matter how much positive information is provided. People do have a right to their opinions, but I think they should look at the data before making up their minds. Those types of allegations stir up a lot of emotion and fear.

274

Father Patrick was bombarded with inquiries, as was Gail. No comment was the word from the archdiocese, so no comment was also the word from my former bosses, at least until the case resolved. There were some parents in the school who disagreed with that approach, but never mentioned it to Father Patrick or Gail.

Upon conviction, Father Patrick sent out a memo to the parents explaining my removal from the facility immediately after the original accusations had occurred back in August. Fr. Patrick encouraged anyone who might be concerned that their children were harmed to let him know. Not one parent or student came forward saying I'd hurt them or their children. Many called up to offer their support, shock and outrage.

Nikki had to keep soldiering on during this entire process. She had to let the staff know I was convicted. Most already knew because some co-workers attended court and word spread quickly. The support continued.

Being jailed was the same for her as it was for me, the only difference being that we occupied different universes. Nikki wanted to help me and would do anything she could in her efforts. This woman knew no boundaries.

*

Her first big challenge was trying to get my medication to me. I was on anti-anxiety medication and a couple days without it had left me feeling shaky. When I talked to Nikki on the phone, I asked her if she could bring my meds up to the jail for them to dole out to me.

When she attempted this, the deputies in the lobby turned her away.

"We use our own meds here," they said. "Take these back home with you."

Undeterred, she went home and called the jail administration to find out her options.

"Sure, Mrs. West," she was told. "Bring the meds up and we'll make sure Mr. West gets them."

Okay. She brought the meds back up and dropped them off with the lady at the front lobby.

The next day, she received a call from the jail. "Get back up here and get this medication, we will not give it to him."

Nikki was becoming very frustrated but headed back up and asked why, after being instructed to bring in the medication in the prescription vials along with a note from the doctor, they were still being denied.

"That's not our problem," the deputy yelled.

"I'm just trying to help my husband," Nikki meekly responded. "He needs this medication for anxiety, and he's been without them for two days now."

The deputy informed her again that I would be seen by a jail doctor and given jail meds. **"We have a lot of prisoners here and he'll be seen when he gets seen."**

They told her to stop bringing the medications. It would have been nice if the right hand knew what the left was doing. She left in tears, vials in hand.

This was another privatization in the jail. More cash for the county. It's Capitalism at its finest: To hell with the public. The jail food? Privatized. The jail doctors and medicine? Privatized. Same for the phones. The county spends little to get these items and then turns around and charges the inmate sixty plus dollars a day for lodging. Outlandish phone bills, cheap lousy spoiled food, and cheap clothing and bedding. Those all contributed to the bottom line. So you didn't think you would have a debt for being in jail? Think again. I would have to deal with that upon my release. You didn't walk away from these fine lodgings without paying the price: Mentally, physically and monetarily.

*

These were not the only challenges awaiting my wife. She had an outstanding lawyer balance for Michael and the bumbling firm. She also had fees staring at her from the court. Victim's right fees, state and local fees for prosecution and the regular bills of day-to-day life. We had two cars sitting at home but now only needed one insured. She had to pay the monthly house payment along with utilities and groceries. That was a tremendous amount of pressure after relying on two incomes for the last five years. She could have quit, chalked up her losses and let me go but she didn't. We'd only been married for five years. I owe that woman my life. Nikki paid the fees and had her car stored in her Brother Fritz's garage. Nikki dealt with Michael and his outstanding balance. Nikki made the payments and kept everything together. Every dollar she had saved in a lifetime including retirement, savings and endowments all went to legal fees and court costs. Luckily, blessings came with donations from family and friends.

Who says it's only the jailed who suffer? The tremors are felt over a large swath. I wish people would think about that when they want to trump up charges against someone. Nikki visited me every week in jail and made sure I had money in my account for the commissary store, which allowed me to buy treats, paper and pencils. She also had to deal with my sentencing, which was scheduled for January fourth in front of Taylor. This woman would do anything for me. Words couldn't describe my love, my gratitude and great fortune of having her in my life.

*

How do you deal with your mate's incarceration? Each night you go to bed worried about them. Every morning you wake up with that same worry. Luckily, my mother stayed at our house with her. This is important, as both of them would cry at the mention of my name. This was not something that was easy to talk about with other people. Nikki was a very private person. Those wonderful women were scarred emotionally. They leaned on each other for the duration and beyond. I think the bond they built together was indestructible. How much can one person stand? How long before you lose your mind and go nuts? Apparently a long time, because my wife was still with me. Even after all the difficulty.

Sometimes I think things happen to help us. You've heard the adage, "what doesn't kill you only makes you stronger." Those other situations that were placed before Nikki kept her busy, distracted and motivated. Everything she was going through made my life as a prisoner easier to swallow

*

Nikki continued to take my calls every day. She also visited me weekly. Visitation was not easy for her. The visitors were treated in much the same way as prisoners; pat downs, cramped elevators and deputies with bad attitudes. Nikki had trouble with closed in areas. That was about as closed in as it could get; no windows, dark rooms, fenced corrals, and locked doors in dark areas. My wife never faltered when it came to my situation; our situation. Nikki would listen to me when I cried. She would listen when I whined and moaned about my jailing. When I look back, I can't believe how selfish I was. Remember, when something bad happens, no matter how many friends you may have, family will always be there. Let's be glad that we are stuck with them. We should always treat them well.

There was one school parent in particular who really understood our trouble. Her brother had been incarcerated for four years because of an alleged incident from *six years earlier*. How sad was that? She burned a tea candle every night in memory of him while he was away. She gave Nikki a box of these candles so she could do the same thing. This was one of the sweetest things I had heard. What a stand-up parent.

*

Who knew how many candles Nikki would have to burn? I suppose we would find out in January. In the meantime, she continued to do her wonderful work while I tried to get used to my new digs.

"In prison, you get the chance to see who really loves you."
    -Suge Knight

Rules and Regulations

For better or worse, I was in my new, yet temporary home. It was certainly not where I would want to spend the rest of my life. It was dirty, unkempt, and had an odor similar to the tanks, only not as intense. Counting me, the cell consisted of two other white men, four black men and one Hispanic. This would change every day. I never saw a cell stay the same for more than a day and a half; it was a constant revolving door. To me it was another sign of how corporate our prison system was in its effort to collect the county dollars.

*

I would say that jail consisted of 75% African-American, 15% Hispanic and 10% white. This is a figure I came up with by noticing the people who came in and out, and during my trips out of the cell, which were rare. I kept a log at the beginning of my incarceration, but so many inmates changed, I couldn't keep up. Out of everyone involved, 75% of the crimes committed were drug convictions. There were also a decent number of sex offenses, robberies and drunk driving. I would find that most of the younger kids were assault type crimes and most of the older folks made up the drugs and drinking. Sex offenses were all encompassing as far as age

281

brackets were concerned. The younger crowd liked to talk about why they were in jail.

The best thing I could do was not talk about my crime. This would result in daily fights. If anyone pressured me to come clean about my crime, I'd tell them assault. I didn't feel like defending myself on a daily basis. One thing I did find funny, however, was that they had a wing in the jail reserved for sex crimes. I wasn't placed in this wing. I could only figure that because I was a misdemeanor case, I was locked up in this location. I ran into some of these sex offenders on trips to the clinic or visitation.

*

A huge secret to making incarceration more bearable was to develop a routine. I woke up, washed, shaved and read. I watched a little television from time to time, but I would mostly read, and of course, write.

The jail had a library cart that came by once a week, so I could take my allotment of three books and spend a majority of time on my bunk losing myself in a story. As it would turn out, I was able to read thirty-two full-length novels and a number of short stories and biographies while jailed. It was mostly Stephen King. I think I read close to his entire collection, except for those that weren't available. Upon release, I would finish King's library. I also read a lot of Dean Koontz and a couple from John Grisham. There was nothing like losing yourself in a good story. Reading their tales was a lot like watching a television program. The writing was so vivid. The wonderful folks at St. Paul were also sending me

reading materials and pamphlets for the study of the Catholic
faith. I intended to become Catholic, joining my wife who
already was, after my release. The jail chaplains would only
let a few items of this material trickle in to me. It was
addressed to me, but apparently, it had to be shared with
others in the jail. The chaplains made that decision for the
church.

*

I would talk to a few inmates from time to time. There
were some legitimately nice people in jail. There were also
some mean, nasty people. I met my share of both. We
sometimes played cards or dominos, usually after dinner.
Sometimes I sat and wondered, "What do I do now?" There is
only so much reading, card playing and talking you can do.
Writing helped immensely. I was able to release some stress
by putting my thoughts and feelings down on paper. It never
stayed too boring for too long. There were always people
upset or angry with others, which usually resulted in fisticuffs.
In the meantime, the clock moved slower than a snail on
sandpaper.

When inmates had fights in the cell, it was considered
entertainment. You didn't attempt to break these fights up. It
didn't matter how much blood was spilled or even if you
thought someone might die. *Do not get involved.* The
thinking was that these grown men would fend for themselves.
Let 'em kill each other if they want, but stay out of it. I saw
some doozies. Fights could be over silly stuff, such as an
apple or games (chess was a big fight starter) or two men who

283

didn't like each other for whatever reason. The corner of the stainless steel table served as a very effective weapon on someone's head. It also caused injury that inmates would not have to explain.

"He hit his head on the table," they'd say.

"What am I supposed to do? It's not my fault he slipped."

These were the big excuses. I saw blood. I saw injuries. I did not see death, thankfully. The only time you could even get remotely involved is if the fight was spilling onto your bunk. It was considered excusable if you used your legs or hands to guide them away. If the inmates thought you stretched your boundaries, though, there would be hell to pay. I started in a top bunk so I had a bird's-eye view of the action. When I eventually claimed a bottom bunk, I was lucky enough not to have any fights spill into my area.

*

Top bunks were "rookie bunks." The bottom bunks closest to the front cell bars were the prime bunks, because you could see the television well. You had to be in the cell for a while to get one of these two prized bunks. It was a rotating system. When someone left, a new person rotated into their old spot. This didn't happen for the floor cots or boats as they were called. These were reserved for the youngest cell members (Age 17-20). The kids could get up and down much easier than the old goats. If you could last in the cell for a few weeks, you would have an opportunity for a prime bottom front bunk. I would have mine in two weeks.

*

The laundry bucket and detergent were another major fight starter in the cell. Once a day you were given toilet paper and bar soap. Only once a week did the trusty give you a bag of detergent. Inmates fought like dogs for this. This detergent was brought to you in a small paper bag, about the equivalent of a school lunch sack. The men would save their paper cups from dinner so they could store detergent for their wash. Eight men converged on this sack all at once. I also had to be involved if I wanted clean clothes.

You would think that a civilized group could dole it all out equally. This *wasn't* a civilized group.

"I do more laundry than you," one would say.

"You took more soap than me."

I saw soap fly. One man threw it into another's eyes.

"There's your fucking soap, punk."

Instant fight. It was over *laundry detergent*. More entertainment for the cell.

I would usually get my share so I could wash my clothes once a week. I never had to fight for it because I was in and out like a flash.

Washing was easier, because you did it by yourself. You filled a five-gallon bucket that the jail provided with shower water, add your soap and scrub by hand. After scrubbing, you rinse the clothes in the shower and hang them on a line made out of sheet edges. Allow them to dry, fold them up and put them away. I always did my laundry when I saw no one else near the bucket. I did it quickly and efficiently, and then stepped away. Some guys went in the shower dressed with the

285

clothes they wanted washed. The only problem with that was the itching afterward. If you were going to do this, you had better rinse thoroughly.

*

Cell cleaning was another chore that had its rules. Each morning after breakfast, a trusty brought very mild, heavily watered down disinfectant, a scrub brush and a mop. Your turn for cleaning rotated according to bunks. One out of every eight days, it was your turn again. The reward for cleaning? TV ownership for the day. This, to me, was no reward. I could easily skip my turn by saying, "whoever wants to clean can have my television." This would cause quite a stir, as the men would argue about who it would be. I didn't care. I rolled over and went back to sleep. You couldn't get these cells properly cleaned no matter how hard you tried. You can't shine up shit.

Television meant little to me. Everyone liked sports, so that would usually be on. I liked sports too, so it didn't matter. Besides, I wasn't going to clean a toilet that was being used by eight guys who were carrying who knew what diseases. That wasn't for me. I became nauseated thinking about it. The toilets were nasty. Some guys would actually submerge their full milk carton in the toilet water to keep it cold.

I told one of the guys, "We shit in there, why would you even think about putting your milk in that?"

He answered in an illogical way. "The carton's shut, so nothing gets in it."

Indeed.

*

The rules changed from time to time, but not too significantly. If you followed them, you would be fine. If you thought you were the cell "boss" or that you were above the rules, trouble would ensue. I never had trouble with this. I always let someone else be the boss.

I did remember one instance in which a little skinny guy was being bullied by a big man. Thinking that I could help, I asked the bigger man to kind of lay off if he could.

"Rock boss, huh?" He asked me with a serious look in his eyes.

"No, I just think you'd destroy that dude in nothing flat," I said. "Is it worth the trouble you'll get in?"

I guess he agreed with me because he left him alone after that.

I put myself on the line for that guy. How did he thank me? "I can fend for myself. You don't have to help me," is what he told me in a squirmy voice.

"Not against that dude you couldn't," I said. "Oh, and by the way, you're welcome."

It was the last time I helped anyone with anything. If someone wanted their ass kicked, far be it from me to try to stop it.

"You have to learn the rules of the game, and then you have to play it better than anyone else."

287

Shaun Webb

-Albert Einstein

Medicine?

After a few days in the clink, the Psychiatrist called me to the jail psycho ward for evaluation and medication. It was about time. I had gone awhile without my meds and I was feeling antsy.

I was taken downstairs to a medical facility that served as the psychiatric ward. They placed me in an unoccupied glass cell, which was a ten by ten room, and I waited for my turn. It was very quiet in this cell, almost too quiet. I could hear other inmates singing and yelling in their cells, but it wasn't annoying. If I could have my books, paper and pencils, I might have been good staying in here for the duration of my sentence. I liked the quiet. The main cells were loud and boisterous all day *and* night. My only problem would have been with the over-thinking. I could think myself into a frenzy. Even in the loud cell I occupied, I could get worked up and make myself crazy. It was probably better where I was because I could communicate. I learned to accept the noise and shut it out. I also learned to fall asleep in the loudest of circumstances.

*

After waiting for two hours, they called me into the doctor's office area.

I met an older Indian man who spoke very broken English.

"You name Sean, yes?" He asked. "We now talk OK, yes?"

He was nice enough, and we talked for about thirty minutes or so. I told him about my meds, and what my doctor normally prescribed.

He mentioned that I was listed as a "bi-polar alcoholic" but we knew that already. I was no such thing.

"But it here says yes?"

I told him no one could make that determination within thirty seconds of meeting anybody. He neither agreed nor disagreed. He only smiled.

After asking me a few more questions, he told me he would put me on an anti-anxiety drug okayed (privatized) by the jail. That was fine. Anything to slow down the nerves.

He also asked if I needed any other drugs to help with sleep or to help deal with the experience of being incarcerated.

"I give you drugs for sleep, yes?"

I said no, but I was surprised. They offered any and everything in sleep medication. Ask and you shall receive. If your health care situation stinks in your world, go to jail; they hook you right up.

I completed my interview with this man and was sent back to my cell and sure enough, that very night, I was given my first dose of meds.

*

Each morning at 5:30 and each evening at 8, the nurses make their rounds.

You can hear them coming. **"JOHNSON MEDS, SMITH MEDS, WEST MEDS."**

The guys crowd the front gate for their drugs. Most of these men went to see the doctor and gave him the sob story, "I can't sleep, I'm so nervous."

The doctor says, "Okay, we medicate you, yes?" Some of those men were taking very strong painkillers and sleep aids.

Each time they took their meds, the nurse watched them and made sure they opened their mouths and lifted their tongues. There was such a problem with spitting the meds out and selling them for food or tobacco or whatever else that this had to be done. They could watch all they wanted, though, because these guys were tricky. The second the nurse left, the guy's pop the pills back out. I even saw an inmate go to the toilet and throw it back up. It was pathetic to see the begging other inmates do for that pill. Don't get caught selling your drugs or your cell will be destroyed by the guards, and always remember, the hole awaited you.

*

The nurses weren't the brightest bulbs in the lamp. You had to watch your med cup or you may end up taking someone else's drugs. That happened to me. About an hour after taking my meds, I felt odd and couldn't keep my legs still. I don't know what they gave me, but it wasn't good. I managed to sleep it off with a whole lot of difficulty. I was up and down all night feeling strange. It finally let up after about eight hours.

"Are you alright, West?" One of the cellmates asked me.

291

"Yeah, I'm okay, but this stuff they gave me is no good."

"Sleep it off, West; you'll be better in the morning." I did, and I was.

If you can help it, try not to get sick while you're in jail. I had a cellmate named Moe who was pacing the floor all night long. Finally, at 5:30 in the morning, the nurses came with the meds. We told her that Moe needed help.

She asked him what was wrong and he said, "I have an erection that won't go away."

The poor guy's prostate was going bad on him. His penis stayed erect for six straight hours. The nurse told him to sit tight and she'd get someone who could help. After a few minutes, another nurse showed up and asked Moe what was going on. He told her the same thing.

"Go in the bathroom and take care of it," she shouted. This while using her hand in a stroking motion. Was she actually suggesting he masturbate to make his problem better?

We yelled at her, "This man really needs help. If you don't know what you're doing, find someone who does."

Thirty minutes later, the guards came and removed Moe from the cell for a trip to the hospital. He returned after three days a new man. He had needed emergency surgery for a swollen prostate.

I was glad to be healthy. I would've hated to see what happened if somebody had a heart attack. The mismanagement of medication and diagnosis was not the least bit funny. Someone could die from mistakes like that. A nurse making obscene gestures to an inmate who was obviously ill? Unbelievable.

"The more we do to you, the less you seem to believe we are doing it."

-Josef Mengele

Shaun Webb

Addicting Behavior

I had the misfortune of meeting young men who were addicted to prescription drugs. It was brutal. They had sunken eyes, sores all over their body, and gray-white skin. I cringed whenever one of these guys entered our cell. They looked so weak and feeble. I met heroin users who weren't as sick looking. I swore that these prescription drug addicts were literally days, or even hours from death. I saw zombies in horror movies that looked better.

One cellmate was in jail for giving too much morphine to his friend; thus causing his death. They charged him with distribution of a dangerous substance and transporting a dead body. He tried to get rid of the body by dumping it in a lake. He was facing many years in prison. It didn't seem to sink in, though. He constantly sold his sleep meds to other inmates. (Matter of point; How in the hell did this guy get sleep meds?) What if they died from his stupidity? He didn't seem worried about it. He was a selfish individual with no value for any human life, except his own. The judge in his case gave him a twenty-year prison sentence. Painful, yet deserved.

I met heroin addicts, meth addicts, cocaine addicts and alcoholics. They gave me the motivation not to drink or use drugs. There were hard lessons to be learned in jail. I was never into prescription drugs; only a little grass and a few pills when I was a teen. I liked drinking beer. It was a legal form of self-medication. After my experiences in this jail, though, alcohol would be off my list.

*

One of the big tricks with the jail alcoholic was to fake a bad cough and be given cough syrup for it. The doctor would okay a large bottle of syrup, the nurses would bring the entire bottle and the alcoholic would drink it all. In two or three days, the alcoholic would ask for another. They would keep giving it to them. There is nothing worse than a man in your cell who is drunk on cough suppressant. They hang on you, they stink and they wet themselves.

I vividly remember a guy in our cell that was about fifty or so.

"I could sure use a drink. I could sure use a drink." That's all the man said.

Finally, one of the inmates clued him into the cough trick. After hearing about this, he drank his cough medicine and acted like a complete and utter moron. It turns out he was in for a "driving under the influence" (DUI) charge. He was so drunk at the scene that he passed out over the steering wheel with the car in drive. Luckily, he ran into a ditch, which kept the vehicle in place. The car was rocking back and forth from being in gear. He tested five times over the legal limit. I found it hard to believe he was alive.

Another drunk had killed an entire family: Two adults and two kids. All he cared about, though, was having his finances moved into his mom and dad's account so he wouldn't lose his cash and valuables in a civil trial. It was selfish and arrogant behavior. This man had to be moved to his own one-man cell because of the beatings he took. He didn't want to take responsibility for his actions when it was obvious he was wrong. The other inmates took action on their own behalf. I'm sure the family of the victims didn't mind.

*

I continued to take my meds. I did not sell them. I needed them for my own sanity. No way was I going to be responsible for someone else's bad reactions or, in a worst-case scenario, their deaths.

We're rapidly approaching a world comprised entirely of jail and shopping.

-Doug Coupland

Fan Mail

Giving proper credit and praise to those who supported my family and me was impossible. There was no way I could ever repay those folks in any way that would match their generosity and love. Those people made my stay in the jail far more manageable. Of whom am I talking? The letter writers.

It wasn't only Nikki who wrote me every day, but a huge number of other family and friends. I received mail from people I hadn't heard from in years offering their support. Mail call in jail was every Monday thru Friday at 8:00 p.m. In the first month of life in my cell, I received over two hundred letters and cards from people on the outside.

Anybody who had heard of my incarceration and knew me mailed me. Letters from other states where family members lived and I'd lost contact, wrote me. Well-wishers from other countries like Bulgaria and Canada wrote me. If I knew people who had relatives in these countries, they would let them know and the letters would come. I was overwhelmed and in tears. Many of my workmates stayed in contact with me: Diana and Jillian being the pair who wrote every week. I had no idea whatsoever that people cared so deeply. It helped restore my faith in humanity; to some extent. It would take a lot longer, or never, to restore my faith in the corrupt criminal justice system.

There was a small downside to all this communication, though.

*

Jealous inmates began asking me why I was receiving so much mail.

"Why are you getting all the love?" They would question, "What did you do to deserve special treatment?"

What they didn't know was that it wasn't what I did, but what I didn't do that had brought this attention to me. I would never ask them why they were getting mail. I wasn't the only inmate who had letters delivered.

The largest amounts of mail came at the beginning of my incarceration and on my birthday, which I spent in the jail. All the other times, it was four or five letters a day at the most, and one letter a day at the least. I obviously received mail from Nikki every day. The other writers were spread out through my time in the jail.

Even the guards asked questions. I shrugged my shoulders. I wasn't going to apologize to anyone for getting support from people.

Two guards in particular didn't like my receiving of mail and wouldn't deliver to me on the nights they were on duty.

"No mail for you West, hope you're not too disappointed."

I wasn't. They actually helped to calm the guys who were a little envious.

This influx of communication kept me writing too. I would send a letter back for everyone I received. My commissary cost was largely paper, pencils and pre-stamped envelopes.

By the way, the envelopes said OAKLAND COUNTY JAIL INMATE on them, so we wouldn't be confused about where they came from. Another in a long list of humiliation tactics of which they try to hit you. The more stomped down you are, the better the guards feel.

*

When you write out, you have to balance your letter on the bar outside of the cell so the guards could pick them up and place them in the mailbox for you. I didn't send letters out when the nasty guards worked, because it would probably end up in the trashcan.

Soon I started receiving books from people. The jail only allowed soft cover books DIRECTLY from the publishers, so some people paid a little more to have these sent. My friend Jillian from St. Paul sent me a couple of large sports statistic books, so that would keep me busy for hours and hours. My wife and Mother kept me stocked with paperback novels. It took them quite a long time to find the right avenue from which to order and send these books, as the jail would get fussier and fussier each time they were delivered. The rules kept changing, so Nikki kept adapting.

I can't come close to giving enough appreciation for all the love. I take it and clutch it to my chest. God bless these wonderful people.

"If you want to know who your friends are, get yourself a jail sentence."

Shaun Webb

-Charles Bukowski

Names without Faces

Nobody who was anybody in jail went by their real names. "I'm 'T'"; "just call me 'D'", "What's up? I'm 'Suge!'" Really? You mean like Suge Knight the rap mogul?

I couldn't understand at first why people didn't want to use their birth names in jail. At the risk of sounding racially biased, which I wasn't, 90% of the "Re-named" inmates were black. On very rare occasions, they were white; never Hispanic or foreign, though. The names were either their first initial or first and last initial. I would be "SW" or just "S" if I so chose to be. I didn't. Sean was fine. I'll never forget the young kid who called himself "White Boy." He was probably seventeen or eighteen years old and he was definitely white. I laughed so hard I almost choked on my green meat.

"White Boy, huh? What's your real name dude?"

He tried to be convincing, "I'm White Boy, OK?"

Whatever, the name on his wristband said Oliver. The rest of the time he was there, we called him "fresh dog." He hated it. He wanted so badly to have a nickname of his choosing that it was grinding away at him.

Now mind you, some guys came in and said in a deep voice, "I'm 'T.'" Okay then, you are "T" and I won't forget it. "T" stood six foot five inches tall and could squash my head in his forearm like a grape. Some people you didn't mess with.

With size comes respect. You don't step on Godzilla's tail, lest he exhales fire.

I came to understand that this was a "ghetto" thing. Nobody wanted their real name out in the world because they could more easily commit crimes with less risk.

"Who did this?" The police would ask.

"Well, I saw 'T' run from the scene," would be the answer.

"Who is 'T'?"

"I don't know."

Street cred, I suppose. This goes for whites and Hispanics in some cases, but it's mostly a black thing.

*

Another other thing that I found interesting was that every black man was some kind of family relation to every other black guy.

"That's my cousin, that's my uncle, that's my brother."

Wow. It was like a family affair. Being from the suburbs, I couldn't possibly relate to the "brotherhood." These men are closer to each other than I ever imagined. It was another valuable lesson for me to learn.

*

Ninety-five percent of the black men I met in jail were convinced that the "system" was after them specifically. I'm one hundred percent white, and the system nailed me too. I'm certainly not saying that they don't have a point. Seventy-five percent of the inmates were black. In this day and age, unless you are rich or have a big name, committing crime, no matter what your race, will probably result in your incarceration. I saw black inmates leave our cell on Tuesday, and come back on Friday.

Men from the cells next to us would see a guy walking down the corridor. "Hey 'J', what up doe?" They would it say with swagger. "You back already? No kidding."

I didn't see this with white or Hispanic people.

I would say it had a lot to do with culture, but a lot more to do with upbringing. A bad upbringing usually equals a bad egg. The people you hang around with had a ton of influence on your actions. Gangs raise gang members, and people who are used to a "crime" culture know nothing else. If you can't find work, you steal. If you're not accepted at home, you find a gang. It was a vicious cycle. I couldn't completely understand what it was like, having not lived it myself.

The prejudices run deep with some blacks. Most think that the whites caused all of their problems. They harken back to slave days. That wasn't my personal history, and I had nothing to do with it. When it happened doesn't matter to some blacks; it's your fault today. This was not fair. Because someone has German blood doesn't mean they agreed with exterminating Jewish people. Other culture's bad decisions weren't my doing. You shot that guy, or knifed that man, or raped that girl; be responsible for your own actions.

Yes, all creeds and colors are falsely accused and wrongfully convicted.

"I didn't do it, I didn't do it," was the catch phrase.

It made it tougher for the guys who really didn't do it. Most were guilty but many weren't. Some men made bad choices that they will pay for dearly. The prejudice exists in all areas of the jail experience.

*

"Why can't we watch black television today?"

What is black television? It's television that feature black actors and actresses? If it was, I've been watching black TV all my life. I've never put a color on it.

"Screw Hockey, let's watch Basketball." Why? Because basketball players are predominantly black. I personally like the uniform colors and the drama surrounding the games. If a white basketball player excels it was, "that white boy sure can play." If it's LeBron James or Kobe Bryant, then there's a difference. "Man, that nigga sure can play."

Look out if a black man gets a slam-dunk. Good Lord it was pure bedlam in the cell. It did make the game experience more exciting.

I had never considered myself racist. After some time in jail, I put a little more thought into it. I hoped and prayed that I could look at people in an equal light. We live in a "melting pot" of society that wasn't melting. It had taken me a long time to like basketball again.

The men I got along with best in jail were, in fact, black. I would talk more with them than the white guys. How come? I have no idea. To me, it wasn't a skin color, but what we had in common. I also spoke with some clueless and undereducated white people.

I remember one man in particular. He was white, but he talked with a black dialect and acted as if he wanted to be black. He wore his jail pants real low like black men and younger white kids did.

One day, a colored man walked up to him and asked, "Are you white?" He said yes. "Then start acting like it." Touché. I hardly heard from the white man again.

On another day, two black men had a fistfight over an apple. Following the fight, another black man who called himself "D" stood up and asked, "Why do you guys fight over an apple? You niggers are entertaining the whites in the cell. The whites like to watch two N's fight."

I didn't care what color they were, fighting was no good. In jail, it was normal, but it made me very nervous.

We must also talk about the "N" word. It was a nasty, dirty, disgusting word in my book. I would never refer to anyone as a nigger, and I would be upset if someone else did in my presence. I heard that word so many times in jail it made me cringe. When two black men talk to each other, they refer to one another as "Nigga." It is every bit as common as white guys saying "dude" or "bud." Only one time did I see a white man call a black man "Nigga." It resulted in a black eye for the white man. It was a culture thing and they could have it. I did on occasion hear a black guy call a white guy "Nigga", but that was during fights or when threats were levied.

I guess I'll never get it, but then again, what's for me to get? It wasn't my game and not the way I chose to roll. We'll leave it at that. I did learn a lot about jail "lingo" during my stay. I decided to put together a little "jail thesaurus." If it's ever your turn to do time, you can be better prepared. Black people invented this lingo, white people who want to be black (wiggers), and the otherwise jailed.

*

Nigga- A black friend to a black friend only.
Example: Dat's ma nigga. Or; Shudda fuck up nigga.

N****R- A threat. Very discriminating.
Example: You betta watch out, n-----r.

Minute- A substantial amount of time.
Example: I'm gonna be in dis cell for a minute. (Usually six months or more.)

Second- A less substantial, but good amount of time.
Example: I gotta visit today, see you in a second. (This is less than a day.)

Bra- Friend.
Example: See dat guy over there, dat's my bra. Or; what up, bra?

An' shit (sheet) - Ends most sentences.
Example: I can't take this jail no more. Dis an' shit. Or; Man, dats whack. It an' sheet.

Crib- Home.
Example: I gotta get back to da crib.

Bitch at home- Wife or girlfriend who you can't stand.

Example: Sheet, I got ta get back to dat bitch at home, man.

Boo- Wife or girlfriend whom you love.

Example: Man, I'm missin' my boo. Or; I saw ma boo today.

Whack- Messed up. Bad.

Example: Dis place is whack. Or; what kinda whack sheet is dat?

Blunt- Cigar, cigarette or joint.

Example: You gotta blunt man? I needa get high. Or; I needa blunt, cherry flavor.

What up, doe? - How are you? What's up?

Example: I ain't seen you in a minute. What up, doe?

Aks- Ask.

Example: I needa aks you a question. Or; Did I aks you, beatch?

Mofo- Motherfucker. This can be used in a threat or as friends.

Example: Bring dat mofo here. Or; Man, what up mofo?

Beatch- Bitch.

Example: C'mon beatch, let's do this.

Ho- Whore. Slut. Prostitute. Also can be used when describing girlfriend or wife. Out of their earshot, obviously.

Example: Dat beatch a ho.

Bitch-ass ho - The ultimate fighting words.

Example: Man, you nuttin' but a bitch ass ho. or; Bring it, bitch ass ho! Or just simply; Bitch ass ho!

Tramp Stamp. - A tattoo on a woman's lower back, usually but not always, with the boyfriend's name on it. A colorful display while in the "doggy-style" sex position.

* Please note that black, white, Hispanic and others ALL use this lingo.

*

Daily log 12-18-2005   The food is beyond sucks. I have eaten dried out liver that I liked better. Worked on the book. Got a visit from Nikki and Mom, which really helps. I don't look forward to anything except their visits. The mail is piling in. So much love. Some guys don't like it. Oh well. I can't satisfy everybody.

Dream log 12-19-2005   Begged Father Patrick and Gail for my job back. Tears. Also dreamed I was in a subway or trolley car that wouldn't move. I couldn't get anywhere. I yelled and screamed. It didn't matter, it wouldn't move.

"A man's true secrets are more secret to himself than they are to others."

-Paul Valery

The Three Visits

We were getting closer to sentencing, which was scheduled for January 4th. I knew that Nikki had been communicating with our lawyer about that very subject. The state wanted eighteen months in prison, but the sentencing guidelines, as determined by some kind of points system I didn't understand, called for a maximum of nine months in county jail. Nikki had told me that huge amounts of letters asking for leniency were being sent to Judge Taylor. Some people were hand delivering them to her office. The support was astounding. People were writing that they trusted me with their own children. That's amazing for a convicted pedophile.

I didn't know how much time I would get, but nine months would be the absolute max, and that was unlikely, because this was a misdemeanor (listed felony) first offense. A listed felony means "high-court misdemeanor." It's treated as a felony for sentencing purposes. The rules for sex offenses change almost daily. Whatever is best today for satisfying society's thirst is usually how it works. Some people want sex offenders locked up for good; throw away the key style. I was convicted of touching a breast over a shirt, but it was a fifteen-year-old breast. Society hates it, and in turn, the media runs with stories of sexual deviancy. The worst part was that I didn't touch Blair's breast at all, let alone "over her shirt". I

313

was going over all the scenarios in my head when I was visited by the first of the three dolts.

*

Michael, my less than stellar lawyer, came in to talk to me. I was summoned from the cell and brought into a small side room where he was waiting. I was still very angry with him because of the trial, so the conference was a little tense.

I sat down with him and after our handshake; he went straight to the point.

"Gardner wanted eighteen months, but that was too much, according to the "points for sentencing" scale. I told him a max of nine months was all he could reasonably expect." He continued, "Taylor wanted to give you a year, but she can't go over the guidelines without you having an appealable sentence. She really doesn't like you Sean."

I sharply interjected, "What do I care whether she likes me or not? It's no surprise. She thinks anyone accused of this is guilty, period. She should have disqualified herself from the trial."

Michael continued with his pitch. "I polled the jury after the trial and they didn't believe Blair's parents or her friend Michelle. However, they were uneasy with you because you were fidgety on the stand and you looked at them too much." (Michael had instructed me to look at the jurors.)

Okay, so what Michael was saying is that the jury reached a verdict due to quirks?

314

"Not really," he said. "They think something *may have happened*, but they're not sure what. They split the baby, Sean."

What he meant was that since they were unsure, they acquitted me of the two counts they thought to be the most damaging, but threw the family something to hang their hat on. I really think that if you're unsure as a juror, you *must* acquit. That was reasonable doubt. Michael explained to me that the jury cast a twelve to zero vote *against* conviction for the first and third degree counts right away, and then spent the next two hours haggling over the second count. There were jurors who wanted acquittal on that count too, but they wavered.

"So what am I looking at Michael?" I inquired with a combination of worry and confidence.

Michael countered, "Oh, I would say it depends on the pre-sentencing investigator. He'll be here to see you soon."

He finished his patter, so now it was my turn.

"Good! As for you Michael, you stunk in court and you were nothing as you said you would be. You told me you loved confrontation. Taylor confronted you and you backed down like a beaten dog. You left my wife in the hallway so she missed everything, and then you didn't even mention that she was there." I continued, "You didn't protect me in cross like you said you would. You allowed the jury to hear only half of the fucking story. No wonder they thought something might have happened."

Michael told me to keep going, because it was the time to get it off my chest. He wasn't even listening. He leaned back in his chair and yawned.

I scolded him again, this time to leave. "Get the fuck out, Mike; I'm going back to my cell. See you in court, unfortunately."

Michael heated up; pointing out the huge bullet I dodged by not being convicted of the third degree felony.

"Do I look like I dodged a bullet, Michael?" I pointed at my scrubs. "It was obvious to me in court that a little extra effort would have won a full acquittal. Now I get to do whatever time I'm given, and then go back into the world as a sex offender. **Don't you get it? I'm innocent! Now leave me alone, scram, beat-it.**"

He did and I went back to my cell.

*

Daily Log 12-22-2005: I saw Michael today. He told me Judge Taylor hates me. Negative, negative, negative. Go away Mike- I don't care to talk anymore. More mail squeezed through. It was the Mother lode. Tons of cards and letters.

Dream Log 12-22-2005: Where am I? I don't know where I am. Everything is dark, but I'm thinking, so I must be here. Where is here? I'm really scared. This is too weird. Woke up sweating like crazy.

*

The next day, the second dolt, Detective Smart, visited me. This would be short, but not so sweet. We were in the same room in which I met Michael. I entered and sat down.

"Hello, Sean. I'm here to take a DNA sample by swabbing the inside of your mouth per court orders."

I said nothing and opened my mouth. My insides were shaking violently. I was *livid.* I had never been that mad in my life. Could he tell? I imagined so.

"So, Sean, your sentencing is coming up pretty soon, huh?" Smart asked with a smile.

My reply was pure anger. **"Just take your *fucking* test and I'll go back to my *fucking* cell."**

His eyes widened. "Okay, then," he briefly retorted.

"Yeah, ok," I said, my voice shaking intensely with my words.

He took the test, and I quickly knocked on the door to get out. My thought was to get away from him swiftly. Why should I put myself through that any longer? As I was walking out of the room, I looked up and saw the White Lake Police Chief looking at me with his hands in his front pockets. He had a smile on his face and was rocking back and forth, toe to heel, toe to heel.

"Yeah," I thought, "you really got 'em, huh? You put the big bad man behind bars." I couldn't believe the attitude.

Smart probably thought Blair was lying, but he was doing his job, in his mind. I thought his profession was to seek out the truth, not abuse the system by simply "getting" someone, thus making the public think they're safer. I truly wondered how many other innocent people these over-the-top morons had put in jail. I shuddered at the thought of it. Beyond plain emotion, I started hating these people. I knew the bible said love thy neighbor, but I couldn't help it. I was being severely tested. The feeling was so strong. I hated their guts with my deepest being. Smart would probably get a nice pat on the back for this collar. It was a farce.

*

Daily Log 12-23-2005: Opening up a bit too some cellmates. I trust no one, and never will inside this place. Smart came to take DNA test today and tried to small talk with me. What a jerk. Take your test and leave me alone. This is such a joke. I feel so much hate.

Dream Log 12-23-2005:   Dreamed I woke up at home. Couldn't get out of bed. Wanted to move, but couldn't. I then woke up for real looking at bars in the cell. Very scary.

*

The visit from the third dolt came. It was the pre-sentencing investigator. Three days, three visits and three trips to the conference room. When I met with the investigator, he told me he was a probation officer given the responsibility of determining how much jail and probation time he thought I'd be assigned. He would then forward his findings to the judge as a "recommendation." Good luck there. She already despised me.

He asked me what happened in a boring monotone. I told him I was innocent. He took pictures and descriptions of my tattoos, but only the ones that were visible.

He asked me what I thought of the situation.

"I didn't get a fair shake. I was convicted of a crime I didn't commit," were my pointed answers. "The jury only heard half of the story because my attorney was inept."

I was getting tired of talking about it; of saying, "I didn't do it." These people didn't care. Anyone who was on the punishment side of the system looked bored and wearied when you spoke of your innocence. I guess they hear it every single day. It was hard for them to separate the sincere from the liars. However, if you didn't want to hear my opinion about the case, then don't ask. I'm going to say what I have to say. Some people may not care for it, either.

He wrote and asked questions. He inquired with boredom, "What do you think I should recommend?"

"Freedom," I answered.

He continued to write and ask more questions. "Did you really not do this, or are you pulling my leg?"

I sighed.

He told me he had spoken with my wife and met with the victim and her family and would weigh our comments out to come to his conclusion.

He met with the victim? She's not the victim, I'm the victim and she's the criminal. I was convinced that the decisions were weighed out by listening to the accuser and dismissing the accused. I didn't want to get on the wrong side of this man, though, because he carried weight with the judge.

The last thing he asked me to do was hand write a comment that I'd like the judge to see. Michael through Nikki that I couldn't complain about being found guilty. That would show no remorse and it would hurt me in sentencing. I refused, however, to say I was guilty of a crime I had never committed.

319

I thought up a good way to sound contrite without actually admitting to guilt.

I wrote, "I am very sorry for everything that has taken place in the last few months."

That was it, short and simple. I'm sorry for what has happened. My accuser should be sorry for ruining our lives. I'm sorry she did that. I'm sorry we had to go to trial. I'm sorry my family and friends were hurt. I'm sorry I lost a good job. I didn't have a bit of sorry in me for those that hurt us. I shook hands with this man and that was it. The meeting ended and I was sent back to my cell.

*

Daily Log 12-24-2005: Cellmate asked if I was in for raping or hurting little kids. I told him to mind his own business. I told other cellmates that he was wrong. I'm clamming up. He threatened me, so I stood up and stared at him. He backed down. Good thing because I'm filled with emotion. I don't know how that would come out in a fight.

Dream Log 12-24-2005: I was in a cocoon with my arms and legs pushed together in a fetal position. I wanted to rip out of it, but I couldn't. It was too strong.

Daily Log 12-25-2005: Nice Christmas dinner. A bologna sandwich with beans. Folks, the beans had MOVING maggots in them. That was the most disgusting thing I'd ever seen. Some guys ate that shit. I'm not sure what company the jail privatizes with, but they need to be ashamed of themselves for serving this nastiness.

Dream Log 12-25-2005: I dreamed about my dog and cat. I miss them very much. I hope Dakota is watching over Nikki well. He's such a good boy.

"We would not be interested in human beings if we did not have the hope of someday meeting someone who was worse off than ourselves."

-Emile M. Cioran

Shaun Webb

Sentenced

I was awake at 4:00 in the morning on January 4th for my sentencing, which was scheduled to start at 8:30. I couldn't sleep in anticipation of finding out what my (our) fate would be. Judge Taylor had all the cards in her boney fingers. This haughty, portentous woman could string me up by my eyebrows. Perhaps she wouldn't. Could it be that she had seen the light and would do the right thing? Maybe God came down and softened her heart. *Soften a heartless person? See the light?* I don't believe it in her dark, miserable world. They only way the spirit would touch her were if she spilled a shot of Jack Daniels down the front of her shirt.

I was expecting the worst, only to be happy if it was not as bad. I shaved, showered and made myself fresh and clean for my adventure. I wrote in my notebook and stayed quiet so not to wake the other guys. At about 7:00, I would be taken from my cell, chained up with the inmates who had court, and then led down through the tunnel, which I had originally arrived in.

After what felt like forever, I heard, "WEST, COURT. WE LEAVE IN TWENTY MINUTES."

A few minutes later, the gate opened and I entered the main jail where I started.

"Have a seat, West."

I did. I sat for a few more minutes while the guards gathered the other prisoners.

*

I thought back to a few weeks ago when I started my journey. The suicide room had an occupant and the tanks overflowed beyond capacity. I would come to find out that they were always full ($$$$). After a couple of contemplative minutes, I was chained to the other men. There were six of us going on the tunnel walk: The cold, dark tunnel. My nightmare continued. Maybe I'd wake up from it today.

*

We arrived at the courthouse jails, were unchained and placed inside. It was after 8:00, so I knew I would see my family soon. They were just a few feet away from me now. What a great feeling that was having my Nikki a short distance away. I was thrilled. It had been some time since I'd been in a decent mood, so I felt very reinvigorated.

We waited; 8:30 came and went, 9:30 came and went, and 10:00 came and went.

I asked the Deputy what the hold-up was.

"Taylor isn't here yet. Have a seat and relax, gentlemen."

She's not here yet? The other guys who were waiting with me were getting edgy. What about all the people who were waiting inside the courtroom? How about the other families who were waiting to hear their people's fate? Alas, I forgot. Taylor doesn't care about anyone but herself. I don't understand what gave her the right to mess with people's feelings in that way. The same public that sat and waited voted her into her position. The clock continued to tick and tock. I was anguished and feeling very uncomfortable. It was 10:15 with no Judge in sight.

Finally, at 10:45, the deputy came to get us. We lined up in the hall and were re-chained.

"Watch yourselves guys, Taylor is being a real cunt today," he warned.

Of all days, it especially had to be this one. I'll bet it was *every day* for her. I was no special case. She was a nasty person and that rubbed off on all who "graced" her presence. Too much power and authority created a tyrant.

*

We marched forward into the elevator. My heart raced with excitement. I would see my family and friends. We finally reached the end of the elevator ride. My gosh, it was taking FOREVER. The doors opened and we walked the remaining twenty feet, went through another door and entered the courtroom. The sun that shined through the windows in the hallway was bright. It certainly felt good to see that. I had not seen sun in twenty-five days. I was badly in need of a healthy dose of vitamin D.

I was seated on the jury bench with the other men. We were all chained together. I looked around and saw everybody: Friends, family, and Nikki. I was so thrilled. I even saw a couple of parents from the school, and some of my

St. Paul workmates. They waved at me and blew kisses. "Wow!" was the only way to describe my feelings.

As I perused the courtroom, lightning suddenly struck. There sat Blair, Michelle and Sara Joan. I lifted my handcuffs so they could see them. My heartbeat increased dramatically. I wanted Blair to see exactly what she'd caused. She was bawling her eyes out while her mom stared at me, and then nodded her head in a (matter of fact) *yes* manner. She was so glad to see my doom. It reminded me of an executioner without the mask. In my opinion, Blair was crying because she was causing pain to someone who didn't deserve it. Sara Joan was vindictive, while Michelle looked as clueless as ever: Court jester, if you will. I think it was her mom sitting next to her.

I looked throughout the courtroom again and didn't see one person whom I'd thought were here for them. By the way, where was Carowitz? Apparently, he didn't find this worthy of his time. Another thing that was missing was the engagement ring that had been on Sara Joan's finger during the trial. It looked like the perfect family had returned to their creepy, dysfunctional selves. I looked to my far left and saw Prosecutor Gardner sitting in a chair, eyeing me and laughing. He was obviously satisfied with the verdict. I shook my head slightly and turned toward my family again. There was no need wasting my time on those people when I had all that love on my side.

*

I found out later that Liza had yelled at Blair out in the hallway before they opened the courtroom doors.

It seemed that Blair and Michelle were laughing and giggling like a couple of kids (which they were), when Liza railed into her.

"You're sending an innocent man to jail and you just sit here laughing?" She wasn't finished, "how dare you. What's your problem?"

Other family members pulled Liza to the side and the smile disappeared off Blair's face. She would conveniently turn it into tears before Taylor. Extra deputies had been summoned in anticipation of this particular sentencing, because the courtroom would be filled with spectators. Given the emotional response to the guilty verdict in trial, Taylor must have thought it could be a potentially dangerous situation at sentencing. There was also, I learned later, a number of television cameras and reporters in the hallway as my family waited to enter the courtroom. Their initial fear was that the publicity centered on our trial. We would find out later that the person of interest was Judge Taylor herself.

*

Michael approached me and we went over the Pre-Sentencing investigation results. They were good except for two things; my firing from St. Paul, and the pre-sentence investigator wrote that I had accepted culpability for the crime.

"I will not take responsibility for this." I sneered at Michael yet again, "I'm not accepting responsibility for a crime I didn't commit, Mike."

Michael said it was routine and showed remorse. He also said it would keep me out of prison. How can you honestly show remorse when you don't feel it? Maybe a few extra months in prison were worth my denials. Stand up for what you believe in, and fight the good fight. I decided that that would be selfish to my family and friends, and I hate selfishness. I needed to show class and dignity. No matter how much it could hurt. I'd never felt such hatred. I also wasn't crazy about going to prison. The dishonesty within the court system continued to baffle me.

The other thing I saw on the investigator's report saddened me. It showed that I *was fired* from my job at St. Paul. This stung worse than I could ever imagine. I knew I had to be dismissed, but I didn't want to see the word "fired" on paper. I loved that job and earned every penny they paid me. I wished I would've been given the opportunity to resign first. I really wanted to leave the job on my terms, not Blair's, Sara Joan's or Carowitz's. These people had robbed me of my career. They had completely skewered our future plans.

The investigator suggested four months of county jail and one year of probation. Michael said that the investigator, after interviewing the Radisons and Carowitz along with Nikki and me, said he had a gut feeling that I hadn't committed the crime. This after he wrote that I'd accepted culpability? Judge Taylor thinks I did it, so denying it would be harmful. The rules of the "system" are not just

Mike would use this report as a basis for sentencing. I'd been in jail for twenty-five days, so another month or two wouldn't kill me. It looked good. We only hoped Taylor would agree, but that's like hoping you hit the million-dollar lottery; a chance, albeit very slim. I smiled to Nikki. She smiled back. It felt so warm and reassuring. If not for Nikki and my family, I would've given up all hope.

*

"ALL RISE!"

Boy, I'd heard that enough for a lifetime. It was 11:15, and Judge Taylor finally entered her kingdom. She was two hours and forty-five minutes late this time. Her statement upon arrival: "I'm not late. Don't you people think I have other responsibilities as a judge other than only being in this courtroom?"

She was trying to excuse her behavior in her own mind. Yes, I'm quite sure she had other responsibilities, but court runs from 8 to 5. That was her time to be there. She started her day by berating some of the other attorneys and chewing out some of their clients. She finally reached the sentencing phase.

She sentenced the other five prisoners first before getting to me. Saved the best for last, I figured.

"Mr. Casper, what do you recommend for sentencing?" Taylor rasped.

"Your Honor, we accept the Pre-Sentencing Investigation findings and trust that this will please the court." Casper was sounding robotic and apprehensive. "Mr. West has a clean record up to now. He is a good person caught up in an unfortunate situation."

Taylor looked to Gardner.

"Your Honor," Gardner chortled with a hint of sassiness, "The damage to this young girl is extensive. Mr. West has shown no remorse and is defiant to the court. We recommend eighteen months prison and three years of probation."

"Objection!" Mike yelled. "We were in agreement that Mr. Gardner could not ask for more than nine months per the point system."

Taylor scolded both men and sent them into the hallway to resolve this. **"GO OUTSIDE AND FIGURE IT OUT, YOUR WASTING MY TIME!"**

They had stepped on the witches' broom. The lawyers took two minutes in the hallway, and they returned. Gardner had no choice but to change his recommendation to nine months jail and three years of probation.

It was Taylor's turn again. "Mr. West, please rise."

I did. I looked squarely at Taylor. This time with my chin evenly raised.

"Do you have anything to say for yourself?"

I spoke. "Yes your Honor, I am truly sorry about everything that has taken place." That was all I said, just as I had written it on the piece of paper during the visit from the second dolt.

"I remember this case," barked Taylor. "I found it to be very disturbing."

Disturbing for whom? I wanted to ask, but couldn't.

"I hereby sentence you to nine months in county jail and three years of probation. Does prosecution have anything else?" Taylor requested.

Gardner chimed in again. "Yes your Honor, we also suggest ninety days on a tether after Mr. West is released from jail."

"Absolutely," Taylor gladly muttered. "Ninety days on a tether following release."

She also added court costs that included restitution for Blair's counseling and registration fees. She did everything she could and then some. She went over guidelines by adding the tether. This was appealable, but by the time it was heard, I'd already be off the tether.

"GET THESE PRISONERS OUT OF MY COURT!"

Back to the cell we went. I waved at my family and said goodbye. Nikki was in tears. I was seething with anger.

Everybody left the court. It practically emptied out. Taylor asked her clerk whom all these people were here supporting. He told her they were supporting me. She said nothing after that.

*

We went back to the courthouse jail for a couple more hours, where I skulked and fumed.

"Man," one of the guys said to me, "that bitch done you hard."

I agreed. "Yeah, she did."

Then the man added, "What the hell did you do to get that kind of harshness?"

"I don't know. I guess she didn't like me too well," was all I could muster.

All of us were re-cuffed to be returned to our cells in the main jail, which meant another walk through the tunnel to hell. I was numb and hurt. When I finally returned to the cell, I lay down and went to sleep while sobbing quietly in my blanket. It took a couple of days to get my wits back. What a long, arduous experience it had been.

*

ORDER OF PROBATION

1. You will register on the State Sex Offender Registry upon release from jail.

2. You must complete mental health counseling upon release from jail.

3. You will comply with the electronic monitoring program upon release from jail.

4. You must not engage in any assaultive, threatening or abusive behavior including intimidation.

5. You must not have electronic, verbal, written or physical contact with Blair Radison. You must maintain a distance of at least 500 feet away from her residence.

6. You must find and maintain employment.

7. You must serve your sentenced jail time.

8. You must pay victim restitution.

9. You must submit to HIV testing and be counseled in the dangers of unsafe sex.

10. You must pay State costs.

11. You must comply with DNA testing.

12. You must pay a crime victims Assessment fee.

13. You must pay Court costs.

14. Defendant may motion for work release program after four months in jail.

*

Daily Log 1-7-2006: Well, life after sentencing. It could be worse. We were looking at eighteen months. Ended up with nine. I must keep my head up and be strong for my family. Everyone in our community knows the truth. We are children of God and we will persevere. I truly think Judge Taylor's remarks hurt more than anything else did. She is a menace to our justice system. She didn't like me and that was it. It

333

really had zero to do with right or wrong to her. Shame on her. She ignored justice. I hope she gets burned too.

Dream Log 1-7-2006:   Working for my Cousin right next to our house. The lot there was bought by him and transformed into a nursery. Also dreamed of porno tapes. I'm not sure why. I was also running a hi-lo for my Cousin. I was collecting colorful lilacs for our yard. I slept like a rock otherwise.

> *"The only discipline that lasts is self-discipline."*
> -Bum Phillips

More Challenges for Nikki

Nikki continued being as tough as nails while maintaining her pleasurable demeanor. She had gone through a trial involving her husband, had bills up to her neck and everything that her job entailed. It was embarrassing for her. How many people have to make announcements about their husband's alleged impropriety? She kept her chin up, though. After the trial, she didn't have to make another announcement to staff because it already had spread through the school. Again, she received hugs and love from everyone. Most people knew this wasn't true. If there was anyone who didn't believe us, they didn't say so.

Nikki kept plugging away until more lightning struck. Her dad, who is eighty-one years old and had undergone quadruple bypass surgery several years earlier, had a heart attack. Now she had another tough situation to deal with. I couldn't be there to help her, so she did as much as she could with help from her brother, Fritz.

Fritz was doing what he could to help. He took on a portion of the lawyer's bill, which gave Nikki a great sense of relief; although I don't think she wanted him to do it. Nikki prides herself in taking care of our problems in-house, not having someone else take it on. However, she needed the help. She accepted it with dignity. Had I been acquitted of all charges, the archdiocese would have reimbursed us entirely for the expenditures. Alas, it wasn't to be.

*

Nikki's father had to have a heart catheter inserted into an artery to repair his problem. She stayed with him at his home the first two days after the procedure. She helped him with groceries and made sure he was as comfortable and healthy as he could be. The woman was tireless. A less dedicated person would run for the hills. It was another challenge that would've been a source of intense anxiety for most. In the midst of all this, she was called to jury duty in federal court. As you can imagine, the courtroom was the last place she wanted to be, and her dad needed her. My father volunteered to drive Nikki downtown and keep her company. She was thankful for his help.

Anonymous donors sent money to help with the cost of phone calls and commissary bills. My mom, Step-Dad, Scooter and Liza each helped make payments on the sky-high legal fees. Even my cousin showed up on snowy days to keep the driveway clear. Everyone united to carry us through the storm.

*

While Nikki was dealing with her dad's problem, another demon came along. This time, my mom had been diagnosed with cancer! Now someone else was sick, and I sat on the inside, unable to help while this poor girl had more to deal

336

with. Nikki took my mom to the doctor, chemo and whatever else she needed to do. Everyone in the family again rallied for support.

Here was Nikki's life while I was in jail; Visit me at the jail, take care of her dad, take care of her mother-in-law, send me books, make sure I have money in my commissary account so I can buy goodies AND on top of it all, go to her job. I'm surprised she's still healthy. Good thing she eats right and takes her vitamins every day.

*

Sending me books wasn't easy because the jail only allowed soft cover books *directly from the publisher.* Not many publishers sell books right out of their offices. She sent at least fifty books that were rejected at the jail because the publisher didn't directly send them. The books she had sent were brand spanking new, but not new enough. A very friendly deputy, as a matter of fact, the only friendly deputy, understood our situation and told me about the book situation. He let a couple of books slide through. He explained to me that a few years ago, someone sent books in that had drugs stuffed in the bindings. Somebody else spoiled it for everyone else due to selfishness. He also told me that it used to be full contact visits until some idiot smuggled drugs in for a friend and was caught. Nice going, whoever you may be. Visits were now only once a week and were separated by a fence enclosure to limit contact. The room was so dark and the fencing so dense it was hard to get a good look at each other.

The friendly deputy was very nice to Nikki and my mom when they would visit. He explained everything in a patient, tactful manner. What a rarity, a deputy that helps people. I won't forget him, his manner was extraordinary. He also had me lead the line on visiting day. I swear when it was my time to visit and he was the deputy on duty, we were given five extra minutes. I only wish other deputies would've followed his example. Meanwhile, Nikki continued her hard work and lit a candle each night.

*

On visitation day, which is Sunday, Nikki would leave the house about eleven in the morning for a two o'clock visit. Upon arriving at the jail, she would have to check in at the front desk. The deputies would make sure she was on the visit list before sending her into another lobby that was much smaller and, depending on the amount of visitors, more cramped. She waited there for a quite a while until it was time to move on to the elevators for a ride up to visitation. Nikki hated elevators, and this one was worse than most because they filled it to the brim. Had it broken down mid-floor, she probably wouldn't have visited me anymore. She would have passed out from anxiety brought on by claustrophobia. Thankfully, that didn't happen. After the haunting elevator ride, it was a walk into the visitation room where she waited for me behind a large cage.

On my side, I waited for the guard to come down the hall and shout out, "WEST, VISIT!" When the cell gate slid open, I would walk down the long corridor where the guard waited for me. I was frisked and placed in the small side room where I met the three dolts. Anywhere from ten to twenty minutes later a deputy who had a group already with him picked me up. "Thumbs in your waistband," was the rule they shouted, and we would walk through the jail and head to the visitation area. If you were caught without your thumbs in your waistband, you lost your visit. Every two hundred feet we would walk by a skinny window. All the guys craned their necks for a slight ray of outside light. We finally arrived at the door to the visiting area and waited in line until they let us in. Upon entering, you located your loved ones and entered a gated area opposite a large mesh screen where your people stood. Don't touch the screen and don't touch your loved ones or your visit was terminated and you would lose future visits.

I was always glad to see Nikki on the other side of the screen. She would have a smile and blow me a kiss. I so longingly wanted to touch her. One kiss; one touch of her hand; one *anything*. We visited for a half hour and then it was over. They left the area and I sat to the side with the others until the deputy retrieved us. That's the smooth version. There have been a couple incidents of note involving Nikki or me.

On one occasion, Nikki was filing into the small lobby to await the elevator when a female deputy yelled **"MOVE YOUR ASSES, YOU CAN EXCHANGE PHONE NUMBERS LATER!"**

The people visiting were not criminals, but depending on the deputy in charge, they were treated as such. I would've been surprised if one of them hadn't been punched in the mouth. I hadn't heard of it happening, though, at least not yet.

On a different occasion, we had a very nasty female deputy in charge of visitation. After Nikki and my mom exited the room and waited for the elevator in another glass room, I waved at them. I always did. It was so good to see them. This time though, I was chewed out.

"STOP WAVING AT YOUR PEOPLE! YOU'RE MESSING UP WHAT I'M TRYING TO DO!" she cruelly chastised me.

"Are you joking?" I said, skeptically. "I only get to see them for a few minutes once a week."

Incidentally, I had no idea what it was she was "trying to do."

This blonde haired, fake-boobed bimbo went on, **"THAT'S YOUR PROBLEM, ISN'T IT!"** She continued her blasting, **"IT'S NOT MY FAULT YOU'RE HERE! GO SIT WHERE I CAN'T SEE YOU!"**

She made me sit in the corner like a child with my nose faced away from her. She also tried to take away visits, but the friendly deputy wouldn't allow her to do so.

*

Life in the county jail. The three things we had to look forward to were visits, commissary and mail. Nikki made sure that I had money in my account so I could purchase commissary items. Commissary was a store that came to your cell once a week. You could get candy, tasty food like sausage and cheese with crackers, and toiletry items like shave cream, underwear and socks. It helped boost your morale. You needed something to look forward to or you'd lose your mind. Keep an eye on your stuff, though, because the crooks in your cell would steal it while you slept.

Nikki my love, I was so lucky to have her.

*

Daily Log 1-15-2006: Visiting day! Yea! I always look forward to that. Cellmate unhappy about no work release. He's going on a hunger strike! Easier said than done; but then again, with this food? I'm still waiting to hear if I'm going to be re-assigned to something. I'm still hoping trusty at work release and/or a learning program. Not much more today, later!

Dream log 1-15-2006: Classes at my elementary school. Det. Smart was a teacher and brought a list of my offenses to me. I pushed him away and he left the school. Upon me going back and trying to teach, kids wouldn't react or move. They just stared straight ahead.

> **"Of all the home remedies, a good Wife is best."**
> *-Kin Hubbard*

Ding Dong, The Witch is Gone

It had been about four and a half weeks since my sentencing and our local television news reporters had busted the dishonorable Dorothy Taylor shopping, eating and working out when she was supposed to be working at the court. That was where her highness was when court was in session and people were waiting.

The story played on the news, and I screamed, **"IT'S FUCKIN' TAYLOR!"** when I saw it.

The guard of the day ran into the hall next to our cell and yelled out, **"WHO THE FUCK SAID THAT?"** Nobody spoke. We just looked at each other with shrugged shoulders. **"NOBODY WANTS TO ANSWER? FINE, NO TV TONIGHT, ASSHOLES!"**

Why did this man care so passionately? He unplugged the television and it cost me two candy bars, fourteen total, for each cellmate to keep from getting my butt kicked.

It was okay, I called Nikki and she filled me in on all the wonderful, lurid details. Sure enough, Taylor the nasty judge had been filmed by the local news gallivanting around town on the taxpayer's dime. When approached by the reporter she did the dishonorable thing and LIED: The judge *flat out lied* to the reporter. When he offered to show her the tape he had

343

recorded, she jumped in her fancy truck and drove away like the little weasel that she was.

The story would cost Taylor dearly. She had an appeals court position with the state locked up, but with this nonsense, she would lose it. Nikki told me that the newspapers, TV and radio were all over the story. The public had something with which to sink their teeth.

People in the community were livid. "How dare she go out doing her own thing while I'm waiting for her in the court," voters and taxpayers said.

She was shamed, but not ashamed. Nobody deserved it more. I wasn't the only person to whom this woman was nasty. She liked getting a cheap thrill out of other people's misery and sadness. Lawyers, defendants and families all suffered with this woman in charge.

In the coming weeks, she would have to give up her position on the bench and follow other "interests" she had. Not only did she lose a lifetime position with the state, she was allowed to retire as a judge. She should have been forcefully removed, but this was good enough for me. Glory to whoever caused this. I celebrated by giving everyone in the cell more candy and running my mouth like a crazy man. I didn't sleep that night. The cellmates were laughing at me because I was so thrilled.

Here I was singing; "Ding dong the bitch is gone, that nasty bitch is gone!" It's the little things in life, I suppose. I attributed this nugget to karma. Here's one of the many articles published in our local paper:

*

LOCAL JUDGE UNDER FIRE
Court security takes issue after Judge blames them for recent delays.
By Cari Hopper

Bea Levinson of Waterford arrived in Oakland County Judge Dorothy Taylor's courtroom at 8:30 A.M., January 13 to hear her daughter's sentence. "The courtroom was filled to capacity. People were even out in the hallway," she said.

As the morning wore on, an anxious Levinson, 49, asked the woman next to her, "where is the judge?" Taylor finally arrived at 9:40, Levinson said.

Levinson called the wait a slap in the face. "I was nervous and upset. For (Taylor) to appear whenever she feels like it, it's as though she doesn't respect the time of the families or lawyers defending their clients.

Levinson's criticism adds to the pile of negative publicity laid on Taylor this past week.

On January 19, television station WJAL channel 14 aired a segment showing Taylor over a series of 10 workdays leaving the county courtroom around lunchtime and then going to a spa, heading into a workout gym and shopping at the local mall.

She did not return to the courthouse after the outings.

Taylor defended herself, saying she is a hardworking judge. "My docket is clear and I have a reputation for being a very effective judge. I'm sorry I gave the wrong impression and Channel 14 gave that impression," she said.

345

Circuit court work hours are 8:30-Noon and 1:30 - 5:00, according to an administrative order issued by the court in 2001. As for Levinson's gripe about the long wait on January 13, Taylor blamed the delay on deputies arriving late at the courthouse.

"I wait for security," she said. "We (judges) share security and we have to wait for deputies. Frequently, there's a delay. I don't take the bench without guards in the courtroom."

Sheriff's office personnel were upset at taking the blame. "We don't just bring prisoners to court, but we get a call from the judges telling us they are ready," said deputy Milt McCoy.

In January, McCoy said, deputies averaged 5 minutes from the time Taylor called until prisoners were brought to her courtroom. "That's pretty good," McCoy said.

On January 13, deputies were called at 9:29 to handcuff six prisoners (including Levinson's daughter) and move them from the courthouse lockup to the courtroom.

"We had them in the courtroom at 9:38, said McCoy. "If Judge Taylor is blaming us, our records reflect otherwise."

Oakland County Chief Judge Wanda Pittsfield reports she keeps track of judges' attendance and monitors dockets. "But if someone takes an hour or two during the day, I'm not aware of that," Pittsfield said. "We are all somewhat on the honor system."

But she added that judges don't work 40-hour weeks.

"Many of us are out in the evenings attending meetings or speaking engagements," she said. "(Our work) is not all in the courthouse. It's a juggling act. To do the job right, you must be in the court and out in the community."

Pittsfield said she has a heightened sense of wanting "to see things done properly. It's unfortunate if the public has lost some confidence in us. We do have to answer to the taxpayers."

I'm saddened because we are a hard working court."

Reports have pointed out that there may be more fallout since Taylor was a likely candidate to be appointed by the Governor to the State Court of Appeals.

The governor's office isn't giving any hints of what the decision will become March 9. "This office doesn't comment on any people under consideration for office," said Lisa Barton, the governor's spokesperson.

Law professor Larry Doby said he believes the investigation will have an impact.

"The (report) showing her spending time on personal matters rather than courthouse business raises important questions about her ability to be a judge," Doby said. "In fairness to the judge, she needs to have the opportunity to provide her best explanation for what looks like a breach of public trust. I'm sure the investigation and her response will be weighed by the governor's office and the public if she wishes to run for tenure in circuit court."

-Cari Hopper, Oakland Times

Headlines:

JUDGE SAYS SHE'S NO SLACKER

TAYLOR SAYS REPORT IS UNFAIR

JUDGE SHOOTS HERSELF IN FOOT

REPORT MAY KILL JUDGE'S CHANCES

LONGTIME JUDGE CAUGHT PLAYING HOOKY

My personal favorite: **JUDGE TAYLOR TO RETIRE**

Too bad. I hope she enjoys her retirement with no pension and no insurance. Wow, that's much like my deal. Do you think what goes around comes around? I think it might. Don't let the door hit ya where the good lord split ya!

*

Daily Log 2-10-2006: Taylor's a liar! Taylor's a liar! Taylor's a liar! Now I know why our trial was shortened and everything was so unfair. It was because Taylor is a friggin liar. She was filmed shopping during the time she was supposed to be judging. She denied it! It was right there on tape! In color! Now, did I get a fair sentencing by someone who can't tell the truth? No! Did I get a fair trial? No! Caught red-handed and still denies it. Side note: No razors today-dep wouldn't give them out.

Dream Log 2-10-2006: Taylors a liar! Taylors a liar! Also was given a furlough to travel with my wife.

348

"The temptation to wrong are many; They spring out of a corrupt nature."

-Matthew Simpson

Shaun Webb

Waiting in the Slammer

Despite what you may have seen on television shows about jail, I wasn't raped while serving my sentence. In prison? You could be if you were messing with the wrong people. In county jail there was no chance; at least not without a fight to the death. Jail rape has been played out on the television to look like that was an everyday event. The media likes feeding the public what it wants; violence, debauchery, drama and trash. There was way more fighting and killing in jails and prisons than there was sex. I've heard from guys who did time in prison that it was much easier than county jail. You can smoke, work, enter and exit your cell when you want to, and the guards are much more respectful. The only drawback was that you stayed at least a year, with the average being five to ten years. You also had to keep your mouth shut and avoid gangs.

The worst part of county jail is sitting and waiting. That was all you did, you sat there and waited for something to happen. Some days I would wake up, put my feet on the floor and ask myself "what now." The visits on Sunday, commissary on Wednesday and the evening mail were my saviors. You could make your life a lot easier if you found a routine. My sentence called for two hundred and seventy-three days in the county slammer. I was to be released at the

351

end of July, if all went according to plan. I would read and write as much as I could.

*

I took trips to the clinic. That was the jail doctor's office. I met some nasty nurses in that place. You meet many nasty folks when you're incarcerated. I had to be tested for STD's (sexually transmitted diseases) per my sentence, and this was done at the clinic located within the jail walls. They called me on three different occasions during my stay, every time at two or three in the morning. They were a twenty-four hour clinic doing business in jail. They deducted ten dollars ($) from your "bank (commissary) account" for each clinic visit. They also deducted five dollars ($) for each prescription. It wasn't a horrible thing if you have the cash in your account. If you didn't have the cash, they billed you later when you were released from jail.

When you arrived at the clinic, they placed you in a glass cell that was much like a waiting room. You sat there until you were called, and then followed the guard to the patient room. The benches in both waiting areas were made of wood and had multiple carvings in them. You had to be careful, or you could catch a splinter scooting over for someone.

There were fights in this area, too. I saw two heavyweights go at it. It was a very rough and scary battle. These two were at least three hundred pounds each, so every punch shook the cell. Minutes later, the guards came and broke it up. They wanted everyone in the waiting room to write a statement about what they had just witnessed. They promised us we

352

could keep the pencils after we wrote our statements. Everyone wrote a statement all right, but it had nothing to do with the fight.

I was eventually called on and had to get my STD check, which included an HIV (AIDS) screening: All this for being convicted of touching a clothed breast. I had to remember that Taylor sentenced me, and she went rough. Before I knew it, the nurse pulled my scrubs down, grabbed my penis and stuck a cotton swab in it.

"OUCH! That burns," I protested.

"If you didn't go messing around with little girls, this wouldn't be happening, now would it?" she hissed. The nurse continued, "If you're going to be a pussy about this, I'll tell the court that you refused the tests. Watch what happens when they strap you down on a table to get it done."

I countered. "You can take your samples. I'm not here for trouble. You just surprised me was all."

There were some unhappy people working these jobs. In fairness, I'll bet they had to deal with some real losers. I wished they would try to go easier, though, as I wasn't one of those scummy people.

Later during the same clinic visit, they brought in this foreign man wearing orange. I was against the wall with my thumbs in my waistband when a guard walked up to me and said, "See that guy? He's a pervert, messing with kids online. They know how to take care of him in prison."

So I asked, "What did he get convicted of, internet porn?"

"Oh," the guard says, "he hasn't been to trial yet."

"What?" I thought to myself, "He's guilty until proven innocent?" It was more ignorance in an otherwise oblivious "system." The poor guy probably didn't have a chance in hell whether he did it or not.

*

I found out that they brought the women down to the same clinic. They were housed next to us with a large plexiglass divider between the cells, which was smoked over to block the view on both sides. No matter, the males had managed to scrape a dime-sized hole in the smoke so they could see next door.

One guy said, "Look here, look at this!" We took turns looking in the glass and the girls were putting on quite a show involving the female human anatomy. I only looked for a second. The guys lined up like slobbering wolves. It was as if they'd never seen a woman before. They could have the peep show, it wasn't for me. It was weird and uncomfortable.

*

Daily Log 2-21-2006: One of our cellmates, Doug, used to criticize another cellmate for hoarding food, begging and hustling in the cell. Now, after that guy leaves, Doug was doing the exact same thing. We were giving him crap about it. The new cellmate called himself "white boy" we renamed him "Fresh dog." Many laughs.

Dream Log 2-21-2006: Let's see... I was scuba diving with Boa constrictors and large frogs. The Boas were coiled up and quiet and the large frogs were coming out of the goop in the bottom of the pond. Angelina Jolie was swimming around in the pond with little snakes all around her. Hot!

"Jail is much easier on people who have nothing."
-Bernhard Goetz

Shaun Webb

356

Exercise (Your Demons)

Recreation and exercise is what I needed. I had been in the cell for two months and we were offered our *first* trip to recreation. It was supposed to be for one hour EVERY day, but it didn't turn out like that at all.

We arrived at the gym and I started walking around. "Uh-Oh, that's a Cramp. Owww, my Back. Ouch, my feet hurt."

This was from being too sedentary for too long. After fifteen minutes, I felt horrible. I had to sit for the rest of the hour. The other guys struggled too. They tried to play basketball, but the nets are lifted to twenty-five feet so no one can hang themselves. Good luck with your jump shot; better luck with your suicide.

I would be given sixteen more recreation days between February and July. It turned out that the gymnasium was usually full of overflowing ($$$) prisoners, so that severely limited our rec time. I still went when the chance presented itself, because I wanted to walk around and stretch my body out. I had to get some exercise.

*

Speaking of the gymnasium, one day, the guards were walking through our cellblock with a jail "inspection" team when one of our inmates lost it.

"GO TO THE GYM, IT'S FULL OF PRISONERS!" He yelled. **"WE DON'T GET ANY REC TIME!"** I could see that this was not making the Guard too happy.

"OUR FOOD SUCKS, WE'RE TREATED LIKE SHIT, IT'S WORSE THAN A DOG POUND!"

After the inspection, the guard returned to thank the inmate for his opinions.

"FUCK YOU!" the inmate roared.

The guard calmly countered, "Pack your shit, your outta here." We never saw that inmate again. He went to the hole.

When the weather turned nice, we saw some outside rec time. I enjoyed sitting in the outdoor area taking in the breeze even though you were caged in. The guards must've thought we could fly. The entire four brick walled area was about one hundred feet wide and long. The walls themselves were twenty-five feet high. It would be very difficult to climb up unnoticed. Even if you made it that far, your next hurdle would be a very thickly fenced wall-to-wall cage. If you made it past that, you would find yourself standing on the middle of the jail roof. The point was, if you wanted to escape from here, forget it

During outdoor recreation, the guards sat on the roof all around you and watched. If it was nice and they were in a good mood, they let you stay out a couple of hours. The guys could play kickball or basketball, this time with normal height nets. If I felt like it, I would bounce a ball off the brick wall. It was better than nothing. The aches improved as I moved around more. Walking in place in the cell also helped. It wasn't much and it wasn't often enough, but it was necessary to keep you from going nuts with cabin fever.

"He who has health has hope; and he who has hope has everything."
     -Thomas Carlyle

Shaun Webb

360

(Mis) Behavior

You needed some kind of activity to release the stress and pressure that was pent up inside your body and mind. The county didn't offer any other form of stress relief except recreation (rare) or trusty work (even rarer). I had heard about the many programs available to inmates to assist rehabilitation: Counseling (none), school courses (none), work release (very limited) and boot camp (eliminated). Have no fear, your tax dollars are not "wasted" on rehab or helping prisoners prepare to be contributing members of society. Jail was all about punishment and breaking people down. The human spirit is indomitable, though, and man finds a way to survive in the harshest of circumstances. The human spirits in jail would figure it out, albeit sometimes in very violent or non-productive ways. Whenever you cloister eight men together in a small cell, bad things are bound to happen. Occasionally, though, the inmates would use their heads to come up with some good ideas.

I was astonished with the engineering skills displayed by some inmates.

*

Shaun Webb

If any of the men managed to get tobacco or marijuana into the cell and didn't have a lighter, they would use a tried and true jailhouse method. These guys would take a deck or two of playing cards (purchased through commissary at five bucks a deck) and twist them up until they were tight, slender funnels. They would slide them together until they formed a solid stick. It was all held together by sheet string and when finished, measured about fifteen to twenty feet long. After piecing this contraption together and wrapping it with sheet string, they would take an eraser and two pencil leads and put them on the end of the stick so it formed a double prong. Next, they took toilet tissue, wrapped the end of the "fork," allowing enough room for the prongs to stick out, and stretched it across the hallway outside of the cell and into the open electrical outlet. When they managed to get both prongs stuck into the outlet, it would cause a spark and voila, the toilet paper lit on fire. They pulled it back and lit their smoke or whatever else they had. The stick also doubled as a television remote control button. Ingenious! It didn't stop there. The jail would occasionally serve greens, a kind of spinach-like vegetable. Some inmates were so desperate to smoke that they would dry them out, roll them up with book paper and then smoke 'em down. The smell was horrid. They lit them with the electric plug method. The guys would cough their brains out on every puff.

Unfortunately, some of the inmates made bad things, like weapons. A few men knew how to take apart a razor, remove the blade and put the razor back together. I still read about throat slashing and sliced wrists to this very day. The guards rarely checked when you gave the razor back after use. If they

362

did, though, and found a blade missing, your cell would be shaken down. Toothbrushes were used to make "shanks," or sharp devices used for stabbing. The toothbrushes issued were only three inches long, but it was enough for a bored or troubled prisoner to fashion into a weapon. The guys would burn and melt the plastic part of the toothbrush, form it into a point, then dip it into the cold toilet water for maximum strength. Anything made of plastic, hard or soft could be formed into a shank using the "melt, form and dip" method. Thankfully, I was never a victim of a stabbing or cutting.

Boredom, I think, was a part of the reason for this misbehavior. Human beings can only sit idle for so long. They needed activities so they could use their hands and energy. Jail offered very few alternatives to keep one busy. Once or twice a month they had church services, and they had a school class for a tiny percentage of inmates who qualified. Unless you could get work as a trusty, you figured it out for yourself. I never qualified for any programs because I was labeled as a bi-polar, alcoholic, sexual predator. I wasn't allowed to do anything except sit.

I signed up for some of the programs numerous times until I had a guard tell me, "This cell is the best it's going to get for you."

At least they let me know so I wouldn't keep asking and hoping for the opportunity. In my sentencing, Taylor said I could motion for work release in four months. The deputy told me to forget about that, too. It was not a possibility for "my kind." I tried to be persistent.

The guard finally asked me, "How many different ways do you have to be told NO?"

He warned me not to ask again, or I'd go to the hole.

*

The very best parts of jail were the cook-ups. We would use our clean soap dishes to chop up sausage and cheese that we purchased from the commissary store. We crushed bags of nacho chips and mixed the concoction together on the stainless steel table. Whoever our cell cook was would save empty milk cartons and stuff them full with toilet paper. He would light them and put them on a ledge under the table. You had to make sure that the toilet paper was vented so the fire would stay lit longer. If you twirled the paper around your hand, pulled it off and stuffed it in the carton, you would have a fire that would burn for five minutes straight. We needed about ten of these to have a complete cook-up. As the fires burned down, you pushed the carton off the edge and into a bucket of water, and then replaced it with a new burner. The table would turn into a griddle and we would pour the food onto it. After about ten to twenty minutes of turning it over, you had the tastiest chip dip in the land. You could put it on bread, dip with chips or just eat it with a fork. You had to contribute something to get in on it though. I always gave part of my share to the guys who couldn't afford anything. Don't get caught cooking up, though, or your whole cell would go to the hole.

Cellmates created many items with the material we had on hand. I was amazed. If they would use this ingenuity in the real world, they could make something of themselves. I think it all came down to laziness. Some of these guys could be inventors or have good jobs using their hands and minds. Where jail could serve to re-hab and teach, it failed by strictly punishing. We wonder why the recidivism rates are so high.

*

Daily log 2-23-2006: Up at 10:00 today. Inmate in the Pods (middle of jail) hung himself after being sentenced to twelve years in prison. Now the deputies are making sure that all the curtains, blankets and lines are down. The jail seemed lax about the rules until someone died, and then they're pricks for a couple of days. Matt (cellmate) was sentenced to six months of boot camp today. We'll see if he makes it. He's afraid he'll get beat up. I would say his chances are better than average.

Dream Log 2-23-2006: I was talking on the phone with 911 and telling them that a murderer was after me. The next thing I know, I'm talking to the murderer. Police ran him off, though. Our cat is sliding down a chute into our basement. I'm at my brother's house; I'm sleeping in the rafters.

"No man chooses evil because it is evil; he only mistakes it for happiness, the good he seeks."
    -Mary Wollstonecraft

Shaun Webb

Shake It Down

Every cell in the jail had a shakedown now and then. How the shakedown went depended on a couple of things: First, were you suspected of hiding something? If the guards think you were, you would be shaken down. Second, was the guard a bully who takes joy in intimidating others? If he was, a shakedown will very likely occur and it would be a complete disaster.

During a shakedown, everyone was removed from the cell and placed in a holding area down the hall. All contraband was removed. This included the television remote sticks. The curtains that blocked the toilet area so you could relieve yourself in peace were cut down. The curtains were made out of torn bed sheets. We exchanged laundry once a week; that included bed sheets and jumpsuits. The guys would rebuild on the next laundry day.

If a bully guard did the shakedown, you returned to find every single person's personal property dumped from the cardboard boxes they were in and kicked into the middle of the floor. You would spend hours sorting it out and arguing about whose stuff belonged to whom. They wondered why prisoners were sometimes violent. This was one reason. I thought it to be disrespectful and cruel, but we were in jail, so you had no choice. We were consistently reminded that we made the choice that landed us here. It was especially hard when you did nothing wrong, but were treated in such a demeaning way.

Most times, the shakedowns were generally uneventful. You could easily restore your curtains and re-make your cots.

Shakedowns were what made me the most nervous about being in jail. I always felt that the ripping away of your privacy and integrity was an intimidation tactic. I hated it. If I were one of these guards, I would never want to be on the prisoner's side of the fence. I swear some of these glorified turnkeys were bullied around when they were younger and someone was going to pay the price. A little respect for a human being goes a long way.

*

It was well into March and I had about four months to go before I would be free again. This was when I had my first cellmate altercation.

For some reason I was arguing with a guy nicknamed Chappelle (we called him that because he looked just like Dave Chappelle, the comedian. Even the guards called him Chappelle) about some stupid subject when he slammed his fists onto the stainless steel table and called me a baby raper. I could feel my blood boil when he said those words. I was going to have my first fight in jail. The noise he made was so severe that the guards came running with whistles blowing. The next thing I knew, I was pinned against the cell wall by some big burly guard while the rest of the guys were cleared

368

out. The brute cuffed me hard. I instantly lost the feeling in my hands. I was led out by my arm to the meeting cell. I didn't know where Chappelle ended up because things happened so fast. This guard questioned me and he finally believed that neither party had thrown punches. I was told I was being moved to another area. The guard uncuffed me and had me go into the empty cell and pack my personal items. I did so, and then followed him to my new digs. On our way, I saw Chappelle sitting on a bench next to the tanks. He had all his stuff, too.

He smiled at me and said, "See ya Sean."

The guard then yelled at him, **"SHUT THE FUCK UP CHAPELLE!"**

On our way to the new cell, the guard said that if I had kicked his ass, he wouldn't have penalized me. I told him he got there too fast. He laughed. I didn't. Chappelle was going back to the tanks to wait for another open cell. After my "no contact" fight, I entered my new home labeled AB2, found a vacant top bunk and sobbed into my blanket until I fell asleep. My wrists were bruised from the cuffs, as were my arms from the guard's tight grip.

*

Getting in fights was not the only way you could be moved to a new cell, or new area, as situations dictated. For instance, there were prisoners that entered the cell fresh out of "boot camp," which was a three-month program at a military style facility outside the jail that supposedly helped younger kids build some discipline while shortening their sentences. When these kids were not "good enough" for this camp they were taken back to jail and placed in general population with us. However, before returning to jail, they were beaten to a pulp. Some of these kids had bruises from head to toe. They would say that they took daily beatings and harsh treatment. One kid said he was handcuffed to a bar in the toilet area for *fifteen straight hours.* What's worse was that he was placed in a position where he couldn't sit or stand (hunched over). He said it was the most painful experience he had ever had.

Every morning started with all the guys being lined up completely nude and inspected by the guards, male and female. One of my early cellmates was physically pulled off a toilet by a female guard while in the middle of a bowel movement. He said his underwear was filled with his own feces for the rest of the day. I believed him because that was a story that seemed to be common among returnees. Those guards were sickened perverts. I thought the jailers were supposed to help these boys. It was another excuse to beat on them and get away with it. It was a form of torture and mental humiliation. A couple of inmates made it as far as the *day before* graduation, only to be told they were not going to make it, and sent back to jail (with a beating) to finish their entire sentence. Those kids were devastated, and many of them had parents or guardians that were going to attend the ceremony. Thank God, this practice has since been dis-banded. The county says it was because of money woes. It was *really* all about lawsuits brought on by injured prisoners. Two inmates actually died at this facility. So much for their rehab. I'm certainly glad I was not a boot camp candidate. My thinking

was that I would have quit early on and been sent back to jail:
With a beating, of course.

*

Daily Log 3-12-2006: I hated it in my new cell. Maybe I just
needed to get used to it. I didn't want to communicate with
the cellmates at all. They were in their own worlds. I tried to
keep my focus, but it was awfully tough when you're in a
place you didn't belong. This sucks and I hate it. Hate it.
Hate it.

Dream Log 3-12-2006: I dreamed I put hamsters and guinea
pigs in a fish tank and they lived. They had gills that kept
them breathing. Maybe that was how it was for me in this
new cell. I thought I was going to drown but I didn't.
Sometimes I wished I would've.

*"It is men's own mind, not his enemy or foe, which lures
him to evil ways.*
                        -Budda

Shaun Webb

Closer Yet

Ah! Spring was in the air. I knew this because the bullying guards took pleasure in reminding us every day.

"It's beautiful outside, why are you guys just sitting in here?"

I didn't let it get to me because I was over halfway through with the jail part of my sentence. I became more and more anxious as the days went by. A big reason for this was that you thought something else might come up, like new charges that would keep you in the joint. It wasn't all far-fetched thinking. I was already in a mess for a crime I didn't commit. Why couldn't it happen again? I met men that, weeks before their release dates, caught a new case. One man caught a case three days before his scheduled release. He had been in for forty-nine weeks. The guards took great joy in telling you that you weren't going home. Who trained these guys? The Gestapo?

*

I kept up with my writing and my reading. All my letters home, jail logs, and writing about my experiences within the system served as good therapy and contributed to my mental welfare. If I could live it, why shouldn't I be able to write it?

373

I would wait until three and a half years after my release to share my story. It took that long to try to relax myself enough to go over it all again. The anger, anxiety and fear consumed me for a very long time. It still consumes me, but in a more positive manner. You could call it the ultimate learning experience. I do believe I suffered from Post-Traumatic Stress Disorder due to the entire experience.

*

Daily Log 3-20-2006: So many days go by, moving us ever so much closer. The end is in sight and will come. I had to take one step at a time. This could be done. Without support from the outside, I couldn't even begin to imagine how much tougher this would've been. Some people had the personality to handle it. Some, like me, abhor it. Home was just around the corner.

Dream Log 3-20-2006: I see a game, but can't seem to play it. Storms are coming through. Lawn, garden and house are involved. Everything was so broken up. I was in a mental ward being told to stop walking on the carpet. Strange non-sensical words on the walls. Very odd indeed.

"There is no medicine like hope, no incentive so great, and no tonic so powerful as expectation of something better tomorrow."
-Orison Swett Marden

Violence and Mental Health

They placed a new man in our cell that seemed to be troubled. He thought that George Bush had pointed missiles at our cell and that we were going to be destroyed. The man seemed to be terribly troubled about this.

He mumbled to himself on his bunk and started talking to us about strange things at strange times. In the middle of the night, he woke up cellmates to tell them whatever came to his mind. Some people you didn't bother while they slept, or any other time for that matter. Who knew what kind of damage some pissed off inmate would do. This new inmate didn't seem to have fear. The man was scary (and scared). He woke me up on his fifth night in our cell to tell me he was an oompa-loompa from Wonka's Chocolate Factory and that he needed brains to put in the big mixing vats at the factory.

I told him to go back to sleep. I reasoned with him, "sleepy brains are no good; you need good, solid, wide awake brains to mix in the vat."

"Yeah," he whispered, "I think you're right." He went back to bed.

I needed to tell a guard about this person. I thought he was in the wrong wing of the jail. He needed a psychiatric unit. The next morning, when the guard of the day came through, we, as a cell, told him that this inmate was nutty and needed to be cared for on a closer level.

"What's the matter guys, can't handle a guy who might be a little strange?"

"Mr. Guard, we are not trying to rattle your chain or mess with you, he really does need help."

"He stays. I don't want to hear another thing about it. Whoever says the next word is going to the hole for a week," the ignorant numbskull yelled.

Fine, we'd try to deal with this mental case ourselves. There were no guarantees that he'd be safe in this cell.

A few days later, this man finally lost it. He kept screaming in his cot about the missiles that were going to blow up our cell.

"I'm scared, I'm scared, help me!" He begged.

One of the guys told him to stifle it. He jumped off his bunk, yelled about being scared again and attacked *ME*. What in God's name had I done to deserve this? He was frightened and he was swinging. I could see the fear in his eyes. I bear hugged him and forced him onto the table. I was big and he was small, so it wasn't too tough to hold him steady considering my weight advantage. A couple of inmates came over to help while a couple more yelled for the guard of the day.

The next thing upset me terribly. One cellmate helped by pinning his arms down, while another pinned his legs.

"Hit him Sean, beat his face in." The angry, evil words shocked me.

I was heated and made it clear. "No way am I hitting this guy. He's being held down, and he didn't mean to attack me. He doesn't even know where he is; he's sick."

I would be upset for days. I couldn't believe how cruel and repulsive some people were.

The guards came and took him away. It was too bad it came down to that. It didn't have to. He should have been unharmed in a rubber cell from the start. The check-in people rated me a bi-polar alcoholic; how did he slip through? A couple of days later, the original guard, who we complained to, was on shift. One of our cellmates piped up about what happened and that if the guard was doing his job, it wouldn't have been an issue. Our cellmate spent the next two weeks in the hole for "insubordination." You have to keep your mouth shut no matter how screwed up you may think things were.

*

Daily Log 3-24-2006: The dep's really needed to chill out on the inmates. Some of those guys who have a little power were very abusive with it. They're insecure and therefore want to punish others for their own mental shorts. (Or penile shorts). You never know when you'll see these guys on the outside, so you should, at least attempt to show some respect. The inmates are getting fired up. No books and no recreation for a while = rowdy inmates.

Dream Log 3-24-2006: Razors were being dropped off in everyone's lawn. We had a certain time limit before they would be picked up. I stole two razors from a deputy locker.

When I noticed they were handing them out I quickly threw
the stolen ones back into his locker. Countryside house with a
two-lane highway and woods. Ahh!

*

More fights, more arguing. Big guys beating up little guys.
"Fuck you" this, "fuck you" that. I had never heard the word
"fuck" so frequently used in so many parts of speech. Verb,
adjective, adverb, noun. It was a wonder word in jail jargon. I
was seriously getting sick of being stuck in the same cell with
these jokers. It insulted my intelligence. I was certainly not
the smartest cellmate, but some men here don't seem to want
to be a part of normal society. Some of those guys
understandably came from very difficult backgrounds, so
"mean" was ingrained into their psyches from a young age.

I didn't have an answer for the violence. I shook my head
and sighed. I did a whole lot of that while I was in jail.

*

One day we were gifted with another troubled inmate. He
was in jail for assaulting his wife. He sat on the edge of his
cot and rubbed his chin repeatedly. He didn't seem nuts as
much as he appeared aggravated.

I asked him if he was okay. His response?

"Do you think my wife is out sucking some strange man's
dick today? Do you think she's cheating on me? I'll kill her
when I get out of here."

Sorry I asked. Anybody that tried to talk to him would be given the same reaction.

One inmate said, "How do I know what the fuck she's doing? When I get out, though, I'll look for her. She sounds like fun."

A beating ensued. This jealous inmate pulverized the smart-mouthed man. When he finished, he sat back down on his bunk and continued rubbing his chin. It was as if nothing happened.

He did say, "When I get home, I'm going to beat her ass just to make sure she knows who the boss is."

I continued my card game and minded my own business.

After my release, I read in the paper that he had killed his wife. He beat her to death with a baseball bat. What a shock. He was given a life term in a prison somewhere. I often read about former inmates in the local paper who were getting into trouble for some horrible crimes of torture, rape and murder. Since the jailers believed in punishment and humiliation first and re-hab never, it should come as no surprise that when some of these guys get out, they go back to the same life with a renewed anger against the "system."

Some inmates needed help. They wouldn't be able to function in society without proper counseling. They aren't given the tools to cope with life on the outside. It burnt me up when I read about the jails wanting to ease the inmate population due to money woes or overcrowding. The public cries out, "don't let these creeps go free!" In some cases, they should be worried. The release of inmates would be much more effective if they had a support program or re-hab to assist them. The "system" is backward, broken and in dire need of repair. The politicians who have never spent one minute in jail think they have all the answers. They don't. Personally, I think anyone wanting to be a prosecutor or a judge should be required to spend thirty days minimum in jail, incognito. They would have a very different outlook upon release. Maybe they themselves would shout out for change. They also may relax their "punishment first" stance.

*

Daily log 4-1-2006: No more violent behavior! I'm tired of people putting their hand on others. Nobody had the right. Especially when they were 2x the other person's size. It hurts my spirit to see stuff like that going on in front of me. Lest I forget, the average I.Q. is about 65 in this joint. (It was that bad) But what I really want to know is; why do the guys have to say what town they're from during a fight? You know, I'm from the LBC, oh yeah? Well I'm from the ATL. For God's sake, just fight.

Dream Log 4-1-2006: Wild night of dreaming. Dreamed I was in the movie "IT". Balloons chasing me. (Ghosts?) Bullies trying to steal my car but I beat them up. I hit a guy with a shovel. Went to St. Paul and spoke with everyone. (Diana especially). Met someone in the school. Walked by a teacher's room but didn't see her. Told everyone I couldn't help Fr. Patrick anymore. A very intense and real feeling.

"I hate to advocate drugs, alcohol, violence or insanity to anyone, but they've always worked for me."
                        -Hunter S. Thompson

Laughter, Weight and the Hole

I could taste the freedom. The life I had been forced to live was going to change again. How would I handle it? I wasn't sure, but I knew it would be better than jail. I had one more trip to the clinic between April and July. I'd shot up to two hundred and eighty pounds. Way too many cook-ups and candy bars combined with little to no exercise. I started at two hundred and forty. That was forty pounds in five and a half months. The inmates and I would try to do some working out in the cell, but if the guards caught you, they made you stop. There was a steel bar over the toilet area that men used for chin-ups. You could do sit-ups or jumping jacks, but if caught, the guards would make you quit. It reached the point where you didn't try, for fear of living in the hole.

*

Daily Log 5-5-2006: Finally shaved today. I grow facial hair very quickly. 276 lbs. That was a huge no-no. I've gone on a milk-lunch-dinner diet. I will lose at least 20 lbs. before I come home. Then I will deduct to 220 lbs. before this diet ends. I will now sit down and read instead of eating.

Dream log 5-5-2006: I punched Blair's boyfriend in the nose, then told him I didn't touch his girlfriend. I also denied the accusations to Judge Judy. She was no help. She said the girl was under stress. Even in my dreams, I can't catch a break. I also found two cute little puppies. They ran under a fence to reach me, but one fell in water and drowned. I was very sad. I also saw Beezer, my old Doberman Pincher. I was hired by a company and trained by "Wes"? Dreams were very vivid and well organized.

*

Living in the hole was hell even hotter than what we had experienced! This was strictly what I'd heard, not what I'd experienced. The cell is an eight by six, so it was short and skinny. It had a tiny cot, a toilet and a small sink, so your limited space became even more limited. When you entered, you went through a sliding gate, and then walked twenty feet further to reach the door to the actual cell. It was a steel door with a six inch by six-inch window on it. When you look through it, you see very little. There were no televisions, books or even writing. You sat in this cramped space for however long they ordered. You aren't advised of the time, so you lose track. I hear that some men came out weary, and not as willing to break any more "rules." I was glad that hadn't been a part of my experience. The guys who spat at or tried to assault guards most often ended up there. I behaved myself for the most part; give for a small fracas or two. The hole wasn't something I was interested in experiencing. It was used as a constant threat by the guards during my incarceration. I couldn't imagine not being able to read or write, or even talk for a week or more.

*

Unbelievably, a couple of funny things did happen at the jail. I still laugh when I think about it. Don't get me wrong, just because I remembered it and chuckled doesn't mean I missed it. The few instances of levity helped to release some of the pent up tension. Without some laughter, I think I would've become depressed. Some unfortunate men had targets seemingly tattooed on their foreheads, and were the main receivers of the practical joker's wrath.

For instance, our shower sits at the middle rear of the cell. A shower curtain held up by a sheet string blocked it. You had the only real privacy while in the shower, so men tended to take advantage of it. One day a younger man, somewhere in his early twenties, went into the shower. After thirty minutes, he was still in there. We asked if he was okay and he said yes, so we shrugged and went about our boredom. Suddenly, the string broke. It revealed the inmate with his back to us and going to town, if you catch my drift. He had no idea for twenty whole seconds that the curtain had fallen. One arm was up on the wall to support himself and one hand was taking care of his business. He must have finally felt the breeze, because he turned around; mid-section completely lathered up, and quickly grabbed the curtain. He struggling to tie it up and finally succeeded, but at that point, the whole cell was in stitches. It was another twenty minutes before he worked up the nerve to come out. He went to his bunk and curled up into a ball. We told him it was okay, you gotta do what you gotta do. That was why we wore flip-flops in the shower.

Bryan, a very funny cellmate then made an announcement.

"Everybody needs to leave that damn thing alone 'till ya get home."

Laughter lifts the spirits- even here.

*

Daily Log 5-23-2006: Fat boy fell last night. He weighs too much (450) it took four of us to pick his ass up. We managed to get him to the table. He's okay, just too big for his own legs. I've finished reading my 23rd novel today. They moved the jealous guy into another area. That in itself calmed the cell down. No more chin rubbing, staring and muttering.

Dream Log 5-23-06: Nikki called me and told me that the pets were going to die any day now. I asked her if she was sure about that. She told me I needed to get home soon and re-energize them. What a scary dream that was. I also remember something about playing baseball, but I didn't know exactly what it was.

*

Other horseplay included cold water over the shower curtain and toothpaste on your head while you slept. Cruel, but sometimes funny pranks were often perpetrated on the weak guys.

386

Doug, a tubby inmate, was relentlessly picked on. The younger guys are the practical jokers. They will only pick on the small, though, which left me out.

Every time poor Doug took a shower, cold water was splashed on him. **"GODDAMN IT,"** he screeched, **"YOU FUCKING ASSHOLES."**

I couldn't help but chuckle. *(Shame on me for that.)* Doug was waiting for them one day, though. When they went to dump on him, BAM, Doug opened the curtain and while stark naked, doused both of them with a bucket of cold water. It was worth mopping up the cell for that one. Both young guys had soaked jumpers. They were upset about this. Tough luck. They got what they deserved. Doug was a good sport, but they pushed him too far.

The straw that broke Doug's back was when they painted a smiley face on his baldhead using toothpaste. Obviously, Doug was sleeping at the time. After he awoke, it took him *three hours* to notice. When he did, he requested to be moved and was granted his wish. I hoped he did well. I personally found Doug to be a very nice man. .

*

The laughs would continue. From time to time, we would be entertained by the arrival of a group of troubled kids who were lined up in front of the cell so the inmates could "scare" them. These kids weren't going to jail *yet*, so a little discouragement was in order. The guard would tell us to whoop it up as loud and obnoxiously as we could so to upset

387

the young men. I took no part in this. I sat and watched, shaking my head as it was being done.

The predominate phrases were; "You gonna be my bitch!" or "Come here, ho, and bend over for me."

I thought it made the guys in the cell look like a bunch of animals. Some of them were, but they should have at least some self-respect. It was, however, very comical to watch. One kid wanted the cell open so he could fight with an inmate. I guess the tactic didn't work for everyone. There will be a place here for him soon.

*

Daily Log 6-16-2006: Went to outside recreation today, but it was cut short because Fat-Boy called the female guard a derogatory name for a woman's genitals. Nice going. What a loser he is. I can't wait until he's gone. We are moving into the 30's of days remaining. I'm trying to contain my excitement.

Dream Log 6-16-2006: Our cell was the boy's restroom next to Nikki's classroom at St.Pauls.
The guard would not give us razors and we grew very long, stupid looking beards.

**"Prison makes you a much better judge of character.
You pick up on people much faster."**
-Suge Knight

Hope, Friendship and Human Touch

It seemed like a long time since I arrived in December. I had missed Christmas, Easter and the Fourth of July. I also missed my daughter's tenth birthday and my own forty-year celebration. The last month would feel like "double time." I didn't have a lot to complain about because, with good time figured in, I'll have spent seven and a half months total in jail. Good time was five days per month if you stayed out of trouble. Find trouble; lose good time. Some innocent men have spent ten, twenty, even forty or more years in prison. When you read about someone being cleared and released after many years, it was very rare event. The system doesn't like to admit their mistakes. If it jails one innocent man in order to incarcerate one hundred guilty ones, the system considers that a huge success. ($$$$)

I'll never forget a fellow inmate once telling me, "Sean, I'd rather be carried away in a casket by six than to be judged by twelve."

I agreed with that, especially after my jury experience. I never wanted to go back to jail and I had no confidence in the system as it stood.

Before my trial, people tried to help cheer me up with their positive reinforcements. The best one I heard was that a jury

389

would rather set a guilty man free than send an innocent one to jail. I'm living proof that it wasn't true. It was a commendable attempt to comfort me, and I do appreciate that. Nevertheless, it all depended on the jurors. There was no method to the madness. If you had a conservative jury, you'd probably go to jail. If you were lucky enough to have a liberal group, then you'd probably be okay. The best jury to have would be a sensible one. Good sense beats politics any day, as far as I was concerned. I wasn't privy to the "sensible" jury, but it could have been so much worse. I could be looking at another fifteen years, minimum.

*

Daily Log 7-1-2006: First day of July! It wouldn't be long now. The days would move quickly, I hoped. We had a new kooky cellmate with us. He said he sometimes talked to death, but death didn't want him yet. The classification people needed to be more careful with their diagnosis. Someone was going to get hurt.

Dream Log 7-1-2006: I was carrying two glasses of wine through the house. A celebration I assume. The rest is foggy. I do remember driving somewhere, though. I don't know where.

*

Bryan was the elder cellmate. He made more sense than any of the other men I had bunked with up to now. He was very much like a father figure without being bossy. If you misbehaved he would yell, **"KNOCK THAT SHIT OFF!"** He would have to tell me this often throughout July because I was going out of my mind over being released soon.

"WEST, KNOCK YOUR SHIT OFF. YOU'LL BE GOING HOME SOON!"

He always said it with a smile. He mentored some of the younger inmates who would come through. **"COME OVER HERE YOUNG FELLA AND HAVE A SEAT, I WANT TO SPEAK AT CHA."**

I really enjoyed sharing a cell with Bryan. I wished I'd met him sooner, but that was jail life: No promises and no guarantees.

Bryan still had another six months to go after my departure, but he was a grizzled veteran who wasn't stressed by his situation.

"AIN'T THE FIRST TIME, WON'T BE THE LAST!"

I wrote a couple of letters to Bryan after I was released. I never heard back from him, but I believed we all disappeared back into our own worlds. We probably wouldn't get along on the outside because our lives were so different. Still, I truly appreciated meeting him.

*

Daily log 7-12-2006: I'm jumping out of my skin. I was so ready to go home and settle down again. We had two young cellmates who recently joined us. They stayed up all night and argued with the cell next to us. They also kept saying the stupidest jokes ever. I was sick of wristband check. I was also tired of the guards referring to us as gentlemen. It was patronizing and they knew it. Maybe when they say, "wristband checks, gentlemen." We should say "no problem, turnkeys." Urg. I hate it here.

Dream Log 7-12-2006: I was walking up the sidewalk to our house and saw all the yellow ribbons wrapped around the trees. I also saw my dog's face. Good boy, Dakota.

*

Father Patrick came up to see me on July 14th. That was wonderful. Since he was a Priest, I was allowed to meet with him in a small holding cell in the hallway. I was so excited when I saw him. It was everything for me not to burst into tears. He put his hands on mine and I felt his strength rush into me. I believe priests have special power. Father Patrick exudes hope. It was also the first time in seven months that I felt the caring touch of another human being. The isolation in jail was another layer of the psychological punishment meted out. I talked with him as long as I wished. He stayed an entire hour. We talked about everything. He noticed I hadn't missed a meal. What was I going to do with no exercise? He also noticed that I looked happier. Part of that was going home and another part was his visit. I did express my disappointment with losing my job. I wanted to go back to my second home at the church. He told me that new challenges awaited me. It turned out that St. Paul was simply a stop on my road through life. When he had to leave, I was sad, but only for a few minutes. I knew I'd see him again very soon. I went back to my cell feeling much more relaxed and content: Only two weeks to go.

*

Daily Log 7-21-2006: I'm not kidding. They gave us spoiled cole slaw. It smelled like old shoes. The drugged out crack head in the cell next to us started yelling at me during chow today. Apparently, he thinks I'm the one turning the TV up loud when he was sleeping. I don't touch, nor do I care about the fucking TV set. He only had one or two teeth left. Bryan said he'd take care of those for him if he'd like. Very funny stuff.

Dream Log 7-21-2006: I saw Blair playing ball with my daughter. I told Blair to get her ass away from her. Blair cried as she gangled away. Gangling is when you walk with your head a foot out in front of your body while your knuckles drag on the ground behind you.

"That's all a man can hope for during his lifetime - to set an example - and when he is dead, to be an inspiration for history."
   William McKinley

Welcome Home

"Oh my God, Oh my God, it was finally time to leave."
My body tingled with excitement and anticipation, but my
brain worried that someone or something would appear at the
last hour to halt the process and leave me here longer. You
have to wait until 11:59 P.M. on the day you're leaving to go
home.

"GODDAMIT WEST, CALM DOWN!" Bryan said.

I couldn't. I was every emotion wrapped in one. It was an
indescribable feeling to be freed from jail or prison. The long
time-out was ending. I could actually touch my wife and hug
my family. The whole day was like a huge blur. I didn't
remember much of it.

*

I heard the guard; "WEST, PACK YOUR SHIT, YOU'RE
GOING HOME."

"Oh my God, Oh my God." I gave my box of goodies to
Bryan and he told me to take care and don't come back. We
hugged and I said my farewells to the other guys. The cell
gate slid open and I went down the narrow walkway for the
last time. No more keys dangling at a guard's waist, no more
disgusting food and no more mean guys to deal with. No

more being ordered around by bullying guards. I heard Bryan yell in the background,

"THAT'S A WRAP WEST!" Yes it was, Bryan; for good.

*

Daily Log 7-27-2006: Last Day! Guards were being jerks, but I didn't care. Our guard turned off the TV and said we could have it again tonight if we were "good." Kiss my ass guard. I wouldn't say it, but I'd think it. Some people have to be mean, I guess. Oh well, see ya tonight!

Dream Log 7-26-2006: I drove to Texas. Friends of ours were driving to Dallas. I gave them a remote control for a TV and told them they could tune into Dallas programming! I begged Nikki to drive to LA with me.

*

I walked into the jail hallway and the guard checked the box I had with me. I was frisked, as if I'm going to do ANYTHING to screw this up. I walked with the guard to the elevator, and we went downstairs to checkout. This was also a process. I had to switch my jumper for my real clothes: One more nude encounter for the road. After changing, I sat at the checkout window until the guard was ready for me.

Finally, after twenty minutes, they called my name. I was given whatever money I had left from commissary, and I was

396

also given a plastic box which contained my things which were confiscated upon entering.

"Hey," I said, "My suspenders are missing. Those were fifty dollar suspenders."

I knew right then that the deputy who checked me in after the trial took them.

The guard said, "Someone must have stolen 'em."

"Really? You don't say?" Whatever, I just wanted out. I hoped the guard who stole them didn't accidentally choke himself with them. That would be a shame.

I was led to a large garage door somewhere in the back of the jail. On our way, a couple incoming inmates called me Drew Carey, because I'd gained so much weight and wore glasses similar to his.

"Hey, Drew Carey, you goin' home?"

I smiled. The door slowly creaked up and WOW! The cheering was incredible. there were balloons, people, signs. Here we were at midnight and the lot was overflowing. It was so overwhelming. Nikki ran over, thrust herself into my arms and cried harder than ever. She had a very tight grip on me. My daughter joined her, grabbing around my waist, also crying. I slowly looked around and the reality of freedom began to sink in. There was my brother and Liza. There were our school friends. Oh my gosh, there was my step-dad I call papa, who *really is* married to my mother.

"Hey! Where's my mom?" I wondered aloud.

Nikki told me she wasn't feeling well and had to sit in the truck. I walked over and looked at her. Tears were streaming down both our faces. She was there even though she was battling cancer and chemotherapy. What could I say? I had an amazing group of family and friends.

There were two other people outside waiting for their family member to be released, and they couldn't believe the amount of people and support awaiting me.

"Are you having a party or something?" They lovingly chided. "Got any cake?"

Even the deputies in the jail were surprised at the number of people waiting for my release. It was a very unusual occurrence.

I looked at Nikki and my family and friends and yelled out, **"LETS GO HOME."** More cheers followed. Even from the folks on the wait for their people. It was so exciting. What a feeling!

"When the prison doors are opened, the real dragon will fly out."
   -Ho Chi Min

III.

Shaun Webb

Freedom AND Punishment

The first thing I did when I arrived home was lay face first in the lawn. It felt so good, and it smelled so good. The grass was dewey, and the feeling of nature was invigorating. I took off my shoes and socks. Walking through the yard with bare feet was splendid. I smelled the flowers; I looked at everything with a smile that had been missing for months. I wasn't supposed to walk around my yard when I arrived home. A probation officer told me earlier that I was to drive straight home and go straight in the house because I was to be tethered the morning after release. *I was still being punished.* Your sentence doesn't end until the sex offender registration period ends (25 years). However, I didn't see any probation officers waiting in my driveway. I imagined they were all in bed sleeping. I had to stop and smell life for a moment.

*

Kisses for everyone. I kissed Nikki repeatedly. I kissed my daughter repeatedly. My Mom, Liza; kisses for them too. I would've kissed my Brother or Papa, but hey, I'm excited, not crazy; hugs and handshakes for them.

We talked and laughed, we enjoyed the human contact renewed. We stayed up until three in the morning catching up. We talked about the trial and the sentencing. Liza was very vocal in her discontent. She couldn't believe what had transpired before her eyes and said they would've had to drag her out of the court screaming. It was certainly understandable.

"You took it better than I would have," Liza said.

I offered her an explanation, "I wanted to keep my emotions somewhat in check because the judge would be sentencing me and I didn't want to make it worse than it already was. I quietly expressed my discontent by commenting to the jury on my way to jail. I was hoping that it didn't hurt me too severely."

I think my actions may have been damaging, but who knew for sure.

My brother was his quiet self, taking in the information as it came. He had never been much for words, but you could tell he was pleased with my release. My poor mom sat and smiled even though she was horribly uncomfortable from the chemotherapy treatments she was undergoing. Nikki was excited to see me and stayed close to my side.

How could I ever forget my best buddy, my Siberian husky named Dakota and my cat, Maggie, greeting me in their aloof manners. Dakota appeared not to care much, but I know he did. He licked me, wagged his tail and went back to his laydown spot. He kept his beautiful blue eyes on me all the while. I knew he was smiling. He seemed satisfied that I was home. My cat looked at me, took a sniff or two and apparently re-accepted me into HER home.

Overall, I think the pets were glad I was back. I missed seven and a half months of their lives, which was almost seven years for them. Nikki explained to me that she thought Dakota longed for me. He would sit at the front door for hours every day waiting for me, before finally giving up after three and a half months. He then endured eye trouble, which Nikki said was a runny, red, sore looking problem. She bought eye drops from the vet that did help. Our vet said she had no doubt that my dog missed me quite a bit. Nikki agreed. When I came home, the eyes improved greatly. He was nine years-old and arthritis was kicking in. Dakota never regained his health fully and passed away in January 2010. I would never forget him or stop loving him. He watched closely over Nikki while I was gone. He was and will always be my very best friend. He did his job well and deserved his rest.

*

Papa told me that Nikki couldn't sit down for two minutes all day. He said the second Nikki's butt would hit the chair; she would pop right back up because she remembered something else. She had the house decorated for my arrival. Happy fortieth birthday was on one banner, Christmas and Birthday gifts lined up on the floor. There were welcome home banners, we love you banners, and balloons on the ceiling. It was everything and more than I ever expected. What a wonderful woman, that wife of mine. I can honestly say that I felt that same excitement she did while waiting for that cell gate to open.

Nikki told me she had invited all of our friends for a coming home party, which would be in a few days. I couldn't have been happier. I had my first post jail meal of French fries, a double hamburger and a big giant diet Pepsi. What were a few more calories? A slight stomachache followed, but this time I had antacid to relieve it. I smoked a cigarette, which I wished I wouldn't have done, but I'd quit on my terms, not the counties; a poor excuse all the same. I loved every puff. I needed to quit, or I'd be joining heaven sooner than expected.

Everyone left and we could finally get a little shuteye. In the movies, the happy couple always makes love upon being reunited. Nikki and I snuggled as close as we could and giggled ourselves to sleep. I was in my bed with my wife, my daughter and the pets close-by. I had to be up in a few hours because reality would again be waiting. I had to be somewhere early.

"We can be thankful to a friend for a few acres, or a little money; and yet for the freedom and command of the whole earth, and for the great benefits of our being, our life, health, and reason, we look upon ourselves as under no obligation."
-Lucius Annaeus Seneca

Monitored

Upon waking, it took me a few minutes to get used to my surroundings. I had been sleeping behind bars for so long, that my room seemed like a luxury suite. There were no jingling guard keys or thoughtless inmates yelling. I had learned to sleep with all the noise. I enjoyed a hot cup of coffee and a newspaper; the little things that I had sorely missed.

It was 6:00 and I needed to be to the probation department for my first meeting. A few months earlier, I had been visited by a probation officer in jail, and was told to report to their building by nine o'clock in the morning the day after my release. If I were late for my initial meeting, I would be in violation of probation and would face more jail time. That wasn't for me, so I'd be early. I wasn't going back to that dungeon. I would rather die. This same probation officer had told me to go straight home and stay in the house upon my release. I'd keep my little yard walk a secret; no harm, no foul.

*

We arrived at the old brick building, located right next to the circuit court. I was told to sign in and that someone would be out soon to see me. It was tough going back there the day after my release. Emotions ran high.

The place was filled wall to wall. There weren't enough seats for everybody. It was another example of the overcrowding and the understaffing. It turns out I didn't need to rush down there because I wasn't called in until noon. It seemed like everyone in this snail-paced system was late. My dad had come to the house that morning and accompanied me through the process. Being an ex-cop, he was more familiar with the routine.

When I was finally called, my dad was asked to stay in the lobby as I was led into an office by a man named Mr. Davis and was told to have a seat. He appeared quiet and timid. It seemed to me he was overwhelmed. He had me pull up my pant leg, and he placed a tether on my ankle. Next, he went over all the rules of probation. Did you know that if you are with someone, or at someone's house and they have a gun, with or without your knowledge, that was an automatic five years in prison, no question's asked? I had never hung out with anyone who had guns, but I never thought of the hunters and collectors in my family. My dad and brother both had weapons in their houses, so I had to pre-empt my visits until probation ended.

My report date was once a week on Wednesday and I would meet with Ms. Milner. I hoped my probation officer would be a little more humane than the people I had encountered thus far. Mr. Davis told me he would come to my house within an hour to set up the tether system. I thought I was all set. Just strap it on and go. I was wrong. I still had a lot to learn about the criminal justice system. My dad asked if he could take me out to lunch before he took me back home.

"I'm sorry, no," was the short, simple response.

Mr. Davis arrived the minute he said he would and was surprised to see all the balloons and posters. I was naive about those probation officer's attitudes. I was sure the man had seen and heard it all. Every excuse that could possibly be offered probably was. He did tell me it was an impressive looking welcome. He had business to take care of, though, so that was all he said about it.

I was hooked up to the tethering system using a large black machine that was connected to my home phone. Your home phone was the counties connection to you. Mr. Davis had me walk to each corner of my house, upstairs and downstairs. Apparently, this system programmed my ankle device to the black contraption as I walked around. He finished quickly, reminded me of the rules and then told us to have a good day. That started my new career as a tethered ex-con. I was confined within the house; No backyard, no walk to the mailbox, no porch.

*

ELECTRONIC MONITORING AGREEMENT

1. You must be in the confines of your residence during the times designated by your supervising agent.

2. You must only go to work or a designation authorized by your agent when you leave home.

3. You must maintain electrical and compatible telephone service at your residence.

4. You must not have or use "call forwarding" service.

5. You must have a private, single line with no options and unlimited calling capability.

6. You must not have an answering machine connected to your phone.

7. You must not have a cordless phone IN your home.

8. You must leave your telephone free from use for twenty consecutive minutes each hour.

9. You are responsible for any charges that result from the use of the monitoring equipment.

10. You must not remove or damage the leg transmitter or monitoring equipment.

11. You must respond personally to telephone calls to verify your presence in your home.

12. You authorize the Department of Corrections to enter your home at any time.

13. You are responsible for all monitoring costs.

14. You must submit your telephone bill each month to your agent.

15. You must contact your agent for any curfew changes.

Failure to comply with these rules will result in criminal prosecution.

"There is nothing anyone can do anyway. The public has no power. The government knows I'm not a criminal. The parole board knows I'm not a criminal. The judge knows I'm not a criminal.
-Jack Kevorkian

Shaun Webb

Compliance

A couple of days went by and it was time for the huge homecoming party that Nikki had organized. Everybody I knew, and even some I didn't know, showed up. What a support group that was. They were so encouraging and grateful that I was home. The parent who had given Nikki the candles to burn came over. Teachers, friends and family all showed up; the people who believed in me. I knew I was looking pale and overweight, but no one said a word about it. Everyone who was there mentioned the same thing; that I'd been railroaded and had no doubt about my innocence. That was definitely nice to hear. I expressed all the appreciation and thanks that I possibly could. There weren't enough ways to properly express gratitude to everyone.

Our party lasted all day long and into the evening. People kept showing up. By the time the last person left, I was completely exhausted from re-explaining my "adventure" repeatedly. I was pleased to be home so I could talk to everyone in person. I had to let them know how crooked and unjust I believed our system was.

The next day, Fr. Patrick came over along with a few of my former workmates from the church. They seemed very happy to see me and wanted to look at the tether on my leg. "Does it make your leg itch? Is it tight? What if this and what if that?"

411

I answered all their questions with enthusiasm. They were curious about it. I would have asked questions, too. I would answer hundreds of questions in only a few days. People wanted to know what jail was like. Many expressed shock by the disparity between what they read in the newspaper and the reality of the experience. Society had better pay attention to the problem, because one in thirty adults in the USA will be incarcerated in their lifetime. That ratio keeps increasing and you could be the next statistic. I would not recommend it to anyone.

*

Wednesday came around and it was time to meet my new probation officer. I went very early so I would be there when the doors opened at 7 a.m. It was a smart move, because I was able to sign my name on the top line of the sign-up sheet to see Ms. Milner.

At 8:15, she called me in.

What a scowl she wore on her face. "Sit down," she snarled.

I smiled and asked how she was doing today, but all I received was business talk.

"Mr. West, did you have any police contact this week?"

"No."

"Mr. West, have there been any changes to your situation?"

"Uh…no?"

"Mr. West, have you been complying with the sex offender registry requirements?"

"Umm…yes, of course."

"Do you have any questions?"

I did, but was afraid to ask. I figured I'd learn more by listening. "No," I said.

"You will see me every Wednesday until you find work," she ordered, "then you will see me every two weeks after that. Got it?"

"Yes, I think I follow."

She gave me a work search list and told me I could leave my house from 9 a.m. through noon every Monday, Tuesday and Friday. I was also allowed to attend counseling every Wednesday from 5 p.m. to 7 p.m.

"If you leave your house at any other time, I will violate you and you will go to jail. I don't fool around Mr. West. Don't test me."

"Okay, I've got it."

Trust me, I had it. I wasn't going back to that hole, ever. She ordered me to the local police department to be officially registered as a sex offender. That would start yet another new adventure in my life, one that would continue to bring pain and heartache. First, however, I was to be sent across the parking lot to the jail collection department.

"Life is not a matter of place, things or comfort; rather, it concerns the basic human rights of family, country, justice and human dignity." **-Imelda Marcos**

Pay Up

Across the parking lot I went. My next move was to stop at the courthouse and figure out what I owed in jail restitution. It was very difficult to enter the building again, as the sting of the trial and jail were haunting these hallways. I could feel my heart beat faster and my blood pressure rise. I saw deputies and those cold prosecuting faces when I walked down the hallway. No smiles or even head nods, only straight-edged looks. No matter, I had business to complete, so I needed to stay focused on the task.

At the collection window, I was confronted with yet another "learning experience" and a bill from Oakland County. Now mind you, we have paid tens of thousands of dollars in defense, court costs and fees, along with victim's rights fees. The tether I was on was costing eleven dollars a day. We paid that in advance. It cost us nine hundred and ninety bucks. Money, money, money was what they wanted. The "system" survives by eating your future. ($$$$)

I met a woman at the "jail restitution" office within the courthouse and she brought me into her personal office to calculate the latest in our ongoing series of bills.

"Let's see," she said. "Add this; carry the two, this plus that. Alright, that'll be fifteen thousand, one hundred and ninety dollars please."

415

I shrieked, "SAY WHAT?"

She explained, "Yes sir, that's sixty two dollars a day times two hundred plus days in jail. I think that's right."

"We can't afford that," I countered. "We spent between thirty and forty thousand on everything else. We're broke."

"Well Mr. West, what do you earn," she asked.

"Nothing yet," I said.

"Oh, you're not working? Well, that's different. Let's re-figure this."

She asked me about our bills. She also wanted to know about gasoline, child support and whatever other bills we owed or paid monthly. I told her everything. She re-tabulated on her computer and countered at twenty-five hundred dollars.

"Can we go lower?" I asked.

"Okay, twenty-two hundred and that's it."

I agreed. What else could I do? She explained to me that the county figures everyone jailed making one hundred thousand dollars a year. Those prisoners? Some of them may be lucky to make that in a lifetime. She then told me to pay ten bucks a month until it was paid, no interest accrued. Fine. It would take a long time for them to get the cash. The way I figured it, they could wait as long for their payment as I spend on the degrading sex registry.

*

The whole jail and prison system was a business. Your sentence of record was only a small part of your punishment; the degradation, isolation, financial blackmail and branding of parolees are the offenses that cause ultimate disrespect for the system and inability for the accused to re-enter society successfully. Men and women go back into jail because they didn't pay restitution. They incur yet more additional debt, and when released, steal and mug to get the finances to pay those debts. They can't get real jobs because they're labeled as a felon or pedophile and no one will consider hiring them. Meanwhile, the county is sending them more bills.

"People," says the system, "we have big costs with electricity, food, clothing, etc."

Everything was privatized. The county gets those items at dirt-cheap rates. The food had maggots in it, the clothes and linens were old and crusty, and electricity was minimized by giving each cell one small light. There was also minimal heat and no A/C. The public knew nothing of that and knew no better. I realized what big business was all about.

Sentences in the USA are about seven times longer than that of most European countries! It wasn't because Americans were slow learners; it was "free enterprise." A longer stay in jail means a higher bill. Which means more ($$$$) for the hungry system.

Don't forget the taxpayers who share the burden. Our taxes include mils for the "corporation." Yes, I said "corporation," because that was exactly what it was.

The prison population has more than doubled since the 1980's, and continues to climb. This wasn't only by crime, but by *design*. The more people you incarcerate, the more ($$$) goes into this entity. You actually have to do less today to be incarcerated than ever before

"Greed is the inventor of injustice as well as the current enforcer.

-Julian Casablancas

The Sex Offender Hit list

Since I lived in Waterford Township, I did not have to deal with the White Lake PD any longer. The "crime" had occurred in White Lake, but I was a Waterford resident, so I dealt with their police department to verify my address on the sex offender registry.

I showed up at the Waterford PD and went about my registry requirements. My father, the former Waterford cop, accompanied me. I was to initial a checklist indicating that I understood my responsibilities as a sex offender. I then had my picture taken and was told I must come up once every three months to verify my address FOR TWENTY-FIVE YEARS! In addition, I had to pay a thirty-five dollar processing fee ($) for the "privilege" of having my name on this list. A drop in the bucket compared to all the other fees.

If I missed a verification date, I would be considered non-compliant and subject to a felony. The penalty for non-compliance ranges from community service to as much as ten years in prison. Some of the restrictions I lived under include, but weren't limited to; not living within one thousand feet of a school or park, not going in any school without letting the principal or dean know I was there, not loitering by bus stops or areas kids "frequent." Those were the main rules I must follow; there were plenty more being added every year. This affected my ability to attend my child's school conferences and events, and even my own ability to attend college. If a child was to turn up missing in my neighborhood or a neighborhood near me, I was subject to an *unwarranted* search of my residence. That's right, no warrant needed, a violation of a basic civil right. More of our freedoms legislated away from us. I was officially considered a threat to the community, and the laws for me were different. It was a shame because I really thought kids were great. I had worked with or near them almost all of my life, and have always been a loving and attentive father to my own child.

*

A week after my release, we were visited by Child Protective Services. This was to determine if I was going to be allowed unsupervised visits with my daughter. The woman from CPS already visited and interviewed my ex-wife, who was supportive of me seeing my daughter with no limitations.

The CPS woman was very nice and respectful towards us. She interviewed Nikki, my daughter, and me. The questions for my daughter were about telling the truth and if I'd touched her in any "funny" ways. My daughter said she understood the difference between truth and lies, and said no "funny" touching had ever occurred.

Nikki's interview was uneventful, except that she told the woman that I was innocent, and that the courts and punishment were over-the-top. I told her the same thing. She liked our house, too, which I think was helpful. She commented about how clean and tidy it was. Presentation was 75% of the battle.

After the interviews, she said that she saw no reason to dissolve any visitation rights. She advised us to have another adult present during my visits until my probation ended (28 years?). This was only to be cautious. She promised surprise stop-ins from time to time to check up on things. It had been years since her visit, and there had been *zero* surprise checks. You somehow feel like their watching you, though. It was a different world now.

Let's not forget the added bonus; getting to have my smiling face on the national sex offender registry along with the state registry for the next twenty five years. This was so our neighbors would feel safer, I suppose; or so they could beat, kick, spit at, or even *kill you*. It happens every day here in the good old US of A.

*

SEX OFFENDER REGISTRY CHECKLIST

- I understand it is my duty to register as a sex offender. Failure to do so will result in criminal prosecution.

- I understand that I must register for a period of twenty-five years or a minimum of ten years after being released from prison, whichever is longer. I understand that registration will be for LIFE for a second or subsequent conviction of a registerable offense or for a first conviction of the following: Criminal Sexual Conduct 1st Degree, Criminal Sexual Conduct 2nd Degree (person under thirteen), Kidnapping, Child Kidnapping, Child Sexually Abusive Commercial Activity or the attempt of any of the above.

- I understand that within ten days of changing my residence, I must report in person to the local law enforcement agency, sheriff's department or State police post having jurisdiction over my residence and provide the new address. Failure to report will result in criminal prosecution.

- I understand that within fourteen days of moving into this state, if I am registered or required to be registered as a sex offender in another state, I must register as a sex offender at the local law enforcement agency, sheriff's department or State police post having jurisdiction over my residence. Failure to comply will result in criminal prosecution.

- I understand that ten days prior to changing my residence to another State, I must report in person to the nearest State police post and provide my new address. Failure to do so will result in criminal prosecution.

- I understand that I will maintain a State ID card with my photo as proof of my identity as a sex offender. My photo will be used for identification on the sex offender website.

- I understand I shall pay a one-time $35 fee for registration.

422

- I understand that my fingerprints shall be taken and maintained at the State police post.

- I understand that I shall register with my local police department within the first fifteen days of January, April, July and October. Failure to comply will result in criminal prosecution.

- I understand that if I attend an institution of higher learning, I shall report my name to the main office of the institution and let them know I am a sex offender. Failure to comply will result in criminal prosecution.

- I understand that I am not to live within 1000 feet of a school or learning institution where minors are present. Failure to comply will result in criminal prosecution.

- I understand I shall NOT loiter at known drop-off and pick-up points for children such as bus stops or places where children frequent. Failure to comply will result in criminal prosecution.

- I understand I will have no contact with the victim of the listed offense. Failure to comply will result in criminal prosecution.

- I understand and initial all lines, thus complying with the requirements of the Sex Offender Registry.

FAILURE TO COMPLY WILL RESULT IN
PROSECUTION.

"All propaganda has to be popular and has to accommodate itself to the comprehension of the least intelligent of those it seeks to reach."
                                    -Adolph Hitler

No Fair

The sex registry was THE worst part of the entire experience. It was a lifetime sentence. I was to be on this registry for twenty-five years because I was convicted of "Hand to covered breast." On the registry it said CSC 4TH (VICTIM 13-16). That could mean anything to a layperson. Some people perceive 4th degree to be the worst conviction. Regardless, I was lumped in with violent rapists and horrible child molesters.

*

People who refer to that registry don't know what the particular crime truly encompasses. I contacted or attempted to contact State Representatives and persons in Congress. They didn't want to hear about my problem. If they bothered to write back, it was something to the effect of; "We are sorry the system failed you, please consult an attorney. We cannot comment because we are not lawyers."

I often forgot that their "tough on sex offenders" stance was part of what got them elected in the first place.

They knew the system was flawed, but they weren't going to risk their political futures by railing against it.

The Sheriff for Oakland County discussed putting special tags on license plates to identify sex offenders. After some deliberation among the "powers," along with public clamoring against it, they decided that it wouldn't be fair to someone driving the vehicle who was not an offender. It was also mentioned that it could get someone hurt or killed, but that was an afterthought.

More offenders and more inmates meant more money and more jobs. The individual states are awarded a sum of government money according to how many sex offenders they had on their registry. Newspaper reporters wrote about the subject often, and many had even said that the system needed to be changed. The primary argument was against Romeo-Juliet romances being turned into sex crimes. The Adam Walsh act had been adopted in most states (with a government bonus=$$$$$) to the states that signed it into law. While it dealt with the Romeo-Juliet situations, there was still much work to be done for all others, including the falsely accused and cases where no evidence exists. Since the passing and adopting of the Adam Walsh Act in Michigan: Another John Walsh baby; I was moved to a Tier 2, one being the lowest and three the worst. My registration period changed from four times per year to only twice.

The way it helped with the teen-agers was as follows:

If a girl that were below the age of consent, and her boyfriend less than three years older, it wouldn't continue to be a crime. If the girl was twelve or younger, though, then it was a crime no matter what the age of the boy.

*

Meeting other offenders at probation also opened my eyes. I met an eighteen year-old kid who, when he was sixteen, had sexual contact with his then fifteen year-old girlfriend. Her mom complained and he went to prison for two years. He was just a kid. He also had to live on the registry for LIFE. Hopefully the passing of the AWA helped his situation.

Do those types of mistakes made by young people need to be dealt with so severely? The law said a fifteen year-old cannot consent to sex, because their brains were under-developed. They can, however, consent to murder and be charged as an adult. Does that make sense?

I also met a man who urinated on a tree, and was allegedly seen doing so by a fourteen year-old girl who cried to her mom that she saw his penis. Her mother pressed it with authorities and he received two months in jail, ten months of probation and twenty-five years on the registry. Try getting a job, or applying for school. You're treated differently when people see you on that sex offender site. A scarlet letter would be worn on the offender's forehead.

I knew there were plenty of creepy people out there doing disturbing things to children. I didn't ever condone that behavior. We do, however, need to update the registry and make a *fair* tier system of some sort. A specified number of years with no police contact should allow removal from the list. There should be some means of redemption, but we're living in a "punish at all costs" society. There are hundreds of thousands of people on the sex registry in the USA. What happens when it reaches one million? One and a half million? Two million? At the rate they are adding people, this will happen by 2020. Do we then strip all kids from their parents?

427

Perhaps parents will give up their kids in fear of being charged with a crime. Kid's lie. Some kid's lie to exact revenge or because they were angry. It happens every day.

Until people speak up, it won't change. When one or more of the lawmakers or their family members makes the list, they might have more to say.

"Do not dwell in the past, do not dream of the future, concentrate the mind on the present moment."

-Buddha

The Grieving Process

I was very disappointed with our defense counsel in the case. After seven and a half months in jail, and waiting for our emotions to settle down, there was no choice but to file a grievance with the State's Attorney Grievance Commission. When I looked back and read some of the documents that were involved in the trial, I had to scratch my head. During the prelim hearing, Prosecutor Gardner *led* Blair straight into every single answer. She never replied to anything other than by saying yes or no. Gardner would then make suggestions as to what her answers should be, i.e. Do you mean "yes" or do you mean "no?" Michael should have vehemently objected. Even if overruled, it would have shown up in the court documents for a potential appeals court ruling. The same thing happened during the trial. Michael rarely objected. I think he objected two times total and only one of them showed up on the transcript. The situation was getting more crooked by the minute. Not one time were Taylor's rants documented. Nikki and Danny were left out in the hallway. No involvement whatsoever. Not one single character witness called. Bert Doylan never showed up in court except for the day I was arrested and arraigned. All those items were grievances in our book.

Nikki had contacted Michael directly after sentencing to find out about the appeal process. Michael told her we could appeal the sentence because Taylor went over the guidelines with the tether, but not the trial. He said there was nothing to appeal regarding the trial, because he had done such a stellar job, and as far as the sentencing was concerned, by the time the appeal was heard, the sentence would be complete. Nikki, still shook up from the outcome of the trial and facing thousands of dollars of lawyer's fees, was not in a position emotionally or financially to make a decision to appeal within ninety days, the dead line required for a *mandatory* appellate hearing. The system had already failed us once. Why would we have hope for an appeal? That seemed unlikely to be successful according to our counsel.

*

We sent a request to the grievance commission and they mailed us the necessary paperwork for processing our case. We responded by citing our three biggest complaints. Please note that we could not grieve against anything in the pre-lim hearing, because the commission deals with jury trials only. Take a moment and read Nikki's letter. It best explains our stance. The following is the real letter as written:

Dear AGC,
I have delayed writing to you in order to ensure that this communication will be based on logic and fact, not on emotion. We were extremely disappointed with the manner in which we were represented in Circuit Court. In our initial

meeting with Michael Casper and Bert Doylan, we were told
that:

1. This would come down to a "he said, she said" case, so
character witnesses, especially Sean's ex-wife, would be
particularly important. Testimony from me, his wife, was
discouraged as I would be considered "too close" to give
believable testimony. It would be imperative that the jury "get
to know" Sean.

2. Mr. Doylan was an aggressive attorney who would be at
all of our court appearances. Some "background" work would
be done by Mr. Casper in order to "keep costs down" for us.

3. Responses to the states attorney by the defendant should
be as brief as possible- yes or no without explanation. Our
attorney would then cross-examine and bring out the details
needed to give the jury an honest and complete picture of the
actual circumstances surrounding the allegations.

The reality of the court experience was extremely different.

1. Despite our submission of at least fifty people willing to
testify on our behalf, including Sean's ex-wife and daughter,
co-workers, his immediate supervisor, young women who he
had direct contact with in the school.....there was only one
witness called to the stand, a Private Investigator who brought
nothing as to Sean's character. Even Sean's physician offered
to testify as to Sean's anxiety disorder and unlikeliness to
commit such an act, but she was not even considered. In
addition, I was left sitting out in the hallway throughout the
trial, in case I should be needed as a witness, and was never
called. I had been told up until the day of trial my testimony
would not be used, and my placement out in the hallway
robbed my husband of the support of my presence- both for

431

himself and the visual re-enforcement that would have given the jury. The prosecutor's closing argument admonished the defendant for not having a single person-not even his wife-speak on his behalf!

2. Mr. Doylan signed on as Sean's legal representative and appeared with him at the arraignment. That is the last time he appeared in court with us. This felt like a "bait and switch" tactic. The seasoned lawyer made promises, and then once paid, switched representation to a less experienced lawyer. Mr. Casper was clearly intimidated by Judge Taylor.

3. When questioned by the State's attorney, Sean responded as instructed in simple yes and no answers; e.g. was she ever at the garage? Yes. Did she enter the garage? Yes. On cross-examination, he expected to be able to clarify the facts: she went to the garage for supplies, she never stepped beyond one foot in the door, and the door was always open. Mr. Casper did not cross-examine at all! The jury was left with only half the story.

If it wasn't for the obvious lies we were able to prove with the tattoo photographs, I shudder to think of the outcome of the trial with such inadequate representation. I write today because I am very concerned about future parties who may come to this firm for representation, particularly others who have been accused of acts that they didn't commit, as in this case. A conviction, even a fourth degree misdemeanor, results in not only excessive jail time and probation, but twenty five years to life on a sex offender list that black-balls you from employment, many aspects of your child's life, freedom of movement, housing.....the results are devastating.

Respectfully submitted,
Nikki West

Mr. Doylan was required to respond to the commission and explain his stance per our allegations. Mr. Doylan did so by saying that we never insisted on him, in particular, defending us. He also went on to say that we were angry because of the conviction and were taking it out on his firm. He finished by explaining how decorated he and Michael were in the lawyer world and that he had his own radio show.

In other words, Mr. Doylan lied exactly the same as Blair had. He would take no responsibility for his actions and it was our problem.

Nikki and I all but begged Michael to bring up character witnesses. He stated in his report to the commission that it may have hurt our defense. How? By having a fifteen year-old student testify that I was well mannered and never inappropriate? By having my ex-wife or doctor testify that they thought this not to be indicative of my personality? Michael was afraid because he wasn't prepared for a cross examination by the prosecution.

We hid nothing, nor did we have anything to hide. He tried to ride on the coattails of the tattoo, but he could've done so much more.

Here is a word-for-word copy of the findings we received back from the commission:

Dr. Mr. and Mrs. West,
The commission is authorized to investigate and when necessary prosecute charges of attorney misconduct. After

433

preliminary investigation and careful review of the materials presented in this file by the commission's staff, it has been determined that matters raised in your request for investigation will not be pursued further.

Our office feels Mr. Doylan has answered your allegations adequately. I am enclosing a copy of the answer for your review. We will take no further action.

Please be advised that we consider this matter to be closed. I hope this letter adequately explains our position in this matter.

Very truly yours,
Attorney Grievance Commission

It was okay because we let Bert and Michael know that we weren't going to be pushed around. They had a letter sitting in that office that, rest assured, will be reviewed when other people file against this firm. It will eventually happen. It wasn't quite over for Michael and Bert. Although it would not affect them directly, we were fully intending on appealing the entire trial to the State. That would mean that their conduct would come to the forefront again. We would have to hire a new, and hopefully better, attorney, and place our hope once again in a system that had failed us continually.

"The more lawyers there are, the more people are out there to encourage others not to go to law school."
-David E. Kelley

434

Appealing To a Higher Power

We talked to a friend and were directed to a man named Marcus Hydeman. Mr. Hydeman was a well-respected defense attorney who began his career working as a prosecutor in his county. He also had the misfortune of working with former Judge Taylor both when she was an attorney and a judge.

Nikki and I met Mr. Hydeman at his office and went over everything. He had me bring all paperwork that pertained to the trial. I really liked him. He seemed sincere and made no promises. He explained to us that this could go either way, but he really thought our chances were good. He felt like we were given the short end of the stick and wanted a chance to help. He gave us a substantial discount on his usual fee and allowed us to make payments on the balance.

Mr. Hydeman shook our hands and told us he would get back with us in a couple of weeks. Nikki and I left and hoped for the best. We knew this wasn't a "timely" appeal, meaning that we could have had an automatic hearing if appealed within ninety days of sentencing. We were banking on a "non-timely appeal" or, an appeal filed after the ninety-day automatic appeal period expired, but within the first year of sentencing. The appeals board didn't have to hear us, so it was up to Marcus to convince them of the worthiness. We needed to trust in him.

435

*

We received a call from Mr. Hydeman a couple of weeks later asking us to come to his office. We reached his office and sat down with him. He again told us he felt we had a good chance of being considered. No promises, but better than fifty-fifty. He then presented us with a hefty document of over five hundred pages. Overwhelmed by the size of the document, he explained to us the main arguments in layman's terms. I have broken the word-for-word document down to one subject at a time as follows:

ARGUMENT I

APPELLANT WAS DENIED HIS SIXTH AND FOURTEENTH AMENDMENT RIGHTS TO A FAIR TRIAL AND DUE PROCESS OF LAW THROUGH; A. MISCONDUCT OF THE PROSECUTOR WHICH CONSISTED OF PERSONAL AND UNSWORN TESTIMONY INTO THE PROCEEDINGS; AND B. DEFENSE COUNSEL'S FAILURE TO TIMELY OBJECT TO MOST OF THE INSTANCES.

1. An improper comment by Mr. Gardner not based on evidence:

"The effects are going to last for Blair a lot longer than that."

Two incidents during trial.

2. During direct questioning of Mr. Carowitz, prosecutor elicited Carowitz's personal belief as to Blair's veracity by asking if Blair was "more honest now," then when she talked to him originally.

The question of Blair's veracity was a question for the jury. Mr. Carowitz's beliefs are not probative and are beyond his competence as a witness.

3. In argument, the prosecutor gave unsworn evidence or medical testimony addressing female genitalia: "There was going to be no evidence of DNA on Blair when the police got involved in July or August. There was going to be no evidence of him penetrating her with his finger. And not to be indelicate, even if police had found out about the case within 24 hours and had her taken to see a doctor, there was not going to be any medical evidence."

Mr. Gardner had no jurisdiction as to medical analysis and cannot argue as such.

4. Unsworn information given to the jury by improperly bolstering Mr. Carowitz's statement:

"Mr. Carowitz says he called a litigating attorney, let me explain what a litigating attorney does. He sues on behalf of another company against another company with regards to contracts and property disputes."

Mr. Gardner has improperly bolstered Mr. Carowitz's statement by explaining to the jury a litigating attorney's work. This example supplied unsworn evidence.

5. Prosecution bolstered the testimony of Ms. Radison:

"Do you think Sara Joan Radison sitting here on the witness stand is a woman who for her own gain would put her daughter through a trial talking about being sexually assaulted? Does that seem like the kind of person that she is? That's an evil person, someone who'd do that to her own child. That woman seemed like a woman who's concerned about her daughter, who was upset that she didn't make the right decision when she should have in terms of telling people, and a woman who supported her daughter, a young lady who she found to be truthful."

The prosecutor's arguments not only presented unsworn evidence and opinion, but also improperly injected personal belief. The defense counselor only objected to one of the five instances listed above, therefore robbing defendant of his constitutional rights to a fair trial.

ARGUMENT II

THE TRIAL COURTS REFUSAL TO ALLOW ADEQUATE INQUIRY SCHOOL RECORD INFORMATION ABOUT THE COMPLAINING WITNESS WAS AN ABUSE OF DISCRETION WHICH DENIED APPELLANT HIS SIXTH AMENDMENT RIGHT OF CONFRONTATION, AND FOURTEENTH AMENDMENT RIGHTS TO DUE PROCESS OF LAW AND TO PRESENT A DEFENSE.

1. Blair's motives, mental state, and credibility, were all inherently at issue in the case. It was a "he said, she said" scenario where the "she" testified that Mr. West was the only, or one of the only people she could talk to, or who would listen to her. Obviously, her mother's boyfriend and Mother were not viewed as confidants during the years at issue. Her

best friend, Michelle, only received a small bit of information on one occasion. It is not unreasonable to think that Blair, who acknowledged that she was looking for attention from a man, and for someone to listen, may have confided in a counselor or other figure at school. The defense moved for an in-camera inspection, and the information could have provided valuable and relevant information, or it may not have provided anything useful. In any event, the trial court should have reviewed the materials to make that determination. The state cannot arbitrarily deny a defendant the opportunity to present exculpatory evidence.

We request this Honorable Court grant Sean Albert West leave to appeal, or, alternatively, order such peremptory relief as is fair and appropriate.

Respectfully Submitted,
Marcus Hydeman

*

It was as an amazing document. The guy was trying to help us and more importantly, he believed in us. Was there a chance we could have a new trial, but in a fair and unbiased courtroom?

Marcus explained to us what he would've done if he had been our defense. He would never have divulged any information to the prosecution about the tattoo on my thigh. He said that it did not fall under the discovery aspect of the trial, because it was a distinguishing mark she herself would have known about had she seen it. Thus, he would have led the questioning to the dropping of the pants until he would finally ask her about the mark and the location. Had she then said I had a tattoo on my penis, he would have marched me into the judge's chambers and had me show the judge and prosecutor my penis, not my leg. Upon seeing that a tattoo wasn't there, he would have required prosecution and the court to advise the jury of this finding. He would have given Gardner an opportunity to drop charges. Had he not, the jury still would have just heard from Gardner and Taylor that the plaintiff did, in fact, lie. The tattoo would never have been mentioned.

Marcus said the next step would have been suggesting perjury against the plaintiff, thus possibly causing her unraveling on the stand. Mr. Hydeman also said that Nikki would have testified and he would have lined up fifty character witnesses: teens, parents and co-workers to testify as well. If Taylor would've challenged it because of whatever reason, he still would have made it clear to the jury that they were here to testify on my behalf.

*

We waited with baited breath. I crossed my fingers and hoped. It would be our last shot at it. We wouldn't take it the next step, which was the State Supreme Court, because we were tired and broke. Family and friends contributed to this appeal cause because they felt so bad for us. A trip to the highest court would've cost thousands more. We had nothing left. We would accept this decision and lay down our arms.

440

The decision came. Allow me to share the appeals court statement in its entirety:

Mr. Hydeman,

We have reviewed the case of appeal and find it does not merit consideration.

The Appeals Court

*

That was it. That was all it said. It was almost like being smacked across the cheek with a wet leather glove. What an absolute joke. Mr. Hydeman called me and apologized. He said he didn't even think they read it. (They don't have to) It was one more disappointment. You'd think we would have learned our lesson by now.

Marcus excused the rest of the debt because he thought we were given such a raw deal and he offered to represent us should we ever pursue an expungement in the future. I'm sure he would've won all three acquittals in court. Thanks Mr. Hydeman, your effort was outstanding. Time to try moving on now.

"An appeal is when you ask one court to show it's contempt for another court."
-Finley Peter Dunne

Shaun Webb

Life, Work and the Difficult Pursuit of Happiness

We tried everything short of the Supreme Court, so it was time to forget it and get on with life. Try finding work when you're a sex offender. Best of luck to you.

"Yes, Mr. West, you're very qualified, but your background check shows a sex offense, sorry. Sorry, Mr. West. Sorry, sorry, sorry."

That was how it went. My probation officer became angry with me on my fourth visit, because I wasn't finding work.

"I have sex offenders under me who are finding work. Why can't you?"

If they're finding it, I wish she'd tell me where. I'd gladly go apply at these places. I went online. I applied at over eighty jobs in the first two weeks. Nothing. Not only was I a sex offender, but I was wearing a tether which restricted the hours I could work and required me to report during normal working hours once a week. I felt like the system was doing everything in their power to make it more difficult. I was giving up. I thought I'd be retired at forty-one. It angered me because I could imagine that Blair was *la-de-daing* through her life without a care in the world. I tried not to think about it, but it takes up residence in your head. I wanted revenge. I wanted to see the evil family suffer, which would've brought

443

me great joy, but I had to re-adjust my thinking. As much as I would've liked to face them, I wasn't going to jail again. I had to trudge on, frustrated or not.

Finally, after a month and a half, a friend from the church called and said I would be given a job with his company. I was happy. It didn't matter what it paid or what I had to do, I just needed some stability. I began working with this company and stuck with it for about three months. Mrs. Milner, my probation officer, called me on only my third day of work and left me a message to call her back. She had a problem with me and I was in trouble.

"Great," I thought, "what did I do this time?"

I called right away, and she told me she was testing me to see if I would, in fact, call her. *Stress for nothing.* It was another form of bullying. I would've complained to a higher up, but I probably would have been in trouble for that. Some people really do get a kick out of watching other people suffer.

*

October came and I was about to be released from my tethering. I showed up to probation and the strap was cut. It was another step out of the way. I needed to make it through two more years of probation visits and my sentence would end; except for that registry. That was another twenty-four years.

I had my freedom. I could go to the store, or drive around in my truck and go wherever I wanted to go. I still couldn't leave the state until probation ended. That was fine, as I needed to work.

444

*

The next thing that happened was the break I was looking for. Fritz called me and said he had pulled a few strings with some union locals and I was going to join a labor union. That was terrific news. I would work at large car factories for union wages. The only drawback was that layoffs occur from time to time. If I could work six months a year, I would make as much as I did in a full year at St. Paul. The only thing left to do was to let my current employer know what was going on and to give him a little notice that I was leaving.

I went into his office and the secretary was sitting at her desk, but the rest of the office was empty.

"Where is everyone?" I asked.

She said that they were all out working and I'd have to catch up later. The next thing she hit me with was a bit of a shock.

"Sean, I know were alone in the office. You're not going to rape me are you?"

"WHAT?" Why would she say a thing like that? I asked her, "Why did you ask me such a scary question?"

I knew the answer, but she replied, "I saw you on the internet sex offender list. I'm nervous around you."

Funny, she wasn't nervous for the first two and a half months, but now that she'd seen me on that stupid site, I was suddenly poisonous.

"Don't worry, I said, I'm not a rapist. In fact, I'll leave now."

I made sure I didn't leave myself in a situation where I was alone in the office with any person ever again. Heaven forbid any more false allegations would occur. I let the assistant manager know what she'd said to me. He didn't, or couldn't, say a whole lot. "I'll talk to her Sean, don't worry about it."

Easy for you to say; try going through it.

No matter though, because I was called by Fritz's company and I was going to work starting the following week. I'd finally found my current boss and told him I had this opportunity. I thanked him so much for giving me a second chance. That wasn't good enough. He chewed me out for not giving him notice that was more advanced. I told him the day I found out about the new job, which wouldn't start until the following week. There was little choice, because I *was* going to this new job. They offered the money and insurance I needed to support my family. This boss called me later in the evening to chew me out some more. He should've been ashamed of himself. There was an opportunity to do better for my family and myself. I let him know that I would work the week if he wanted me to, or I'd go away. I worked the week, but it was horrible. Apparently, everyone I worked with learned of the sex offender situation, and they wouldn't say one word to me. Everyone has a cross to bear and as far as I'm concerned, mine is like everyone else's; "t" shaped. I ignored them in return. I couldn't worry about everything that everyone thought about me. It was turning me from mild-mannered into mean.

*

I started work with Fritz' company in the winter of 2006 and I loved it. I was a real union guy. I went into large factories and cleaned up after millwrights, ironworkers, electricians and riggers. The job was physical and I was good at it. That gave me confidence. My weight started to drop and I was happier. Money came into the house and life was getting back on track. I was so pleased that Fritz did this for me. It truly was a blessing. He was another person to whom I couldn't possibly make this up. It was wonderful when people, especially family, rallied around me. My probation officer was also happy. I had a new female officer and she was very nice. I saw her once every two weeks for a while, then after I worked steady for a few months, she knocked down the visits to once a month in person and once a month by telephone. I continued to work steady until August of 2008. Life seemed to be returning to normal. Then the sex offender registry reared its ugly head again.

*

I'd worked at the same factory for almost ten months, or since November. We were being laid off no later than October, so I figured I could make a few more bucks in the month or so before this happened. Then she came along, another person in a seemingly endless line of people. The troublemaker was a cleaning girl for this factory. She had no business with me at all, and I rarely talked to her except to say hi when I passed by her. Here's what happened:

I urgently needed to use the restroom one day. I approached the restroom and noticed she was cleaning it. I asked her if I could have only thirty seconds or so to do my thing.

"**No**, can't you see I'm cleaning? Go find another one," she scowled.

The "other" one was about the equivalent of two city blocks away. I begged her.

"**NO**," she spit.

I angrily told her; "You know what? If I wanted to go right now while you're cleaning, I'd just do it." Then I left. My words came from anger.

I managed to make it to another restroom, but it was close. She could've let me go. She was being nasty to me on purpose. I'd find out why.

This woman started spreading around the plant that I was a sex offender. My stomach knotted as people would approach me with this newly found information. I used to talk to a labor girl who was on the job with us, but worked for a different company. I was no longer allowed to talk with her per her bosses. The laborer I worked with stopped talking to me. I was called into the main office to explain the "sexual harassment" that this cleaning girl complained about. I told them what happened and was told not to worry about it, that this girl was being vindictive and had a reputation for this kind of gossiping. I was getting nervous and uneasy, though.

I was told to go back on the job and ignore her, so I did. Somewhere around late August, or early September, Fritz pulled me off the job. I asked him why, and he told me there was no sense in tempting fate because the job would be ending soon anyway.

"You know how the "he said, she said," shit goes, Sean."

I do, but I wasn't going to back down. I had every right to work and make a living. Those without sin!

Come to find out, she had complained about being "uneasy" around me because I was an offender. She hardly ever saw me. Her boss called me and apologized. He said he felt horrible because he thought I was a good person who did a nice job and deserved a second chance. I told him there were no worries and thanked him for calling. The job was ending in two months anyway. He fired her two days after I was laid off. This hadn't been the first time she caused trouble. It was another reminder to me how quickly life can change from good to bad, and how far reaching the effects of the published registry could be. Should I retrain for a new career? What college would allow me to attend? What profession will allow me to enter?

The economy tanked while I was laid off, and unemployment had been my saving grace. I kept looking for work and hoping for an economic upturn so work would call me back in. I have confidence that this would happen. When it does, I will go in with my head held high. I refuse to be intimidated.

"He that is taken into prison in chains is not conquered, though overcome; for he is still an enemy."
-Thomas Hobbes

Shaun Webb

450

Paranoid

When the phone rang, I literally shuttered. When a car pulled in the driveway, I uncharacteristically stressed out. I was fearful because I knew someone could be completely innocent, yet be charged *and* convicted of any crime. I grew up the child of a police officer and I was in fear and suspicious of them. I had been traumatized and it affected me even five years after the fact. I said I wouldn't be scared or intimidated, but sometimes I was very leery.

I saw a court mandated counselor who told me I had Post Traumatic Stress Disorder. I was constantly looking over my shoulder. It was a scar on my psyche. Blair talked about how it had been a nightmare for her. That was only because she felt the guilt from the untruths she told. I felt it because I knew it could happen at any moment. All it took was an allegation.

*

I heard a story while in jail that made me shiver. A gentleman was accused of raping a child. He served twenty years in prison, all the while insisting he was innocent. Upon his release, he tracked down the accuser and her family and shot them *ALL* to death. When he finished the job, he called

451

the police himself to tell them what he'd done and waited for them to arrive. He went back to prison satisfied with his revenge. While I do not condone that type of behavior, it doesn't surprise me in the least.

I tried to keep my head above water. I worked when called on by my brother in-law's company. It had been a rough year because of the economy, but I trudged along.

I verified my address with local police once every three months. I continued to check and make sure I was compliant. I did everything I was supposed to do to stay on the right side of the law. If not for a couple of understanding people, I would never have gone back to work at all. Rest assured that that registry definitely kept me from getting a job on my own. Supposedly, there were good people out there who would take a chance on you, but they're rare. Nobody wanted the headache that came with hiring an offender. People find out and they talk. Employers find out and they fire you. It was a nasty circle indeed.

It was very frustrating for my family too. My daughter seemed okay, but she had suffered a lot through all of this. She was without her father for seven and a half months, and I could no longer freely attend her school events. I didn't feel comfortable allowing any of her friends to stay overnight or even visit at our house. It spooked me too much. She lived with her mom, so sleepovers had to take place there.

Nikki tried to stay positive. She was a very bright woman with a good head on her shoulders. I tried not to talk too much about our ordeal, though, because it was also very painful for her. There have been times when she's had to hush me mid-sentence because she couldn't take it. I understand and attempted to watch what I said involving any part of the situation.

Court and crime stories fill the papers and mass media: To Catch a Predator, Court TV, Forensics, CSI, America's Most Wanted. Although they were good shows that do catch a lot of criminals, I couldn't hear; "we got that scumbag/dirt bag/whatever bag off the street," one more time. I didn't even bother to watch "Cops." I have learned much dislike towards the police. When I heard about or saw what I perceive to be police brutality, I cringed. I tried to stick with the lighthearted stuff. I also watched sports, even though it took me three years to like basketball again.

It was a big change to your thinking and the way you conducted yourself. I wasn't nearly as friendly as I used to be and that was too bad because it rubbed against my grain. I was very careful not to brush against people in crowded areas. You never know.

My tastes had also changed. I liked hard rock music very much, but since my release from jail it had been more of a meaner, metal edge that appealed to me. From Aerosmith to Slipknot and from Pat Benatar to OTEP has been the progression. I can't explain it except to say that the harder, nastier beat and angrier lyrics seem to say more to me than they used to.

All facets of my life have been affected. Living in this world was almost too much to bear. I have to believe that with bad eventually there came good, so I hung in there. It was a huge test, though.

"We gain strength, and courage, and confidence by each experience in which we really stop to look fear in the face... we must do that which we think we cannot."

-Eleanor Roosevelt

I Weep for the Future

What was in the future for us? I don't know. I wish I could see what lay ahead. Had I known what was going to happen to me up until now, I would've been much better prepared and probably could've put up a better fight. I can tell you that I think more about situations and consequences than I ever used to. The scenario of this case runs through my mind every single day. Would I be in a different situation had I followed my gut instinct more often? I could have hired a different lawyer, possibly female, and been found guilty of each charge or even acquitted on all counts. If I had ignored Blair completely, would that still have happened? My thinking was that it would have because of my actions in telling the company about the theft. It was my guess that life wouldn't be nearly as interesting if we knew everything in advance.

What if all my career windows close because I was labeled? What then? Would I lose everything? The secret for me was to not allow my life to slam shut. I would try to persevere no matter what the circumstance. I wouldn't quit trying to move ahead. Thank God I wasn't in it alone. Thank God for my family and friends who truly believed in me. I couldn't imagine having to deal with it by myself. I would probably go insane. It affected Nikki, myself, my daughter and everyone close to us. I believe more than one person involved with that mess has learned lessons. I would like to say that the whole experience had made me a better person, and it did, but not in every way.

*

I used to feel that it was every man's duty to help and care for those in need. My "apostle's creed" had unfortunately changed. I wouldn't put myself out there for other people I wasn't sure about, or didn't know. I wouldn't stop to help if someone had a flat tire. If someone was being mugged or hurt and it didn't affect my family, or me I'd move in the other direction.

"Turn the other cheek," was my new motto. I was sorry I felt that way and it hurt me to my core, but society and the system had taught me to behave in this manner. No way was I taking any chances with people I didn't know. When I went to work, I toiled and stayed silent. If I went to the store, or the bank, or wherever, my mouth stayed tightly shut.

I was at a convenience store getting coffee when I looked to my right and a young woman, obviously harboring a black eye mixed with tears, asked me to help her.

"My boyfriend beat me up; could you take me to the police station?"

I ignored her and acted as if she was talking to someone else.

She walked up and pulled me by the arm. "Please, sir. I really need help."

I looked at her and said, "call 9-1-1," then bolted out of the store as fast as I possibly could.

It was a shame. I hoped she was okay. I was quite sure someone helped her at some point. It wasn't going to be me, though.

*

The windows on my vehicle have been waxed with the word "Pedophile", and I've been threatened with physical harm on more than one occasion. I've been asked to "step outside," so I could be slugged in the mouth. I was worried it would continue.

I remember when I was helping my cousin at his company, a bully that worked for him happened to be married to a woman I dated TEN years ago. He walked up to me and said, "I'm gonna kick your fuckin' ass!" I asked why. "You know why you son of a bitch," he fumed.

I thought he was mad because I had dated his wife before he ever met her. He told me to leave the premises.

"NO!" I protested, "I'm standing right here speaking with my cousin; you cannot, and will not, tell me what to do."

We stood toe to toe until we were separated and went our separate ways. I would find out later that he and his wife saw my picture on the registry and *assumed* I had *raped* a girl between the age of 13-16. It didn't matter that there was no description of the crime. Anything from urinating in public to actually raping a young person, there was no way to tell what the crime actually encompassed. It was an assumption made by someone without checking the facts.

No wonder I was jumpy. It was a surprise that more people on the registry (some have) hadn't been badly injured or even killed. I hoped it didn't come to that. Vigilante justice was even worse than our current system. I remain worried about the future. Will I someday be severely hurt or worse, murdered? Would somebody, somewhere, feel that they needed to take justice into their own hands and carry out a hit on me? I couldn't know, but I sure hope that wasn't not the case. Ignorance is bliss.

"I think my attitude towards human beings has changed since I left prison."
> *Jeffrey Archer*

Epilogue I

Nikki and I sit down together every morning to read the newspaper. This was when the frustration begins once again. I had to put the paper aside to collect myself, as the news is filled with allegations, sex crimes, murder, arson, and many other bits of cruelty that men perpetrates upon one another. Nikki, ever the understanding and attentive wife, discusses these matters with me and tries to soften the blow of a world seemingly gone mad. It wasn't as if it used to be when I was a kid running around my neighborhood trying to rustle up a sandlot game of baseball. What has happened to brotherly love, understanding and most of all, forgiveness. People nowadays are judgmental and unyielding. Nikki tries to assure me that these issues are the anomalies, not the typical disposition of the public. The anger settles, but I was still troubled by all the bad news and negativity engulfing today's world.

*

I spend much of my time blogging about the falsely accused and attempting to help right some of the wrongs in our society. I feel these issues need attention. If I could help one person who has felt the cold grip of our "system," than I'd

459

done something good. I stood firm in my beliefs, and *would not* give in to a governmental machine that sucks the rights and liberties out of American citizens every day.

I saw congressional representatives and women constantly using the sex offender as a tool to win elections. If they said they would be tough on the offender, the public gave them their vote. SO's aren't allowed near parks, schools, bus stops, or anywhere children frequent. What the lawmakers didn't look at were the statistics, which painted a very different picture then the fear-mongers did. Predators are different then sex offenders. Predators are just that; predatory people who seek out children to groom and abuse. Sex offenders may be on the list for urinating in public, having a Romeo-Juliet relationship or even mistaking a person's age. (Although no one mentions that young people often lie about that).

More and more, SO's are being forced away from cities, towns and small municipalities. People get a false sense of security when the offender is living in the woods (Florida), under viaducts (everywhere), or are simply dead. We criticize the Middle East custom of stoning an adulteress, but basically do the same thing here. The lawmakers will tell you that we're more civilized then those countries. Are we?

Epilogue II

Consequences (What goes around, comes around)

I watch life happen. I mind my business and watch people destroy each other, and themselves. I see the news, I read the paper and I hear things. I listen.

*

Dorothy Taylor had been dismissed from her throne and denied her bid for State Appeals Judge. A direct result of her missing court time and then lying about why. Being her abhorrent self-cost her dearly. Her arrogance and self-centered attitude bit her hard. Good riddance. I couldn't imagine the injustices that would occur with her on the appeals bench. Some people didn't belong in positions of power. Dorothy Taylor was a prime example. She once put a man in prison for fifteen years after a fifty-five minute sex case trial. He won his appeal and will have a brand new trial with a different Judge. His chances for acquittal increased tenfold.

461

*

Ronald Gardner had been fired from the prosecutor's office because of his ineffectiveness. A new County Prosecutor was voted in, and Gardner was the *first* to go. I was so glad someone recognized his shortcomings as a lawyer. He would try for a laughable run at Judgeship, but would be soundly routed on voting day. (2% of the vote). Mr. Gardner railroaded more than one man into a wrongful conviction. He had been a part of the counties sex crime unit, but deserved to be sitting at a desk doing paperwork instead.

The County Prosecutor who had been voted out of office had a reputation for pushing cases that were obviously fraudulent. He was facing a judicial discipline board for his outrageous conduct.

*

Detective Mike Smart's wife *accidently* died in their house. Of course, it was written in the papers as an accident. Mr. Smart claimed that they had to run their vehicle *in the garage* because of a low battery charge. I told him on the way to District Court that his car needed some work, but he waved me off. I wonder if he regretted that.

Honestly, how dumb did Mr. Smart and the rest of the White Lake Police think the public was? He claimed that she ran the car to charge the battery. Why was the garage door closed and locked? She allegedly died trying to reach the car to cut the engine. Therefore, what they were saying was that

462

the fumes between the doorway into the house and the car door, which was fifteen feet apart, overcame her. She collapsed on the garage floor between the two doors, or about seven and a half feet into the garage. Nobody mentioned that in the newspaper article. Anybody, especially a thirty plus year-old woman, knew how dangerous that practice was. The woman was buried *before* the newspaper article about her death was released. To me, it reeked of suicide, although only one person knew for sure: Detective Smart.

*

David Carowitz dropped dead on a job site in 2010. (Heart attack). He was found at his worksite the next morning. Was I surprised? Yes and no. I myself would have a lot of trouble living with the guilt of sending some innocent man up the river. Perhaps he died of guilt, or maybe it was plain deceit; whatever it was, it was earned in my book.

*

I had a book signing scheduled for a local Borders bookstore near where I live. They invited me, told me to bring posters and flyers for my book and even called me on more than one occasion to make sure I had everything I needed for the event. They ordered twenty books, and all was a go. Then it happened.

The Oakland Press wrote and released an article announcing my new book and event at the store. Two days before the event, I was called by the store and told that I had been cancelled. I asked why.

"We have another event that cancels you out," The woman said.

"That event was scheduled *before* my signing was scheduled, though." I continued, "why would you do such a thing? Over two hundred people are scheduled to come to this."

"Sorry, Mr. West." CLICK.

She hung up. I was saddened and flabbergasted. It turned out that someone, I'll never know who called the store after seeing my article and told them I was a sex offender. It was a case of somebody doing the same thing to me as others did when I was on certain jobs. I didn't know who did it, because people love to do those things behind the security of a telephone, or from a keypad nestled securely in their own house. Those are the people that didn't think SO's should be allowed to recover their lives. To add insult to injury, some of the bookstore employees went to other bookstores around town and asked them to remove my work. None of them did. I called their corporate offices and received four different stories from four different people. Not one of them told me the real reason why I was cancelled. If they had said it was because I was a sex offender, that would be discrimination. Not that it would've helped.

For two full weeks after the cancelled event, the support again showed itself. Many people boycotted this and other sister stores, refusing to ever shop there again. This chain of stores had to file bankruptcy only eight months after the cancellation. I knew it wasn't because of my situation that the stores went under, but hey, one should watch how they treat people. What goes around comes around, and it certainly has come around for them.

Epilogue III (The Death of a Marriage)

My wife couldn't take another minute with me. My mind was in the wrong place and a few years after my incarceration, we divorced. I was diagnosed with Borderline Personality disorder, which I originally thought to be anxiety, panic and maybe a touch of Post-Traumatic Stress Disorder. With BPD, I sought attention anywhere I could find it. Compliments became my goal in life. I wanted everyone to like me and it cost me my relationship.

I fought with Vigilantes, flirted with other women and destroyed an already stressed marriage. It reached a point where people would say and do awful things to assist in the process, but ultimately it was my baby to deal with.

Nikki tried as hard as she could, but it was too much. The Sex Offender Registry, my mental standing and the need for attention by me ruined us. Don't get me wrong, it was by no means all my fault, but I'm able to take responsibility where it needs to be taken. Without the conviction, our relationship would've been tough. With the conviction, our odds were diminished 100 fold. Nikki is quite a bit older than I am which also plays into the parting of ways. We have two different generations of experience trying to become one. It's a hill (mountain) that is almost impossible to climb.

The fact that the registry makes it next to impossible to get a job hurt our relationship, the hatred and nasty talk between

467

myself and the "enemy" hurt our relationship and the constant need for attention on my part *killed* the relationship.

I will never resent Nicki. She did all she could but can do no more. She went out on a limb to hold us together but in the end, it was too much for her to handle. She really does deserve better than what I can give her and it is about time she was given a rest.

I hope for the best Nicki: For you and your life. I'm sorry about everything that has happened and hope you find your way.

Yet more victims of a flawed system.

Facts and Figures

Please take note that these are figures I rustled up via the internet. I have cited all sources at the end of each set of stats, but I do believe that the stats and figures are scewed to some point to make it appear as if the problem is worse than it truly has become. I believe each advocy group has their very own set of numbers and uses them to their advantages. Where a Government anti-sex offender site may have a certain statistic, an anti-Government site may in fact be the exact opposite. I side with most advocy groups; not from simply being a victim of a cold criminal law system, but because I believe the Government spins subjects to their advantage no matter the circumstance. Please feel free to have a look at your favorite sites and see how different the stats are from one another. I think you'll be shocked as well as confused when you complete the task.

* PRISON STATISTICS

The U.S. has an incarceration rate of 743 per 100,000 people (2009): That's the highest rate in the world, an astonishing fact that can't be repeated enough. However, it should be noted that crime in the U.S. in general has decreased over the last 20 years. For example, from 1980 to 2009, the murder rate decreased from 10.2 per 10,000 inhabitants to 5.0

in 2009; the violent crime rate decreased from 596.6 per 10,000 inhabitants to 429.4; and the robbery rate decreased from 251.1 per 10,000 inhabitants to 133. Now, whether or not the improvements are a result of harsher punishment has yet to be proven. For comparison, from 1925 to 1975, the crime rate stayed at about 110 per 100,000 people, excluding those kept in state and local jails.

The U.S. houses a quarter of the world's prisoners (2008): The U.S. population is 311,341,000, roughly 4.5 percent of the world's population, and in 2008, it kept 2.3 million people behind bars. China, the world's most populous country with 1,339,725,000 people, kept 1.6 million people behind bars the same year, though it should be noted that it had hundreds of thousands of people in administrative detention. During America's younger years, it was regarded around the world as more relaxed on criminal justice, hence the Wild West reputation. But as the population has grown, particularly in cities, we've taken more drastic measures to control crime.

The U.S. houses more inmates than the top 35 European countries combined (2010): Europe, which has a denser population than the U.S., is well-below the U.S. when it comes to incarceration rates. In England and Wales, for example, 139 people are imprisoned per 10,000, one of the highest rates in Western Europe. Harsher sentencing in recent years is blamed for the rise in prison population in the U.K. Nevertheless, it pales in comparison to America's rate; only Easter Europe's Belarus comes close, with a rate of 385 people imprisoned per 10,000.

The federal prison population has more than doubled since 1995 (2010): Because the federal system is generally stricter than state systems and has expanded its jurisdiction over certain offenses, it has seen a drastic increase in the amount of people it houses. In particular, an increase in immigration cases since 1994 has been a main contributor, as they accounted for 28.2 percent of all federal sentencing in 2008, for example.

The number of state prisoners declined by 4,777 from December 2008 to January 2010: Possibly due to the recession, many have attributed the decline in state prisoners to large state budget deficits, which have forced states to release inmates to save money. However, according to the Pew Center on the States, the decline actually started just before the economic downturn due to a reduction in the amount of people sent to prison for new crimes, while the number of people released from prison increased. Of course, prison rates vary from state to state.

The most significant decreases in state prison populations from 2008 to 2009 occurred in California (-4,257), Michigan (-3,260) and New York (-1,699): Overall, 26 states saw a decrease in prison population. California led them all, as the state has made an effort to cut the number of low-risk parolees returning to prison by expanding the use of intermediate sanctions. Overcrowding has been a problem for California; so much so that a deferral court in 2009 ordered the state to reduce its prison population by 40,000 in just two years. Michigan has cut its prison population by decreasing parole revocation rates, improving its reentry planning and supervision, and reducing the number of inmates who serve more than 100 percent of their minimum sentence.

The most significant increases in state prison populations from 2008 to 2009 occurred in Pennsylvania (+2,122), Florida (+1,527) and Indiana (+1,496): During the last three

decades, Pennsylvania's prison population has expanded from
8,243 to 51,326. In recent years, the increase can be attributed
to former Gov. Ed Rendell's 2008 moratorium on paroles in
response to the killing of a Philadelphia police officer by a
paroled felon. The state also transferred prisoners out of state
due to overcrowding. In Florida's case, some attribute the rise
to legislators failing to cut corrections spending like in many
of the states that saw reductions in their prison populations.

**Those who have spent time in prison earn 40 percent less
annually (2010)**: Universally, crime is associated with people
from poor economic backgrounds who have few options in
life. In many cases, those who've been incarcerated grew up
around family members and friends who suffered the same
fate. Their ability to escape the rut decreases greatly after
their first offense, as their annual earnings are almost slashed
in half because many employers refuse to hire them. Most
unsettling is the fact that more than half of those incarcerated
were the primary financial providers for their children.

**One in every 28 children has an incarcerated parent
(2010)**: A quarter of a century ago, one in every 125 children
had an incarcerated parent. The rise, of course, can be
attributed to the implementation of harsher laws for lesser
crimes; two-thirds of today's incarcerated parents committed
non-violent offenses. The above stat is one of the most
disconcerting of all U.S.-related prison stats because common
sense dictates that a child's chances of growing up as a
productive, law-abiding adult are greater when both of their
parents play significant roles in their life.

**More than one in three young black men without a high
school diploma are in prison (2010)**: Additionally, more
black men without a high school diploma are incarcerated than

employed. As previously mentioned, it's more difficult to secure a job once a person has spent time in prison, further limiting the options of the already less fortunate. In fact, black men earn 44 percent less after they've been incarcerated, four percent less than the average for all races/ethnicities.

* Sources- Webcite, The New York Times, The Pew center on the states and Pew's economic policy group

Afterword

By Shana Rowan,
Advocate for nationwide sex crime legislation reform.

Sex Offender Legislation in the US
Endangering communities and destroying families

Quick Facts:

A 10-year study by the US Department of Justice, ending in 2004, found the recidivism rate for sex offenders to be between 3.5 – 8.5%. This has been echoed by many state recidivism studies as well, including a February 2012 study from the state of Connecticut, which lists the re-offense rate for sex offenders as a mere 2.7%.

Only 3% of the public is aware that sex offenders have low re-offense rates. 74% of the public claim the knowledge they have about sex offenders comes predominantly from the news media. (Center for Sex Offender Management, 2010)

90% of children between 12 and 17 knew their abuser, 95% of children between 6 and 12 knew their abuser and 97% of children under 6 knew their abuser. Adult victims 18 and over knew their attackers 73% of the time. (US Department of Justice, 2004)

A quarter of all registered sex offenders are children aged 17 and younger. Juvenile offenders account for over a third of all sex crimes committed against other children. (US Department of Justice, 2009)

The public registry and community notification have shown to be ineffective at reducing sex crimes; some studies have found they lead to a false sense of security, which makes the community more vulnerable to sex crimes. (Center for Sex Offender Management, 2001, 2002 & 2007)

Residency restrictions, employment restrictions and "child safety zones" have all been shown to be ineffective at reducing sex crimes. Areas that have enacted such restrictions have not seen reduced numbers of sex crimes, but have seen increases in homeless/transient offenders. Lack of stable housing has been identified as one of the highest predictors of re-offense. (Association for the Treatment of Sexual Abusers, 2010; Center for Sex Offender Management, 2001)

50% of family members of sex offenders report fearing for their own personal safety as a result of the public registry. 86% report that the registry causes stress in their lives and 77% feel isolated. 44% report being threatened or harassed due to their family member's public status as a sex offender. (Levensen & Tewksbury, 2009).

Summary

After reading these quick facts, you may be asking yourself why they aren't reflected in any of the laws in this country regarding sex crime and sex offenders. Law enforcement, lawmakers and politicians continue to tout the importance of the registry; and the constant coverage the media provides us on high-profile sex crimes is just as bad. Why is it that the people we elect to lead and protect our communities have fallen down so miserably when it comes to this very serious issue?

It's important to remember that lawmakers, politicians and certain members of law enforcement rely on the public's approval to remain in their position of power. Make no mistake – these individuals are very much aware of how ineffective our methods for managing sex crime are. Some of them may not know either way, but don't care to find out. Law enforcement needs a steady stream of criminals and victims to pay their salaries. Lawmakers need someone to scapegoat and scrutinize to draw attention away from the fact that since the dawn of the registry and the legislation that followed, sex crimes haven't been prevented. Up until now, they have succeeded with this incredible cover-up. Not anymore.

The key to infiltrating the public approval of the registry is to chip away at its shortcomings. The registry doesn't protect children; it endangers the safety of the children of registrants and ignores the high majority of current and future victims. Our communities are not safer; they are enjoying a false sense of security and empowering predators that have never been caught to strike with ease. Those in power are not interested in child safety; they just don't want you to find out that sex offenders pose little risk to children when compared to significantly less strictly regulated and monitored criminals.

477

If we are a society that truly values civil liberties, family values and the right to live freely, then we must abolish the registry and replace it with a fact-based, carefully thought out system that prevents crimes rather than punishes perpetrators for life. We must remember that behind every mug shot on the registry is an innocent family who deserves safety and rights. We must not be the ones to judge.

Afterglow

A Little about Me

Writing a book gives me the emotional outlet for which I constantly search. I can feel the stress slipping away with every word I type. Writing, for me, is a mentally productive hobby to undertake.

I had dabbled with writing since I was twelve years old, but I never organized my work in a manner that would prompt writing a full-length book. I enjoyed writing about sports. I also liked to write and study professional athlete's statistics and numbers until my fingers hurt. I had memorized every stat from all of my favorite teams and pulled them out of my memory on request. It made watching ballgames more interesting, especially when I could show off to my friends. They would be awestruck by my ability to stay ahead of the announcers during a telecast. Making up my own sports games using my statistical thinking was also something I enjoyed. This, of course, preceded PlayStation and other gaming devices, which kept all the stats for you.

As I grew older, work and raising a family took center stage. There wasn't enough time to do all the writing I did when I was a kid. In time, I found that I missed it. I had some time on my hands between jobs, and figured, why not?

Writing helped relieve some stress that had built up over the years. Anything that would come out of it as far as publishing is concerned would be an added bonus. I don't expect it to be some best-selling novel, but I wanted to get one side of the story out. If this unfortunate situation could touch even one person, then it would be worth it to me.

Reading is also a great way to lift the spirit and help with tension as you lose yourself in something besides drugs or alcohol. I have read my share of novels, and figured I could write my thoughts down by using some discipline and mixing in a part of my imagination. Writing a book now ranks up there, for me, as something everyone should try to do before they die. The feeling you get when you finished the story is beyond description. I was so into this work that at some points I would completely lose track of time, as the story translated onto paper nicely. Hours would pass and I would keep on typing. I had a patient wife who supported the process. It was probably as much for her sanity as my own.

This book, addresses real issues that I, along with society, face today. I'm hoping you the reader will come away with a more empathic and understanding view of how broken and in need of attention our justice system has become. Sometimes the real victim is not so easy to recognize.

Rest in peace, Dakota (1997-2010)